From the Ashes of 1947

This book revisits the partition of the Punjab, its attendant violence and, as a consequence, the divided and dislocated Punjabi lives. Navigating nostalgia and trauma, dreams and laments, identity(s) and homeland(s), it explores the partition of the very idea of *Punjabiyat*.

It was Punjab (along with Bengal) that was divided to create the new nations of India and Pakistan and that inherited a communalised and fractured self. In subsequent years, religious and linguistic sub-divisions followed – arguably, no other region of the subcontinent has had its linguistic and ethnic history submerged within respective national and religious identity(s) and none paid the price of partition like the pluralistic, pre-partition Punjab.

This book is about the dissonance, distortion and dilution which details the past of the region. It describes 'people's history' through diverse oral narratives, literary traditions and popular accounts. In terms of space, it documents the experience of partition in the two prosperous localities of Ludhiana and Lyallpur (now Faisalabad), with a focus on migration; and in the Muslim princely state of Malerkotla, with a focus on its escape from the violence of 1947. In terms of groups, it especially attends to women and their experiences, beyond the symbolic prism of 'honour'. Critically examining existing accounts, discussing the differential impact of partition, and partaking in the ever democratising discourse on it, this book attempts to illustrate the lack of closure associated with 1947.

Pippa Virdee teaches Modern South Asian History at De Montfort University, Leicester. She has been a visiting fellow at the Centre for Governance and Policy (Information Technology University), Lahore. She is the author of *Coming to Coventry: Stories from the South Asian Pioneers* (2006) and has co-edited *Refugees and the End of Empire* (2011). Her academic interests include British colonial history, the history of Punjab and Partition Studies.

From the Ashes of 1947

Reimagining Punjab

Pippa Virdee

CAMBRIDGE
UNIVERSITY PRESS

CAMBRIDGE
UNIVERSITY PRESS

University Printing House, Cambridge CB2 8BS, United Kingdom

One Liberty Plaza, 20th Floor, New York, NY 10006, USA

477 Williamstown Road, Port Melbourne, vic 3207, Australia

314 to 321, 3rd Floor, Plot No.3, Splendor Forum, Jasola District Centre, New Delhi 110025, India

79 Anson Road, #06–04/06, Singapore 079906

Cambridge University Press is part of the University of Cambridge.

It furthers the University's mission by disseminating knowledge in the pursuit of education, learning and research at the highest international levels of excellence.

www.cambridge.org
Information on this title: www.cambridge.org/9781108428118

© Pippa Virdee 2018

First published 2018
Reprint 2018
Printed in India at Thomson Press (India) Ltd.

A catalogue record for this publication is available from the British Library

ISBN 978-1-108-42811-8 Hardback

Table of Contents

List of Photographs

Photographs

List of Maps and Tables

List of Excerpts

List of Abbreviations

AIHM	All India Hindu Mahasabha
CLO	Chief Liaison Officer
DC	District Commissioner
DLO	District Liaison Officer
GoI	Government of India
GoP	Government of Pakistan
INC	Indian National Congress
IOR	India Office Records, UK
MEO	Military Evacuation Organisation
MR&R	Ministry of Refugees and Rehabilitation
NAI	National Archives of India
NDC	National Documentation Centre, Islamabad
NMML	Nehru Memorial Museum and Library
PBF	Punjab Boundary Force
PEPSU	Patiala and East Punjab States Union
PSA	Punjab State Archives, India
RSS	Rashtriya Swayamsevak Sangh
SARRC	South Asian Research and Resource Centre, Islamabad

Glossary

Abadi	Village area.
Arains	Cultivators Vegetable growers.
Arora	Trading/business caste.
Artisans	Classification of people, majority were Muslims. Artisans were usually treated similarly to shudras.
Bania	Merchant class, village shop-keeper or money-lender, originally from Gujarat.
Bazaar	Market place.
Bazigars	Nomadic tribe that live off circus-like performances.
Bigha	A measure of land about 4 kanals or 2,000 yards.
Biradari	Brotherhood or social networks which are often used for marriage and political relations.
Brahmin	Priest/intellectuals; belong to the highest caste, function is to study and teach, to perform sacrifice and other priestly duties.
Caste	System of hereditary social stratification. In Hinduism, there is a four-fold classification of – brahmin (priests), kshatriya (warriors), vaishya (traders) and sudra (labourers). There is also a fifth group at the bottom of the scale and they are considered as 'outcastes'.
Chak	A block of land – a colony village.
Chamar	Menial worker, usually with leather and animal hides. Considered unclean caste/untouchable.
Chowk	Meeting point or main junction like a roundabout.
Crore	Numerical term denoting ten million.
Dargah	Muslim shrines, especially Sufi Shrines.
Dharamshalas	Shelter for devotees at Temples/Gurdwaras.
Doab	Literally 'two rivers'; the strip of fertile land between two rivers. For example, the area between the rivers Sutlej and Beas known as the Bist Doab.

Dogras	The term 'Dogra' refers to an ethnic group that lived in the south-eastern part of Jammu, ruling family of the Princely State were Dogras.
Gali	Narrow lanes.
Ghee	Clarified butter.
Goonda	Thugs.
Gurdwara	Sikh temple.
Guru	Religious leader in Sikhism.
Hakim	Traditional doctor.
Harijan	Term popularised by Mahatma Gandhi for untouchables. Literally means 'children of God'.
Hindutva	Literally means 'Hinduness'; term has been popularised by the Hindu nationalists in India.
Izzat	Honour, prestige or status, often associated with maintaining 'face'.
Jat	Agriculturalist; cultivating caste prominent in Punjab agriculture and within the Sikh community. Also prominent in the military.
Jatha	A group of volunteers for a specific purpose – usually associated with groups of Sikhs.
Kacha/Kachi	Mud houses or those with weak structures.
Kachi abadi	Slum colonies.
Kafla	Foot convoys of refugees.
Katha	Hindu prayer.
Khatris	Trading/business caste.
Khojas	Members of a Muslim trading community who are disciples of the Ismaili Agha Khan.
Lakh	Numerical term denoting a hundred thousand.
Lohar	Artisan Class – ironsmiths/blacksmiths.
Mandi	Market/Market town.
Mandir	Hindu temple.

Maraba	25 acres of land.
Masjid	Mosque.
Memon	Muslim commercial community from usually western part of India. Historically associated with the Kathiawar area.
Mohalla	A residential locality or area of a town.
Nala	Ravine, river bed.
Nawab	High-ranking political/military official, provincial governor or viceroy in Mughal India; later used as courtesy title for member of the Muslim elite.
Rajput	Caste of northern and central India traditionally associated with rulership and warriorhood.
Ramgarhias	Sikh artisan caste, prominent among East African Sikhs.
Sepoys	Indian soldiers originally in the East India Company.
Sheikh	Respectable Muslim.
Tarkhan	Artisan Class – carpenters.
Tehsil	Sub-division of a district in the British and post-independence period.
Vaid	Traditional doctor.
Viswakarmis	Artisan Class – work with tools.

Acknowledgements

The journey towards completing this book has been a long one, perhaps too long. It has been filled with immense feelings of gratitude and fulfilment but at the same time, it has been accompanied by the enormous amount of personal loss too. While the loss can never be replaced those loved ones remain in memory. Like many of those people that I interviewed over the years, their personal loss of friends, family and homelands can never be replaced but they retain fading memories of former lives. This work would not have been possible without the generosity of people who shared their memories with me and opened their hearts to a stranger.

This research was also made possible by funding and support from a number of people and institutions. William Clarke and Robert Oakshot, who set up the Penderel Moon Fellowship in partnership with Coventry University in honour of their late uncle, enabled me to commence my research. They deserve special acknowledgement for this. De Montfort University, where I have been for over ten years, has been enormously generous in supporting my research and allowing me the time to write and reflect on my work. Information Technology University (ITU), Lahore gave me the space in Lahore to complete my research during a visiting post. I am thankful to the many wonderful colleagues I have had the pleasure of working with at all these institutions.

This work would not have been possible without the network of colleagues and friends in the subcontinent. Khalid Mohammed, Punjab University, Chandigarh for providing me with contacts in Malerkotla, Dr Mujahid Hussian for assisting me with the interviews in Malerkotla and Dr M. Ramzan for being kind enough to provide a base for me. Sardar Jodh Singh, my *jija ji*, for assisting me with my interviews in Ludhiana, Iswhar Dayal Gaur for providing valuable thoughts and insights at pivotal moments, and Ajay Bhardwaj for opening new ways of thinking. In Pakistan, I would not have been able to undertake any of this research without the generosity of many individuals: Tahir Kamran who introduced me to the late Bilal Ahmed, who provided support for much of my early research, Ahmed Salim (SDPI and SAARC) for providing so much help in conducting and setting up interviews in Lyallpur and in providing access to his personal archive in Islamabad, Raja Adnan Razzaq for his enormous support in Islamabad, Virinder Kalra, an honorary Pakistani for many, Mohammad Waseem, Tariq Rahman, Ali Usman Qasmi, Ilyas Chattha and many more whom I am sure I have forgotten to mention.

Three inspirational mentors I've had in three cities close to my heart, Delhi, Lahore and Coventry. Pran Nevile for encouraging and supporting me right from the beginning of this journey, thank you for the many wonderful moments we have spent reminiscing about old Punjab. Iqbal Qaiser in Lahore has provided so much of his time in supporting and helping me with my research. His energy and knowledge of Punjab is unrivalled. And Ian Talbot without whose guidance and knowledge I would not be here.

A special note of thanks is needed for the many people who keep the libraries and archives going despite the many challenges they face in the sub-continent. The staff at Teen Murti in Delhi, which was a blissful place to conduct research; it is impossible to forget the many plates of *daal chawal* I had there. The National Archives of India, the staff at the Punjab Archives in Chandigarh and Patiala for trying to help me when things often looked impossible. The National Documentation Centre in Islamabad and the Punjab Archives in Lahore (including the cups of tea) have also provided valuable assistance. British Library and their staff for providing a wonderful environment (and cakes!) for researchers.

There are of course many friends and family without whom our lives would be empty. They play an important part in supporting us. Gulnar for her laughter, Yaqoob for his amazing energy, my yoga buddies for their sparkly sanity, Harry for his unflinching kindness, Victor for his impossible laughter, my family in Chandigarh and Ludhiana who have always supported me despite not always knowing why I spend so much time in Pakistan! Pinky, Tony, Pavan and Gaggun for providing much-needed reality checks and dark humour. And finally, Bilal (in memory), his family and the children in Lahore, who have adopted me as their own and have always provided a welcoming home in Lahore and Rakesh for his timely entrance.

Finally, thank you Qudisya Ahmed at CUP for pushing me to send the manuscript and my mum who would have been enormously proud.

Preface
Memories Create History

It is 5 December 2013 and I have just attended a lecture by Rajmohan Gandhi, grandson of Mahatma Gandhi, at Foreman Christian College, Lahore. He was giving a talk on Khan Ghaffar Badshah Khan, the great leader from the Frontier. At the same time, Gandhi was also launching his book *Punjab: A History from Aurangzeb to Mountbatten*. All these fragmented pieces are brought together later in the day while I am attending a dinner for Rajmohan Gandhi and I sat there chatting with Najum Latif, talking about Indian nationalism, the two-nation theory and Punjabi nationalism. We were meeting after many years; the first meeting was at Government College Lahore while I was doing my PhD on the partition of India. We are conversing in Punjabi and through his stories he takes me back to the days of his childhood in pre-partitioned Punjab, more specifically in Jullundur, where his ancestral roots are. He laments about the state of Punjab and why it should never have been partitioned; he is one of the few survivors of that generation that witnessed this great calamity himself as a child. Uprooted, unsettled, traumatised and ultimately disappointed in outcomes. No politician asked people like him or that generation whether they wanted a divided land. Instead, they were sold dreams, aspirations and division.

Ten years after completing my PhD thesis, I revisit my own work that was never published in its entirety. After visiting Lahore at the end of 2013, I felt that it is even more relevant today. There is a need for many to understand why this happened, though the answers may never be truly known. Many friends and colleagues were still discussing and debating the events of 1947. I also noticed that there seems to be a great deal of interest in partition and what happened in Punjab among many people.

I had a chance meeting with Jamil Khan, another migrant from Patiala and himself an Urdu writer; we had many discussions about partition and why so many people turned to violence. Jamil sahib is still not at peace with this event, which has shaped much of North India and Pakistan. There are fragments of partitioned lives wherever one goes; casual conversations inevitably lead to questions about one's background and then of course, in the distinctly unpolished tones of the Punjabi dialect, there are questions about which side one belongs to? My own identity, as I assert, is Punjabi and I am usually immediately placed in the *doab* and thus the familiar tones to the migrants in West Punjab and home in East Punjab. But as a child of the diaspora, my Punjabi is largely untainted with the influences of (Arabic) Urdu and (Sanskrit) Hindi in modern Pakistan and India. Yet there is immediately a connection with each other, a sense of lost kinship, which is awakened and so the conversation continues to reminisce about lost homes, friends and childhoods abruptly dislocated. The past is unadulterated, pure and happy until the great *halla, batwara, takseem*, or *wand* (partition) came to shatter the illusion. The new imagined homelands of India and Pakistan are then put under the microscope: Was it worth it? There is a question mark over whether it was worth the loss and why Punjab had to pay such a heavy price. This is why individuals like Latif and Khan still lament the politicians and choices they made. The population exchange and territorial division cannot be undone but the greater tragedy is the loss of homelands that people can no longer visit. The strict visa controls mean that the ordinary people still suffer the most because they are unable to visit the 'other' side. Why are we still separated? This is the question many migrants ask.

Indeed, the strained relation between India and Pakistan for the past seventy years has further embedded this trauma. Although there is still much nostalgia about 'my city, my street', as testified by Abdul Haq,[1] the hard border between the two countries has made it impossible for these forced migrants to re-visit their homelands. Instead, memories of that lost youth and place have 'served to reinforce displacement, loss, and anger',[2] even though some people delayed this process for as long as possible. However, it is Sarwan Singh who captures the essence of the issues that have really torn the people that were dislocated. This was also one of the first interviews I did as a PhD student and the gentle sardar, sitting there cross-legged in his fabric shop in Malerkotla, with tears in his eyes, left an emotional impression on me. Poignantly, he talks about his village in Pakistan and his yearning to visit his 'home' again, which will remain unfulfilled:

> The thing that has affected me the most, which I still yearn for is the need to go back to my village and have a look but I am unable to do this. The law does not allow me to go back there to see my ancestral village and meet my friends and others there. This thing I feel I will be unable to complete in my life…Work is good but what happened at that time, the things we saw and experienced, and now when I see trouble taking place then it upsets me. We are settled now everything is fine but like I said it

---

1   Interview with Abdul Haq, Montgomery Bazaar, Faisalabad, January 2003.

2   Jeffrey Diamond, 'Narratives of Reform and Displacement in Colonial Lahore: The Intikaal of Muhammad Hussain Azad,' *Journal of Punjab Studies* 16 (2009).

can never compensate for that time and what is in my heart. The thing that I yearn for, to see my house and my friends.[3]

Many of the people I interviewed vividly remember their homes. They can describe their homes in such detail as if an image has been permanently preserved in their memory. As someone who grew in Nakuru, Kenya, and had to leave as a child, I can relate to those feelings of wanting to see that home once again, just the way I imagine it in my head, but I chose not to, partly because I want to preserve that picture just the way it was, untainted. While the people I interviewed have moved on and they have settled down and created new lives, a part of them still yearns for those childhood memories.

Exploring Partition

In 2001, when I started my PhD, I was a student of history with limited knowledge of partition. Despite being closely connected to that land, I tried to remain an outsider in order to maintain some objectivity. The process of completing the thesis and now revisiting it, I realise now, has left an indelible impression on me and has shaped much of my understanding and growing intellectual interest in the idea of *Punjabiyat*. Punjab was divided to create the new nations of India and Pakistan but the lingering legacy has been one of a communalised and fractured Punjabi identity. The Punjabi Muslim has been absorbed in the Pakistan project and thus hardly speaks his mother tongue, especially the younger generations; the Indian Punjabi has been sub-divided into the Sikh and the Hindu. The Sikh and Punjabi identity has become synonymous to create a Punjabi-speaking state and the Hindu Punjabi is marginalised out and has been absorbed in the Hindutva project. Punjabis as an ethnic group have therefore been divided (and sub-divided) along religious and then linguistic lines. Punjabi as a language is now almost exclusively associated with the Sikh community, yet it is the mother tongue of most Pakistanis who have adopted Urdu as their national language and thereby created a new mother language. The Hindu Punjabis, on the other hand, associate themselves with Hindi; this was of course made easier by linguistic reorganisation of East Punjab 1966. These are simplified stereotypes of the divided people but, more broadly, they are symptomatic of the communalised politics of the sub-continent, and more specifically, they are much more peculiar to the Punjab region. It is difficult to think of another region in the sub-continent that has shunned its own linguistic

---

3   Interview with Sarwan Singh, Lal Bazaar, Malerkotla, August 2001.

and ethnic history in favour of a national or religious identity. The pluralistic region of Punjab that epitomised people like my own mother's generation are fewer and fewer. The convergence of different religious practices is evident in the way many people practice faith. Recent scholarship has been particularly interested in unearthing and documenting these shared religious practices and histories to challenge the otherwise distorted communalised histories. This book is about that period which transformed the land, the people and a dilution of its history which now tells us a different myth and past of Punjab. It is a revised post-1947 history, which fulfils the national projects of Hindu India and Islamic Pakistan but fails to adequately acknowledge the shared cultural roots and traditions of the broader Punjabi community. This polarisation of people is an attempt to homogenise people and endanger the essence of the plurality which has existed in Punjab for centuries.

Over the years, I have interviewed many people about their experiences of partition and the hardships they endured; the responses resonated across borders, regardless of their religion or country. People went through similar process of being uprooted and forcibly removed from ancestral homes, and feelings of dislocation were apparent in all communities. The differences were more at the class, caste and gender to some extent. Through the course of the research, it was clear that the migrants experienced intense trauma arising from loss of life, loss of property and being forcibly removed from their ancestral homes. Even today, some families bear the physical and psychological scars of the upheaval that was accompanied by incomprehensible violence against the most vulnerable in society. This of course raises many ethical concerns about the researcher's role in intruding and evoking old memories. What was also clear to me was much of the research, and indeed, history in South Asia is concerned with the political dimension. This work is an attempt to move away from seeking answers to why and how India was divided (which is done to a limited extent to provide the context). Instead, there is a need to focus on the people's history. This is also in line with current trends in history that is seeking to explore experiences 'from below' or provide a history which connects with the public. The oral narratives and poetry used in this book seek to bridge that gap between traditional history and popular history. These narratives also allow us to understand our own history through the prism of personal accounts and experiences. They are just as important as the 'high politics' because they remind us of the human suffering that was endured in the creation of India and Pakistan.

I wanted to speak to people who experienced Partition and migration first-hand, and record their narratives as opposed to the 'high politics'. Spending time

Picture 1: The India–Pakistan border at Attari–Wagah. The picture was taken in 2006 when trade was still exchanged manually at the line of control.

Picture 2: The Indian Border Security Force in full swing during the daily lowering of the flag ceremony, at the Attari-Wagah border. It attracts many people and is packed with the euphoric patriotism and excessive nationalism.

in both India and Pakistan was a privilege which not many people have. Relations between India and Pakistan often follow a roller-coaster ride where there is little certainty of the highs and lows. When I set out to do my research, I was not even sure that I would be able to get a visa for Pakistan since I was born in India. Having overcome that first hurdle, my first visit to Pakistan was filled with trepidation of the unknown land. Mysterious, because of how my own community's history is shaped by the Muslim/Sikh conflict going back to Mughal India. However, I was determined to visit regardless of the fears, but once I got there, all this vanished. The people I met were so generous and warm, that it almost immediately felt familiar and like home. The shared culture and heritage of the two Punjabs was only too apparent; however, there were clearly differences in the way West Punjab and East Punjab have developed over the past seventy years.

While trying to document that transformation of the land and people, I focused on two localities, Ludhiana in India and Lyallpur (now Faisalabad) in Pakistan because both had prospered economically in the post-1947 period. I wanted to examine to what extent partition migration had an impact on the two cities. I also use another case study, Malerkotla, a Muslim princely state surrounded by Sikh states. This was a very interesting area, because there was hardly any violence in this state during those partition days and in fact it became a safe haven for Muslims fleeing the surrounding areas. In addition, I also focus on women and their experiences because they are often forgotten for their contributions in the making of modern India and Pakistan. Although they have become symbolic of the nation's 'honour', their experiences and impact go beyond that and continue to shape our understanding of South Asian society.

The first aim of this book is to critically examine existing accounts of partition and its aftermath, focusing specifically on the Punjab region. Second is to analyse the diverse historical experiences of partition and its aftermath with the use of localised case studies and personal accounts. The final one is to utilise case studies to bring about a new understanding of the differential impact of partition and its aftermath on the Punjab region. An attempt is made to consider, first, the localised patterns of political authority and how culture impacted on the differential experience of partition-related violence and second, how far the experience of partition and dislocation was a process rather than an event confined to August 1947. For many of the victims, it took many years for the physical process of refugee rehabilitation to be completed. Within this story, it is important to understand the extent to which the input of refugee capital and labour were locally significant in the region's post-partition urban economic development.

Throughout this study, part of the objective has been to chart this change and shift taking place in Partition Studies, the move from high politics to politics from below, a move that has been made possible in part because of this shift in wider history which has begun to envelop social causes and move beyond just the archival record. At the same time, this process has at least democratised the discourse, with a greater diversity of voices emerging and being represented in the history books. But in moving towards a people's history, technology has played an important role – the way recording and sharing devices have transformed our understanding of partition history. A history without hard borders is crucial in providing a new kind of history, a kinder history I hope.

In the past ten years, there has been a plethora of material emerging in Partition Studies. Some of this work is concerned with this new approach, others have continued with the focus on the politics. Yet one aspect is clear: There is still an appetite for material and research on partition. This of course begs the following questions: Why should this be so? Why, after seventy years of this bittersweet experience of partition and independence, should the people be talking about their memories? The answer partly lies in the lack of closure and understanding of why ordinary people paid such a high price. The history books talk of an organised process, controlled by the 'great men', yet few expected the great upheaval, mass dislocation and the violent response to the drawing up of the boundaries. While both India and Pakistan have engaged in projecting a 'nationalist', and thereby, providing the *aam log* (ordinary folk) with a rationale for why this was necessary, neither country can truly come to accept its responsibility and liability in bringing about such carnage and forced migration of millions of people who were uprooted from their homes.

Note on permissions

Every effort has been made to establish contact with the original publishers for works/excerpts for obtaining permission. I would like to acknowledge the following publishers for providing permission to use material/excerpts which have appeared in earlier versions. Taylor and Francis: 'Dreams, Memories and Legacies: Partitioning India', In Knut A. Jacobsen (ed) *Routledge Handbook of Contemporary India* (Routledge, 2015); "No-mans Land' and the Creation of Partitioned Histories' In India/Pakistan', In *Remembering Genocide,* eds Nigel Eltringham and Pam Maclean (Routledge, 2014) and 'Negotiating the Past: Journey through Muslim Women's Experience of Partition and Resettlement' *Cultural and Social History*, 2009, Volume 6, Issue 4, pp. 467–484. *The Oral History Society*: 'Remembering Partition: Women, Oral Histories and the Partition of 1947' *Oral History*, 2013, Volume 41, Issue 2, pp. 49-61. Palgrave Macmillian for: "No Home but in Memory': The Legacies of Colonial Rule in the Punjab', In Panikos Panayi and Pippa Virdee (eds) *Refugees and the End of Empire: Imperial Collapse and Forced Migration during the Twentieth Century* (Palgrave, 2011). Oxford University Press, Karachi: 'Partition and the Absence of Communal Violence in Malerkotla', In Ian Talbot (ed.) *The Deadly Embrace: Religion, Politics and Violence in the Indian Subcontinent 1947-2002* (OUP, 2007). Finally, I would like to thank the *Journal of Punjab Studies* for kindly providing permission to use excerpts of poetry from Volume 13, 2006, which was a special issue dedicated to Punjabi poetry.

Any errors or omissions in this book are of course mine.

Quote by Catherine Hall

'For the most part, however, in all sectors of higher education we remain on the margins. But the margins can be a very productive terrain – a space from which both to challenge establishments and develop our own perspectives, build our own organisations, confirm our own collectivities. The hopes for feminist history in the 1990s cannot be the same as they were in the 1970s for we are living in a very different political world, and some of the harsh lessons we have learned about both exclusivity and marginality must inform our practice in the future. The dream remains – a kind of history that excites and engages, that retains its critical edge, is open to new voices, and always in a dynamic relation to the political world in which we live.'[1]

---

1   Catherine Hall, *White, Male and Middle Class: Explorations in Feminism and History* (Oxford: Polity Press, 1992), 34.

1

Partitioned Lands, Partitioned Histories

Defining the post-1947 relationship between India and Pakistan, and given that seventy years have lapsed, the partition of British India in August 1947 remains a watershed in the subcontinent's history. Underlying this is the juxtaposition of Jawaharlal Nehru's famous 'Tryst with Destiny' speech on the eve of independence, and the millions of people in Punjab who woke up not knowing which country they belonged to. The jubilation of independence was simultaneously marked by carnage, and so the memory of decolonisation/independence/partition varies greatly, depending on which side of the border you were, where you were within that, and who you were as an individual. How have historians captured these experiences and voices?

The actual event or process was marked by one of the greatest migrations in the twentieth century,[1] resulting in approximately 14.5 million people being forced to cross the newly created borders of India and Pakistan.[2] The majority of these people came from Punjab, Sind, North-West Frontier Province and Bahawalpur state on the Pakistani side and from East Punjab, the East Punjab princely states, Delhi and United Provinces on the Indian side. Migration in Bengal was on a much smaller scale in August 1947, although, unlike in Punjab, it was drawn out for many years.[3] The communal violence, which prompted this mass movement, resulted in an estimated death of one million people. This figure continues to be a contentious issue and will be examined in greater detail in chapter four. The migrants experienced intense trauma arising from the loss of property and family members, and, as a result, of being forcibly exiled from their ancestral homes

---

Gyanendra Pandey, *Remembering Partition: Violence, Nationalism and History in India* (Cambridge: Cambridge University Press, 2001).

2 For a detailed discussion, see Prashant Bharadwaj, Asim Ijaz Khwaja and Atif Mian, 'The Big March: Migratory Flows after the Partition of India,' *HKS Faculty Research Working Paper Series* RWP08-029, June 2008, www.hks.harvard.edu.

3 On the Bengal experience see Ian Talbot and Gurharpal Singh, eds., *Region and Partition: Bengal, Punjab and the Partition of the Subcontinent* (Karachi: Oxford University Press, 1999); Joya Chatterji, *Bengal Divided: Hindu Communalism and Partition, 1932-1947* (Cambridge: Cambridge University Press, 1994).

and lands. Sadly, even today, families bear the physical and psychological scars of this forced migration that was accompanied by reprehensible violence and crimes that, as a society, we have not been able to fathom.

Writing Partition History

The celebratory spirit of hard-fought freedom has largely defined much of the official histories produced in India, Pakistan and Britain,[4] and at the same time they have played down the disruption, dislocation and ordeals inflicted on ordinary people effected by Partition. The colonial interpretation is generally viewed through the successful transfer of power rather than the success of the freedom movement. Certainly, H. V. Hodson's account, which utilised the Mountbatten Papers, is an early account examining both the role (and glorification) of the last Viceroy and the success of the British Raj while absolving the corrosive impact of colonial policies.[5] The Indian nationalists, on the other hand, saw partition as the net result of years of divisive policies adopted by the colonial power. These undermined pre-existing cultural unities and social interaction, which cut across religious identity. Pakistani writers understandably focus on the creation of a separate homeland, which arose from the desire to safeguard their community from the 'tyrannical' Hindu majority rule. The ideologically incompatible discourses arising from 'divide and rule' and 'two-nation theory' understandings of partition that followed from independence have been the framework upon which the relationship between India and Pakistan has evolved in the independent history of both nations.[6]

Both India and Pakistan have produced documentation, which despite its biases, is useful to the historian in understanding the communal violence of August 1947. Chaudhry Khaliquzzaman attacked the Congress leadership and Mountbatten for this biased approach and blamed both for contributing to the disorder that resulted in an inevitable partition. Chaudhri Muhammad Ali, in *The Emergence of Pakistan*, offered another Pakistani view of events leading to partition. Central to Pakistani official history is Muhammad

---

4   See further, P. N. Chopra, ed., *Towards Freedom: Documents on the Movement for Independence in India, 1937* (Delhi: Oxford University Press, 1986); P. S. Gupta, ed., *Towards Freedom: Documents on the Movement for Independence in India, 1942-1944* (Delhi: Oxford University Press, 1997).

5   H. V. Hodson, *The Great Divide: Britain-India-Pakistan* (Hutchinson, 1969).

6   S. Settar and I. B. Gupta, eds., *Pangs of Partition, Vol. II: The Human Dimension* (Delhi: Manohar, 2002), 12.

Ali Jinnah's inspirational role in the freedom movement. Among western scholars, Stanley Wolpert provided a sympathetic biography of Jinnah, which attributed him with the single-mindedness and drive to achieve a separate homeland. Yet, Ayesha Jalal, in her revisionist approach, has challenged that very idea and contended that Jinnah's call for a Pakistan was more ambiguous than has been presented.[7]

One of the best-known attempts to document the violence is G. D. Khosla's account which is based on many first-hand accounts of people. It also provides details of atrocities and violent episodes, though largely in West Punjab. J. Nanda also provides a survey of riots that occurred in Punjab and the subsequent rehabilitation of refugees.[8] In Pakistan, there have been a number of government publications that understand the violence against Muslims in East Punjab in terms of a so-called 'Sikh plan'.[9] Saleem Ullah Khan, meanwhile, provides an insightful piece, detailing first-hand accounts of Pakistani refugees.[10] Though this publication, like that of Khosla, has many biases, the combined effect of the two publications at least provides some insight into localised and personal experiences of the frenzied months following partition.

Comparatively, there is much less nationalist writing on the issues of partition's aftermath. Mohinder Singh Randhawa and Bhaskar Rao focus on the epic story of rehabilitation; both were official documents, which portrayed the Indian government's stance and relayed their agenda. Satya Rai in her volume examines the longer term impact of partition, focusing

---

7   C. Khaliquzzaman, *Pathway to Pakistan* (Lahore: Longmans, 1961); C. M. Ali, *The Emergence of Pakistan* (New York: Columbia University Press, 1967); Akbar S. Ahmed, 'The Hero in History: Myth, Media and Realities,' *History Today*, March 1996; Akbar S. Ahmed, *Jinnah, Pakistan and Islamic Identity: The Search for Saladin* (London: Routledge, 1997); Stanley Wolpert, *Jinnah of Pakistan* (Oxford: Oxford University Press, 1984); and Ayesha Jalal, *The Sole Spokesman* (Cambridge: Cambridge University Press, 1985).

8   G. D. Khosla, *Stern Reckoning: A Survey of Events Leading Up to and Following the Partition of India* (New Delhi: Oxford University Press, 1949, reprint 1989); J. Nanda, *Punjab Uprooted: A Survey of the Punjab Riots and Rehabilitation Problems* (Bombay: Hind Kitab, 1948).

9   Government of Pakistan, *Note on the Sikh Plan, The Sikhs in Action*, and *Rashtriya Swayam Sewak Sangh in the Punjab* (Lahore: Government Printing Press, 1948).

10 Saleem Ullah Khan, *The Journey to Pakistan: A Documentation on Refugees of 1947* (Islamabad: National Documentation Centre, 1993).

on the administrative problems encountered in the rehabilitation of displaced persons. The economic consequences of partition have in comparison received little attention, although C. N. Vakil has made a major contribution in this area. More recently, Tan Tai Yong and Gyanesh Kudaisya have attempted to examine the aftermath of partition in their expansive study, which covers India, Pakistan and Bangladesh. Moreover, they examine the transformation of the urban landscapes such as the capital cities.[11]

There have also been a number of personal accounts by British officials. These predominantly focus on the role of figures such as Nehru, Gandhi and Jinnah. A notable exception is provided by the work *At Freedom's Door* by the Indian civil servant Malcolm Darling. He travelled through northern Punjab during 1947, spoke to many villagers and highlighted the anxiety felt by all communities over the imminent departure of British and the ensuing communal carnage that would follow.[12] In the frontline of violence, General Francis Tuker in *While Memory Serves* provided a graphic account of the communal violence during the Bihar riots.[13] Other notable accounts have included Alan Campbell-Johnson's attempt to redeem Mountbatten's role during the events leading to partition. Penderel Moon produced his classic study, *Divide and Quit*, based on his postings in Punjab; in it he questioned whether it was too late for a united India by the time Mountbatten arrived. Sir Conrad Corfield, who was a political advisor to the Viceroy, provided an insider's view of how the princely states responded to British rule and struggled to maintain their individuality. Richard Symonds, who was engaged in relief work in Punjab during the 1947 disturbances, provides a personal account,

---

11 M. S. Randhawa, *Out of the Ashes – An Account of the Rehabilitation of Refugees from West Pakistan in Rural Areas of East Punjab* (Chandigarh: Public Relations Department Punjab, 1954); Bhaskar U. Rao, *The Story of Rehabilitation* (Delhi: Ministry of Labour, Employment and Rehabilitation, 1967); Satya Rai, *Partition of the Punjab: A Study of Its Effects on the Politics and Administration of the Punjab 1947-56* (Bombay: Asia Publishing House, 1965); C. N. Vakil, *Economic Consequences of Divided India: A Study of the Economy of India and Pakistan* (Bombay: Vora & Co. Publishers, 1950); and Tan Tai Yong and Gyanesh Kudaisya, *The Aftermath of Partition in South Asia* (London: Routledge, 2000).

12 Malcolm Darling, *At Freedom's Door* (Oxford: Oxford University Press, 1979), first published 1949, 300–5.

13 General Sir Francis Tuker, *While Memory Serves* (London: Cassell & Co, 1950). Tuker was chief of the Eastern Command at the time of partition. His troops were involved in controlling the riots in Bihar and Calcutta.

which combines insights from 'high politics' with what would now be termed a 'history from beneath' approach.[14]

The main protagonists of independence and mainstay of those focusing on the 'high politics' have also increasingly questioned the role of the leadership. Jalal's 'revisionist' approach examining Jinnah's role has already been mentioned, but ironically, this radical history is now increasingly considered an 'orthodox' account on Jinnah. Mountbatten has also been the subject of debate and controversy. This has arisen from his alleged interference in the partition plan. His influence, which led to the princely state of Kashmir (a Muslim majority state) acceding to India, has also received much attention.[15] Mountbatten's rushed approach to exit India, his bias towards Nehru and his apparent dislike of Jinnah have also been debated.[16] While his supporters see him as someone who was able to overcome constitutional deadlock and oversee the swift transfer of power, his critics hold him responsible for the Punjab massacres.[17] Increasingly over the past seventy years, Indian writers are now much more critical of the founding fathers, Gandhi and Nehru, and more broadly of the Indian independence movement. Following the emergence and the increasing legitimacy of *Hindutva* ideology, Nehru is now openly held responsible for Partition. Writers such as Sucheta Mahajan, however, are more sympathetic and defend Gandhi's and Nehru's position in terms of the limited options that they faced in 1947.[18]

---

14 Alan Campbell-Johnson, *Mission with Mountbatten* (London: Hamish Hamilton, 1985), first published 1951; Penderel Moon, *Divide and Quit* (New Delhi: Oxford University Press, 1998), first published 1961; Conrad Corfield, *The Princely India I Knew: From Reading to Mountbatten* (Madras: Indo British Historical Society, 1975), 15–16; and Richard Symonds, *The Making of Pakistan* (London: Faber and Faber, 1950). Also see further, Richard Symonds, *In the Margins of Independence: A Relief Worker in India and Pakistan, 1942-1949* (Karachi: Oxford University Press, 2001). Symonds also served with the United Nations Commission for India and Pakistan.

15 See further, Shereen Ilahi, 'The Radcliffe Boundary Commission and the Fate of Kashmir,' *India Review* 2, no. 1 (2003): 77–102.

16 Ahmed, *History Today*.

17 Ian Talbot, 'The Mountbatten Viceroyalty Revisited: Themes and Controversies,' in *Mountbatten on the Record*, ed. C. M. Woolgar (Hartley Institute, University of Southampton, 1997), 53–74. Also see Philip Zeigler, *Mountbatten: The Official Biography* (London: Phoenix, 2001).

18 Sucheta Mahajan, *Independence and Partition: The Erosion of Colonial Power in India* (New Delhi: Sage, 2001).

The opening up of the archives was paved by the release of the twelve-volume series, *The Transfer of Power*, which was pivotal for historians to understand the closing chapter of the British in India. The British Prime Minister appointed Nicholas Mansergh the editor-in-chief to oversee the documents from the India Office pertaining to the constitutional transfer of power in India; the twelve volumes remain a treasure of 'high politics'.[19] The availability of Governors' fortnightly reports further encouraged academic attention to shift from the all-India to the provincial level of politics. This coincided with the emergence of the so-called Cambridge School of Indian historiography. They focused on material interests rather than ideas as driving forward politics. Mobilisation was understood in terms of patron–client relations.[20] At the forefront of this shift towards regional politics in the case of Punjab were historians such as Ian Talbot and David Gilmartin.[21] Talbot has highlighted the transformation in the Punjab Muslim League's fortunes in the period from the 1937 to the 1946 provincial elections.[22] This breakthrough was essential for the creation of Pakistan. Other writers more recently, such as Sarah Ansari, have provided valuable insights into political developments in other Muslim majority provinces, in her case Sind, while Joya Chatterji, H. Bhattacharyya, and Taj-ul-Islam Hashmi provide a Bengali perspective.[23]

---

19 Nicholas Mansergh (editor-in-chief), E. W. R. Lumby and P. Moon, (asst. eds.), *Constitutional Relations Between Britain and India: The Transfer of Power 1942-47*, 12 Volumes (London: HMSO, 1970–83).

20 See John Gallagher, Gordon Johnson and Anil Seal, eds., *Locality, Province and Nation: Essays in Indian Politics 1870-1947* (Cambridge: Cambridge University Press, 1973).

21 Ian Talbot, *Punjab and the Raj* (New Delhi: Manohar, 1988); David Gilmartin, *Empire and Islam: Punjab and the Making of Pakistan* (Berkeley: University of California Press, 1988).

22 Ian Talbot, *Provincial Politics and the Pakistan Movement* (Karachi: Oxford University Press, 1988). Also see by the same author, *Khizr Tiwana: The Punjab Unionist Party and Partition of India* (London: Curzon, 1996).

23 Sarah Ansari, *Sufi Saints and State Power: The Pirs of Sind, 1843-1947* (Cambridge: Cambridge University Press, 1992) and 'Partition, Migration and Refugees: Responses to the Arrival of Mohajirs in Sind 1947-8,' *South Asia* XVIII (1995): 95–108; H. Bhattacharyya, 'Post-partition Refugees and the Communists: A Comparative Study of West Bengal and Tripura'; Joya Chatterji, 'The Making of a Borderline: The Radcliffe Award for Bengal'; and Taj-ul-Islam Hashmi, 'Peasant Nationalism and the Politics of Partition: The Class-Communal Symbiosis in East Bengal 1940-7' in Talbot and Singh, *Region and Partition*.

More recently though, scholarly discussion is beginning to explore what may
be considered the peripheries but were nevertheless impacted by the events
of 1947. Thus, there is some interesting work on Assam and the Andaman
Islands.[24]

For both India and Pakistan, it was important to establish an independent
national identity; re-imagining the past and creating a new national history
allowed this new identity to emerge and to reinforce and justify the nascent
nation-state. Thus, the dominance and glorification of the 'great men' such
as Jinnah, Gandhi and Nehru is palpable in the post-independent histories
of India and Pakistan. Despite some important advances in regional studies
as mentioned above, the emphasis has predominately been on why partition
happened, rather than on how it impacted and transformed the lives of ordinary
citizens. Gyanendra Pandey has been particularly critical of this neglect in
historical writing in India, where the 'great man' approach is still dominant.
The blindness to the horrors of partition has also been at the expense of
marginalising these ordinary voices in mainstream history, in which partition
is seen as an event rather than questioning the enormity and widespread
impact this had on the nation-state.[25] The pervasive hold of the national
leadership in shaping perceptions of partition and the relationship between
the British, the Congress and the Muslim League have all contributed to an
obsession with what happened at the top echelons. Moreover, this imbalance
is reflected in the history books,[26] which have for a long time neglected the
heavy price paid by the citizens of the two new nations. This 'curriculum of
hatred' continues to feed religious bigotry on both sides of the border, placing
Hindus and Muslims against each other. Yet, as Mushirul Hasan notes, 'never
before, in South Asian history did so few decide the fate of so many'. For
this reason alone, Nehru, Gandhi, Jinnah and Mountbatten are worthy of
historical interrogation, but conversely, as Hasan continues, 'rarely did so few

---

24   Anindita Dasgupta, 'Remembering Sylhet: A Forgotten Story of India's 1947
     Partition,' *Economic and Political Weekly*, 2 August 2008, 18–22; and Uditi Sen,
     'Dissident Memories: Exploring Bengali Refugee Narratives in the Andaman
     Islands,' in *Refugees and the End of Empire: Imperial Collapse and Forced Migration
     during the Twentieth Century*, eds. Panikos Panayi and Pippa Virdee (Hampshire:
     Palgrave Macmillan, 2011).

25   Veena Das, *Life and Words: Violence and the Descent into the Ordinary* (Berkeley,
     CA: University of California Press, 2006), E-book version, 18.

26   Krishna Kumar, 'Partition in School Textbooks: A Comparative Look at India
     and Pakistan,' in Settar and Gupta, *Pangs of Partition*, 17–28.

ignore the sentiments of so many in the subcontinent...never before in South Asian history did so few divide so many, so needlessly'.[27] Hasan, in this quote, evidently places the burden of responsibility for partition on the 'great men', who needlessly decided to partition India, but in the process it was not just a territorial partition, but also the division of people, emotions and memories.

Writing Fiction

The glaring omission of ordinary voices was filled with the imagination of literature and film. It was fiction that, very early on, provided an outlet to express and share those emotive, traumatic and religiously sensitive subjects that Jalal labels as 'the pity of partition', but too peripheral for mainstream history. Yet, it was the ideal medium for capturing the ambiguities and the shades of grey that could not fit into the overly nationalistic tones. Writers such as Intizar Hussain, Bhisham Sahni, Saadat Hasan Manto, Faiz Ahmed Faiz, Balraj Sahni, Khushwant Singh and Amrita Pritam were writing from their own personal experiences of dislocation and captured the human drama of partition. Manto never shied away from writing about the true depravity of people and he fully exposed the sexual violence associated with partition. As Kamla Bhasin and Ritu Menon argue, 'Partition fiction (and some non-fiction) is almost the only social history we have of this time...it is in fiction, rather than any other genre, that we find an attempt to assimilate the full impact of what Partition meant'.[28] Moreover, they suggest that 'nowhere in the thousands of pages of fiction and poetry do we find even a glimmer of endorsement for the price paid for freedom, or admission that his "*qurbani*" (sacrifice) was necessary for the birth of two nations.'[29]

Although much of fictional writing was done in months and years following partition, it was limited largely within literary circles until writers such as Alok Bhalla published the anthology of partition stories.[30] Bhalla's three-volume anthology has remarkably gathered short stories on partition,

---

27 Mushirul Hasan, ed., *India's Partition: Process, Strategy, Mobilisation* (New Delhi: Oxford University Press, 1993), 42–3.

28 Ritu Menon and Kamla Bhasin, *Borders and Boundaries: Women in India's Partition*, (New Jersey: Rutger University Press, 1998), 22.

29 Bhasin and Menon, *Borders and Boundaries*, 7.

30 Alok Bhalla, ed., *Stories about the Partition of India*, Volume I–III (Delhi: Indus, HarperCollins, 1994).

bringing together writers from different languages to present work which encapsulates and exposes the anger and confusion, the hypocrisy and tragedy of partition.[31] Subsequently, there has been a plethora of translated work in English and also from Urdu to make it accessible in India.[32] There is also now more of an appetite among Punjabi writers to make their work available across the border by publishing in the Gurmukhi/Shahmukhi script.[33]

The universal suffering, the physical and psychological scars, the violent realities, the painful misery of brutalising women's bodies and the disillusionment of the new states are themes which could be explored through fiction without directly challenging the fragile new states. The trauma associated with the partition and displacement is something that both the states of India and Pakistan have shied away from, because this became the necessary price of freedom and separation. For historians, such as Hasan, it is important to emphasise 'the centrality of literary narratives and the role of memory in a historian's attempts to write partition's history from the margins'.[34] Hasan's work, *India Partitioned: The Other Face of Freedom*, published in 1995 remains an important volume in bringing to the fore the literature that has come to be associated with Partition Studies.

Writing New Histories

During the 1980s, a new historiographical school had started to emerge, focusing primarily on narratives that were previously unheard of and silenced. Influenced by Marxism, writers such as Ranajit Guha pioneered the study of Indian history 'from below'.[35] The Subaltern Studies School, as they came to be known, sought to provide an 'alternative' history, away from the populist

31 See further, Jason Francisco and Alok Bhalla, "'Stories on the Partition of India" – A Review Essay,' *Annual of Urdu Studies* X (1995): 208–17.

32 To read further see, for example, Ian Talbot, 'Literature and the Human Drama of the 1947 Partition,' in *Freedom, Trauma, Continuities: Northern India and Independence*, eds. D. A. Low and Howard Brasted (Delhi: Sage Publications, 1998), 39–55.

33 Nirupuma Dutt, ed. and translation, *Stories of the Soil: Classic Punjabi Stories* (India: Penguin, 2010).

34 Sudha Tiwari, 'Memories of Partition: Revisiting Saadat Hasan Manto,' *Economic and Political Weekly* XLVIII, no 25 (2013): 50–1.

35 Ranajit Guha, ed., *Subaltern Studies 1: Writings on South Asian History and Society* (Delhi: Oxford University Press, 1982).

nationalist struggle that was being depicted.[36] They highlighted the role played by popular peasant movements in contrast to the nationalist struggle, which they argued touched only the middle classes and those with political influence. The Subaltern School historians essentially sought to redress the imbalance present in nationalist historiography. Their attempts represented a return to the grass roots and the depiction of politics of the people, who were neither distinguished public figures nor acclaimed freedom fighters, but who did, nevertheless, make a contribution to the nationalist struggle. Most of this writing, however, was limited to the 1920s and 1930s and was criticised for its reliance on the same 'colonialist' sources as those deployed by the 'elitist' nationalist accounts.

By the early 1990s, the impact of this approach started to permeate Partition Studies and resulted in a shift away from the 'great men of history' approach towards a 'history from below'; Regional Studies had already shifted the focus from national to regional politics.[37] Crucially, this approach towards cities has disrupted the concern with the centrality of the nation-state. Works such as Zamindar's,[38] which bring together through personal narratives the story of families divided by partition in Delhi and Karachi, or Talbot's work on the divided twin cities of Amritsar and Lahore travel across and bypass the territorial borders. Similarly, Ravinder Kaur's work on Delhi, my work on Ludhiana and Lyallpur, and Ilyas Chattha's work on Gujranwala and Sialkot

---

36 The term 'subaltern' has been adapted by post-colonial studies from the work originally done by Antonio Gramsci. The Subaltern Studies group were interested in exploring themes such as class, caste and gender. The group was started by Ranajit Guha and at inception included other historians such as Shahid Amin, Gyanendra Pandey, David Arnold, David Hardiman and Partha Chatterjee. Several influential volumes emerged during the 1980s covering inter-disciplinary themes. The following is a small selection of subaltern literature: Ranajit Guha, ed., *Subaltern Studies* (5 vols.) (New Delhi: Oxford University Press); Shahid Amin, *Event, Metaphor, Memory: Chauri Chaura, 1922-1992* (Berkeley, CA: University of California Press, 1995); David Arnold, 'Gramsci and Peasant Subalternity in India,' *Journal of Peasant Studies* 11, no. 4 (1984): 155-77; David Hardiman, '"Subaltern Studies" at Crossroads,' *Economic and Political Weekly*, 15 February 1986, 288–90; and Partha Chatterjee and Gyanendra Pandey, eds., *Subaltern Studies VII* (New Delhi: Oxford University Press, 1992).

37 For example, see Ian Talbot, *Divided Cities: Partition and Its Aftermath in Lahore and Amritsar 1947-1957* (Karachi: Oxford University Press, 2006).

38 Vazira Fazila-Yacoobali Zamindar, *The Long Partition and the Making of Modern South Asia: Refugees, Boundaries, Histories* (India: Penguin, 2007).

present micro-histories of meta-narratives.[39] More recently, Ananya Jahanara Kabir has interestingly merged inter-generational personal accounts with the political ruptures of 1947 and 1971 that transcend multiple locations.[40] The work of visual artists is rarely acknowledged in history but with the passing of fifty years, a number of rich and engaging work emerged. Nalini Malani's *Remembering Toba Tek Singh* and Amar Kanwar's *A Season Outside* show artists working across borders in India and Pakistan and an attempt to re-examine partition history. The Lines of Control project, which began in 2005, brought together several artists, curators, film-makers and historians to investigate notions of lines and boundaries vis-à-vis partition in India and Pakistan.[41]

However, it is the social activists and feminist writers that pushed the agenda into probing a more hidden and traumatic past within history. A key catalyst for this was the chilling similarities between partition violence and the anti-Sikh riots in Delhi that followed the assassination of Indira Gandhi in 1984. Second, and more importantly, the golden jubilee of independence encouraged a reassessment of partition. This was marked with many special publications and it presented an opportunity for introspective and reflective writing that was able to deal with the horrors and violence that accompanied independence. Previously, scholars have shied away from this darker side of partition, but with a new generation of writers, taboo subjects such as violence, rape and abduction were now at last being talked about. Over-layer this with class boundaries,[42] and what emerges is a differential migrant experience and the conflict between the state and individuals. This was visibly discernible in how the process of state construction and legitimisation involved the forcible repatriation of abducted female migrants.[43]

---

39   Ravinder Kaur, *Since 1947: Partition Narratives among Punjabi Migrants of Delhi* (Delhi: Oxford University Press, 2007); Pippa Virdee, 'Partition in Transition: Comparative Analysis of Migration in Ludhiana and Lyallpur,' in *Partitioned Lives: Narratives of Home, Displacement and Resettlement*, eds. Anjali Gera Roy and Nandi Bhatia (Delhi, Pearson, 2007); and Ilyas Chattha, *Violence, Migration, and Development in Gujranwal and Sialkot 1947-1961* (Karachi: Oxford University Press, 2011).

40   Ananya Jahanara Kabir, *Partition's Post-Amnesias: 1947, 1971 and Modern South Asia* (India: Women Unlimited, 2013).

41   Iftikhar Dadi and Hammad Nasar, eds., *Lines of Control: Partition as a Productive Space* (USA: Green Cardamom, 2012).

42   For a discussion on class, see Ravinder Kaur, 'The Last Journey: Exploring Social Class in the 1947 Partition Migration,' *Economic and Political Weekly* 41 (2006): 2221–8.

43   For a discussion on forcible repatriation, see Menon and Bhasin, *Borders and Boundaries*.

Interestingly, in Europe at the same time was the ongoing debate about ethnic cleansing, genocide and war crimes against women in Bosnia. In this case, 'feminist activists made a concerted effort to affect the statute establishing the International Criminal Tribunal for the Former Yugoslavia, the rules of evidence under which rape and other crimes of sexual violence would be prosecuted…'.[44] There was now a wider discussion about the use of mass rape against women in conflicts; indeed Menon and Bhasin note the similarities of the accounts of violence against women in Bosnia and Herzegovina with the partition violence.[45] In both these cases, women are the upholders of community honour and are then tainted by the 'other' and forced to take on the burden of dishonouring the community. Writers such as Menon, Bhasin,[46] Butalia[47] and Das[48] have all led the way in opening the discussion in India about communal violence and its relationship with women and in doing so have made significant contributions to this new history of partition.

Significantly, they have sought to foreground the 'victims' of partition and provide them with a 'voice' by utilising oral narratives as a means of communicating their histories. Surprisingly, personal accounts and experiences of people who witnessed partition first-hand have hardly featured, except from the one-sided accounts by Khosla and Khan.[49] More empathetic and broader experiences have only emerged in the past twenty years which have been far more critical and introspective in understanding the human plight.

What is distinctly noticeable in the 'new history' of partition is that it is largely, though not exclusively, female writers and scholars who have embraced

---

44 Karen Engle, 'Feminism and Its (Dis)contents: Criminalizing Wartime Rape in Bosnia and Herzegovina,' *The American Journal of International Law* 99, no. 4 (October 2005): 778.

45 Menon and Bhasin, *Borders and Boundaries*, 63, ff. 34.

46 Menon and Bhasin, *Borders and Boundaries* and also see Ritu Menon and Kamala Bhasin, 'Recovery, Rapture, Resistance: The Indian State and the Abduction of Women during Partition,' *Economic and Political Weekly* 28, no. 17 (24 April 1993): 2–11.

47 Urvashi Butalia, *The Other Side of Silence: Voices from the Partition of India* (New Delhi: Penguin, 1998).

48 Veena Das, ed., *Mirrors of Violence: Communities, Riots and Survivors in South Asia* (Oxford: Oxford University Press, 1990).

49 Khosla, *Stern Reckoning* and Khan, *Journey to Pakistan*.

this agenda, particularly through the use of oral history.[50] It is perhaps the sensitive and emotive nature of the subject and the attempt to capture life stories and the human dimension that lends itself more easily to the female gaze. More importantly, it has been an active assertion by a new generation of writers to re-orientate our focus and understanding of partition. The feminist embrace of oral history emerged from the neglect of women's voices in traditional sources; oral history has therefore provided an opportunity to integrate 'women into historical scholarship, even contesting the reigning definitions of social, economic and political importance that obscured women's lives'.[51] The centrality of gendered accounts in historical discourse is an important development in recognising and challenging the dominant tendencies in the discipline. In this way, the new developments have brought a welcome shift. More broadly, these accounts have challenged the conventional histories, which marginalised women and other subaltern groups, although as Butalia has argued many of the proponents of the Subaltern Studies saw her as an 'interloper' within the discipline.[52] Paola Bacchetta goes further and suggests that these accounts 'reflect a different kind of subaltern writing that inadvertently challenges almost-established subaltern writing, which…continues to marginalise women'.[53]

Sheila Rowbotham's contention is that women's experiences in historical discourse were often 'hidden' and new methodologies, such as personal testimonies, allow us to challenge 'historical interpretations based upon the lives and documentation of men'.[54] Feminist interpretations that have focused on the plight of women and other marginalised groups, often on the periphery of Indian society, have enabled this reappraisal in partition discourse. It has brought the experiences of women during this traumatic time to the fore and

---

50 For recent example, see Devika Chawla, *Home Uprooted: Oral Histories of India's Partition* (New York: Fordham University Press, 2014); and Anam Zakaria, *The Footprints of Partition* (India: HarperCollins, 2015).

51 Joan Sangster, 'Telling Our Stories: Feminist Debates and the Use of Oral History,' in *The Oral History Reader*, eds. Robert Perks and Alistair Thomson (London: Routledge, 1998), 87.

52 Gayatri Chakravorty Spivak in conversation with Sanjay Subrahmanyam and Urvashi Butalia. *Rewriting History – Writers of India*, accessed 13 June 2017 https://www.youtube.com/watch?v=bjwEujsZyOk.

53 Paola Bacchetta, 'Reinterrogating Partition Violence: Voices of Women/Children/Dalits in India's Partition,' *Feminist Studies* 26, no. 3 (Fall 2000): 567-85.

54 Sheila Rowbotham, *Hidden from History* (London: Pluto, 1973). Also see Sangster, 'Telling Our Stories,' 87–100.

begun to expose the harsh realities of sensitive and taboo subjects such as abduction, rape and violence against women in a predominately patriarchal state and society. Until recently, these subjects remained hidden from public discourse. Although wider feminist discourse has been well developed in pre-partition India, and then also in independent India and Pakistan, partition-related violence against women has remained largely in the shadows of nationalist and political discourse. It has been triumphant and, what I would argue, masculine in its approach rather than dealing with the realities that exposed the brutal, patronising and domineering nature of the state.

There are two distinct features about this 'new history' of partition. First, it has a predominately Indian-centric approach and comparatively little has been written about women in Pakistan (and Bengal). Nighat Said Khan, a Lahore-based activist, conducted some interviews with women, largely in Sindh, but the interviews remain unpublished.[55] More recently, my research has attempted to bridge this significant gap in documenting the experiences of partition and resettlement of women in Pakistani Punjab, especially in terms of how this is recorded in public and private spaces.[56] Second, most of the work so far has attempted to document the plight of Punjabis (including this work). Although the region, it can be argued, suffered the worst of the atrocities, within wider partition historiography, the research is geographically limited. There is of course more work emerging on Bengal and Yasmin Saikia has also been exploring the impact of the 1972 war in Bangladesh on women.[57] But in addition to these accounts, there remain many unexplored histories of lesser known experiences of the upheaval caused by partition and independence. Even Ishtiaq Ahmed's claim at producing the most comprehensive volume on partition largely neglects the new feminist agenda that has re-orientated recent discourse.[58]

Living Histories

The use of oral history in the study of partition has been embraced in recent scholarly work because it has enabled us to understand the impact partition

---

55 N. S. Khan, R. Saigol and A. S. Zia, *Locating the Self: Perspectives on Women and Multiple Identities* (Lahore: ASR, 1994).

56 Pippa Virdee, 'Negotiating the Past: Journey through Muslim Women's Experience of Partition and Resettlement,' *Cultural and Social History* 6, no. 4 (2009).

57 Yasmin Saikia, *Women, War, and the Making of Bangladesh: Remembering 1971* (Durham, NC: Duke University Press, 2011).

58 Ishtiaq Ahmed, *The Punjab Bloodied, Partitioned and Cleansed* (Karachi: Oxford University Press, 2012).

had on everyday life;[59] this is absent in the official records and provides an alternative through which the lived experience can be understood. The use of oral testimonies thus becomes an important source of information as well as allowing us to understand the perceptions and lived experiences of ordinary people. Moreover, as women's voices are often peripheral, oral history has become even more important as it can empower those muted voices that would otherwise remain undocumented.

However, documenting, recording and recounting these stories also presents the researcher with ethical dilemmas. In a recent discussion with Gayatri Chakravorty Spivak, Butalia noted how she went into the research on partition as a feminist and wanted to liberate these women and their silences, but in the process realised the importance of silences. There was thus a great burden in terms of the ethics and responsibility of doing this work.[60] Das also very powerfully questions the complexity and moral dilemma in conducting such research, particularly when we look at them in isolation without understanding the evolutionary discourse that has taken place:

> It is often considered the task of historiography to break the silences that announce the zones of taboo. There is even something heroic in the image of empowering women to speak and to give voice to the voiceless. I have myself found this a very complicated task, for when we use such imagery as breaking the silence, we may end by using our capacity to 'unearth' hidden facts as a weapon. Even the idea that we should recover the narratives of violence becomes problematic when we realize that such narratives cannot be told unless we see the relation between pain and language that a culture has evolved.[61]

Furthermore, this interaction and the interview process itself also create a new historical document 'by the agency of *both* the interviewer and the interviewee'.[62] The interview process is therefore much more complex, one in which the interviewer has an agenda to document an untold story and the interviewees share their particular experience or story. Bornat argues that 'for the oral historians the interview is always more than the recorded and

---

59   Ian Talbot and Darshan Singh Tatla, *Epicentre of Violence* (Delhi: Permanent Black, 2006); Kaur, *Since 1947*; and Ahmed, *The Punjab Bloodied*.
60   Spivak, *Rewriting History*.
61   Das, *Life and Words*, 57.
62   Sangster, 'Telling Our Stories,' 92.

transcribed words, it is a process in which the narrator, the interviewee, is actively constructing and creating an account'.[63] There is also in many ways a power imbalance between the two agents; it is ultimately the interviewer who has the ability to interpret, recount and analyse the interview before narrating it and the interviewee has no power or control over this process. This new approach has enabled historians to broaden what history is about and in many ways, it has democratised history and enabled 'hidden voices' to be incorporated into our wider understanding of society.[64] There is, however, still a dilemma about the use of these accounts and the radical potential of oral history to reclaim the history of ordinary people. Joan Sangster forces us to question the impact of the feminists discourse which 'hoped to use oral history to empower women by creating a revised history "*for* women"' and to what extent this is overstated. She questions - are 'we exaggerating the radical potential of oral history, especially the likelihood of academic work changing popular attitudes?...are we ignoring the uncomfortable ethical issues involved in using living people as a source for our research?'[65] As an oral historian, this is one of the challenges of working with living history. The radical nature, of course, comes from providing space for alternative histories to exist and challenge the status quo. It is these voices that I have attempted to capture, those nuances and fragilities of the human which often get erased in the meta-narratives. Afzal Tauseef was a Punjabi writer and journalist based in Lahore. I spoke with her in 2007 and below is a small extract of the interview in which she is trying to make sense of Partition. Much of what she was articulating has to do with her own experiences and memories, shaped both by the 'event' and subsequently by the 'experience' of living in Pakistan.

> [What made you write about the partition of Punjab?] For me it is different because I am the one who keeps on recalling, keep on thinking about it, keep on questioning everyone I meet and keep on shaking the Punjabi minds about what happened. Why did it happen? Keeping aside the question of 'what happened', more important is that 'why did it come about'. Why did they let it happen? Who did that? Who let it happen? There is no end to my questions, no end. I have seen three generations and this third generation

---

63 Joanna Bornat, Leroi Henry and Parvati Raghuram, '"Don't Mix Race with the Speciality": Interviewing South Asian Overseas-Trained Geriatricians,' *Oral History* 37, no. 1 (2009): 82.

64 Joanna Bornat, 'Oral History as a Social Movement: Reminiscence and Older People,' in Perks and Thompson, 1998, 190.

65 Sangster, 'Telling Our Stories,' 92.

is going towards its end. It was the first generation before mine that got hit directly, second generation was the young ones of that time which was hit badly as well, the child of that age got shattered, what is left is 'we people'. In that way, I have seen three generations suffering, crying, sighing, dying, bleeding, getting lost in memories and feeling homeless. Krishan Chandar was the first to announce 'I have no land' and being disowned by my country, now I am an international citizen. I had been conversing with different people as and when I get any opportunity but nobody has any root cause for the division. I gathered different opinions, amongst them one is from a major intelligentsia that it simply happened because Punjab did not have any leadership. Right, we understand, that means whenever we do not have the leadership we can be exploited at any time by anyone in any way, only for the reason that we do not have any mouth piece to express our point of view. Then what were the causes for not having leadership in Punjab whereas all the major movements, resistance movement, progressive movement, revolutionary and independence movement, were going on. They had deep roots in this soil.[66]

As we approach towards seventy years since decolonisation/independence/ partition (perspectives vary), there are still many unexplored and unanswered areas. Tauseef, who sadly passed away in 2014, had many questions which remain largely unanswered in her mind. She is representative of those many silent voices which moved across new boundaries but could not understand the personal and collective loss paid by millions for this new boundary. By having a more rounded approach towards history, perhaps, we can better understand the complexities surrounding partition. The connections between memory and history are important in appreciating the lived reality of what partition meant for people like Tauseef, especially when the vision sold by the 'great men' failed to deliver the promises made. Although historians, such as Jalal, are critical of the intrusion of Memory Studies into History, especially in terms of how we understand partition,[67] the focus and dominance of 'high-politics' is no longer justified because it neglects the vast changes that have taken place. It forces people to remain focused on the idea of the nation, nationhood, political and religious identities and therefore confines our discussion and understanding. There is a need to move away from this dominant discourse towards a more nuanced, empathetic and localised (micro) history to understand these all-encompassing events.

---

66   Interview with Afzal Tauseef, Lahore, April 2007.
67   Ayesha Jalal, *The Pity of Partition* (India: HarperCollins, 2013), 13, 86–8.

Firoz Din Sharaf

Punjab[1]

Among beautiful lands, Punjab is the most beautiful, friends!
Among flowers, Punjab is a rose, friends!
In the garden, girls swaying on swings like creeping vines.
Freshness of youth surging, jewels sparkling.
Bedecked in diamonds and pearls, with moon like faces, friends.
Among beautiful lands, Punjab is the most beautiful, friends!

Gathering at the spinning session, young girls twirl the *charkha*.[2]
They create beautiful thread with delicate arms outstretched.
Hearts afire, wine coloured lips, friends.
Among beautiful lands, Punjab is the most beautiful, friends!

Rivers bring beauty and fertility to the landscape.
'Sharaf'[3] says, Punjabis walk delicately upon their land.
Of Satluj, Ravi, Jhelum, Indus, Chenab,[4] friends.
Among beautiful lands, Punjab is the most beautiful, friends!

---

1   Firoz Din 'Sharaf', *Joganh* (1932), Trans. Ami P. Shah, *Journal of Punjab Studies* 13, nos. 1 and 2 (2006): 5.
2   Spinning wheel.
3   The insertion of the poet's signature (*takhallas*) is a common feature of Indian poetry.
4   The five rivers of Punjab.

The Treasure within the Five Rivers

The Land and the People

The historic region of the Punjab dominates the north-western portion of the contemporary subcontinent. It is divided into the province of Punjab in Pakistan and the states of Punjab, Haryana and Himachal Pradesh in India. The region itself has many natural boundaries, with the Himalayas in the north, the Rajputana Desert in the south of the Indian Punjab (hereafter East Punjab), and the Cholistan Desert in the south-east of Pakistan Punjab (hereafter West Punjab) leading to the international boundary with India. The region takes its name from the five rivers that join to form the mighty Indus,[1] which flows from the Kashmir region right through the heart of Punjab and into the Arabian Sea. It is therefore often referred to as 'the land of five rivers' – Punjab is derived from the Persian words of *Punj* (five) and *aab* (water). The melting snow from the bordering mountain range and heavy summer rainfall from the monsoon provide the water for the five great rivers.

These five great rivers have dominated the geography, inspired literature, fed the people of this fertile land and, within their flows, carried the tales of love and poetry that feed the emotional and aesthetic needs of the people. Like the land, the rivers were also divided and since partition, only the Sutlej and the Beas flow through East Punjab, while West Punjab has the five rivers flowing through the province, namely the Jhelum, the Chenab, the Ravi and the Sutlej, all tributaries of the Indus.[2] Historically the rivers of Punjab have played an important part in the development of the region under colonial rule[3] and form the backbone of the region.

As a region, Punjab has been home to the first known Indian civilisation in Harappa and many other empires. Punjab formed the main invasion

---

1   Sindhu is the earlier name in Sanskrit in Vedic culture; it is thought to provide the name for both the Indus River and Hinduism.

2   For an in-depth analysis of the geography of the Punjab, see G. S. Gosal, 'Physical Geography of the Punjab,' *Journal of Punjab Studies* 11, no. 1 (2004): 19–37 (Special Issue on Geography of Punjab).

3   Ian Talbot, *Punjab and the Raj* (Delhi: Manohar, 1988), 11.

Map 2.1: The Land of Five Rivers

route to the Indus plains. Consequently, the people of Punjab are mainly descendants of Aryan tribes that invaded India from the north-west.[4] This led to an assimilation of different tribes and many of the great Punjabi castes such as the *Jats* and *Rajputs* are a product of the movements and amalgamation of Iranians, Turks, Afghans, Arabs and the indigenous population. As Malcolm Darling observed while travelling through Punjab just prior to independence:

> In crossing the Chenab we entered the central Punjab, where Muslim and Sikh are as intermingled as barley and wheat when sown together, where

---

4 Aryan is a linguistic term indicating a speaker of one of the Indo-European languages; however, it tends to be used as an ethnic term. Romila Thapar, *A History of India Vol. 1* (New Delhi: Penguin, 1966), 27.

too the Muslim is for the most part a converted Hindu. There are many villages where Muslim and Sikh are of the same tribe, and both of Hindu ancestry, with still some customs in common...The Naib-Tehsildar, a Hindu, joining in, said: 'The zaildar and I are of the same tribe. He is a Bhatti, and I am a Bhatia; our origin is the same.'[5]

Punjabi is the primary language in the region, which is an Indo-European (or Aryan) language and has some similarity with Hindi and Urdu. More popularly, Punjabi is known as the language of the Sikhs primarily because it was given its own script, *Gurmukhi*, by the second Sikh guru, Guru Angad Dev (1504–52). In East Punjab, Punjabi is the state language, while in West Punjab, it is confined largely to being an informal language with no official status despite being spoken by the majority of people. Being a phonetic language, Punjabi is written largely in three different scripts: the Persian script (sometimes referred to as *Shahmukhi*) is used mostly in Pakistan; Hindu Punjabis are associated with the *Devanagri* script; and Sikhs use the *Gurmukhi* script. As discussed in the final chapter, the division of Punjab has also led to the division of language along communal lines, emanating from the colonial period and permeating into the post-colonial. There is, however, a strong culture of oral literature in Punjab and for this reason, it seems that the different 'religious' scripts of the language have not created any barriers. Problems largely emerged when the language became more politicised, particularly in the colonial period; prior to that, Persian would be been the first choice for written Punjabi for everyone; yet this is itself a legacy of first the Mughals and then later the British, who did not recognise Punjabi as the court language for the province.[6]

Prior to partition, more Muslims lived in the areas comprising West Punjab than in East Punjab, though not exclusively. Today, West Punjab is overwhelmingly Muslim, while East Punjab has a majority Sikh population and a sizeable Hindu population and a significant minority of Muslims and Christians. Within this diversity, it is important to remember that before 1947 greater Punjab included the Punjabis of Haryana and the Hill States of Himachal Pradesh; areas which easily get overlooked in contemporary East Punjab and Hindu India. This is a crude way of looking at Punjab because, beyond religion, the people of Punjab share many cultural values. Many

---

5   Malcolm Darling, with Introduction by Ian Talbot, *At Freedom's Door* (Oxford: Oxford University Press, 2011), 69.

6   See further, Farina Mir, *The Social Space of Language: Vernacular Culture in British Colonial Punjab* (Berkeley: University of California Press, 2010).

Map 2.2: Punjab and Bengal in Undivided India

Muslims, Christians and Sikhs trace their ancestry back to a Hindu lineage; indeed conversions were necessary for new religions to take root in the land. Language was a crucial factor in this heritage; it has been a key feature that has helped to connect people. Punjabi writers such as Waris Shah and Sufi poets like Bulleh Shah and Baba Farid,[7] have managed to transcend religious boundaries.[8] The mystical experience of Sufism, Surinder Singh and Ishwar Dayal Gaur suggest, is due to Punjab's 'frontier location and a long tradition of non-conformism' which has made the region 'a fertile cultural soil' that embraced Islamic mysticism.[9] Further, the folk music of Punjab is another

---

7   This is the expression of mysticism within Islam. The Sufi believe in a mystical union between the individual soul and the Supreme Being. Sufi poetry is often the expression of divine love and mystical union directly between the individual and God.

8   Ian Talbot, *Khizr Tiwana: The Punjab Unionist Party and Partition of India* (London: Curzon, 1996), 5.

9   Surinder Singh and Ishwar Dayal Gaur, eds., *Sufism in Punjab: Mystics, Literature and Shrines* (Delhi: Aakar Books, 2009), 1.

composite tradition, binding generations of Punjabis together through the heroic tales of Dulla Bhatti or the tragic romances of Mirza Sahiban, Heer Ranjha, Sohni Mahiwal and Sassi Punnu.[10]

Gateway to India

For thousands of years, the region of Punjab has been the route of many invasions and has been the site of numerous empires. That history is represented in the diversity of people and influences that have come to shape this land of five rivers.

> ...this is the original home of the Gypsies, Ods and Sadhs, the Gurjars, Ahirs and Khatris; here came Skylax, Alexander, Huen Tsang and Fa Hien. Here we saw past the pageant of Aryanism, Zoroastrianism, Hellenism, Buddhism, Islam, Sikhism. How did this land fare under each contact, under each cataclysm, under each fresh revolution in thought and deed? How in its blood and brain it received and integrated something of Greece, Persia, China and Tibet, Arabia, Egypt, Central and Western India?[11]

The Aryans came via the Hindu Kush, perhaps from Central Asia, as semi-nomadic pastoralists living mainly on the produce of cattle. They spoke an earlier common version language belonging to Indo-European family. Romila Thapar views their coming as a backward step, as the Harappan culture had been more advanced, while the Aryan's were pre-urban.[12] The ancient Indus Valley Civilisation (or Harappa) developed in the Punjab region *c.* 2300 BC while the Aryans who arrived in the region *c.* 1500 BC introduced the Vedic religion and Sanskrit.[13] The *Rig Veda* and the *Upanishads,* which belonged to the Vedic religion, were a precursor of Hinduism, both of which were composed in Punjab. The great Hindu epic of *Ramayana* was also believed to be composed near the city of Amritsar. At Kurukshetra, in present-day

---

10   See further three volumes by R. C. Temple, *The Legends of Punjab* (Patiala: Language Department, Patiala, 1963 [original 1884]); and Sohinder Singh Bedi, *Folklore of the Punjab* (India: National Book Trust, 1971).

11   Mohan Singh, *A History of Panjabi Literature (1100–1932)* (Amritsar: Kasturi Lal & Sons, 1956), 2.

12   Thapar, *History of India,* 34.

13   This was the most extensive of the ancient civilisations which developed in the Indus plain (Punjab and Sind). It was a city culture and evidence of early civilisations is found on the ancient sites of Mohenjodaro and Harappa, now in Pakistan. Thapar, *History of India,* 24.

Haryana, Lord Krishna gave his famous message from the *Bhagavad Gita* to Arjuna before the great battle between the Pandavas and the Kauravas.[14] The region thus possesses an association with some of the most defining periods in ancient Indian history.

As North India became increasingly identified with foreign conquests, it strengthened the links with Central Asia, not only bringing trade benefits but increasingly bringing the people closer together. Running like an artery through Punjab, the Grand Trunk Road lay at the heart of this trade and conquest.[15] Rudyard Kipling describes it as 'the Great Road which is the backbone of all Hind'. He writes:

> All castes and kinds of men move here. Look! Brahmins and chumars, bankers and tinkers, barbers and bunnias, pilgrims and potters – all the world going and coming. It is to me as a river from which I am withdrawn like a log after a flood. And truly the Grand Trunk Road is a wonderful spectacle. It runs straight, bearing without crowding India's traffic for fifteen hundred miles – such a river of life as nowhere else exists in the world.[16]

The Mughals used the Grand Trunk route of the Khyber Pass and into the mountainous Hindu Kush taking them into the vast empire that reigned over India from the sixteenth century onwards until the exile of Bahadur Shah Zafar by the British following the mutiny in 1857. Islam, however, first arrived in Sind in AD 711, when Muhammad bin Qasim took several towns and an Arab army arrived via Afghanistan. Later Mahmud of Ghazni subjected Punjab to regular raids and defeats for twenty-five years, often destroying local Hindu states and

---

14   The central theme in the Mahabharata revolves around a power between two families: the Kauravas and their blood relatives the Pandavas. The most important piece within the Mahabharata is the Bhagavad Gita (Sanskrit poem, considered to be the most important religious text by Hindus) which is a dialogue between Lord Krishna and Arjuna. The conversation takes place before the famous battle at Kurukshetra and is centred around the meaning of life. The Mahabharata was composed around 300 BC and forms an essential part of Hinduism.

15   Irna Qureshi and Tim Smith, *The Grand Trunk Road: From Delhi to the Khyber Pass* (Stockport: Dewi Lewis Publishing, 2011), provide an interesting photo-journal look at the Grand Trunk Road, which incidentally also covers the areas from which the majority of South Asian diaspora originate from. Also see Anthony Weller, *Days and Nights on the Grand Trunk Road* (New York: Marlowe & Co, 1997).

16   Rudyard Kim, *Kim* (Oxford: Oxford University Press, 1987), 57.

converting people. But it was not until the Mughals established their power that Islam really took root in the region.[17] Babur, a descendant of Timur and Genghis Khan, came first with his march across Punjab to take Lahore in 1524. Two years later, the Battle of Panipat,[18] in present-day Haryana, confirmed Mughal control of India. This resulted in nearly 200 years of Mughal rule in Punjab ending with Aurangzeb in 1707. During this period the Punjab region changed considerably, including the advent of a new religion.[19]

Guru Nanak (1469–1538), born in Talwandi and died in Kartarpur, both in present-day West Punjab, preached a new type of religion. It was partly born out of the Bhakti movement,[20] and essentially rejected the rigidity and compartmentalisation that both Islam and Hinduism preached. It found resonance with people and thus established a following, which eventually developed into Sikhism. The growth of the Sikh faith was set in the backdrop of the rise of the Mughal Empire. The increasing intolerance preached by the last great emperor Aurangzeb is intrinsically linked to the move towards violent confrontation between the Sikhs and Muslims. It culminated with the battles between the last Sikh Guru, Guru Gobind Singh (1666–1708), and Aurangzeb (1618–1707) in the seventeenth century. During the chaotic and confused period that followed the death of Aurangzeb, Punjab witnessed the decline of Mughal influence and the rise of the Sikhs as strong contenders for political dominance.

---

17   To read further about the Mughal period, see Satish Chandra, *Essays on Medieval India History* (New Delhi: Oxford University Press, 2003); and M. Athar Ali, *Mughal India: Studies in Polity, Ideas, Society, and Culture* (New Delhi: Oxford University Press, 2006).

18   Panipat is 85 km north-west of Delhi and is close to the area where the great war in the Mahabharata took place. Babur also defeated the forces of Ibrahim Lodi at Panipat.

19   For good understanding of medieval Punjab, read Ishwar Dayal Gaur, *Society, Religion and Patriarchy: Exploring Medieval Punjab through Hir Waris* (Delhi: Manohar, 2009).

20   The Bhakti movement spread throughout the subcontinent from *c.* sixth to sixteenth centuries. There were many strands to it, but saints such as Nanak and Kabir were critical of the dominance of Brahmanical ritualism, formality and exclusivity. There are two main perspectives on Sikhism: first the 'Syncretic' view, which sees Sikhism being influenced by external factors such as Arabic, Farsi and Guru Nanak's contemporaries such as Kabir and Namdev. Second, there are those who view Sikhism as an independent and separate religion with little in common with either Hinduism or Islam.

Though the Sikh religion had grown considerably since the days of Guru Nanak, it was still a minority community. Under the leadership of Guru Gobind Singh, it had acquired a more militant and aggressive character. This was to inject a sense of heroic pride in the small community that later led to the emergence of the young leader, Ranjit Singh (1780–1839), in 1801.[21] Under his reign the Kingdom of Punjab flourished, which gradually extended to include parts of Afghanistan and Kashmir. Ranjit Singh had ruled in the name of the *Khalsa*[22] and was personally a devout Sikh, yet tolerant and encompassing of the ground realities.[23] His death in 1839, however, created a power vacuum, and the factionalism among the Sikh chieftains and the omnipresence of the expansionist British power led to the two Anglo-Sikh Wars of 1845–46 and 1848–49. Finally, the kingdom of Ranjit Singh collapsed and independent Punjab was annexed by the British in 1849.

Importantly, Punjab was the last region of the Indian subcontinent to fall to the British Empire. Equally interesting is that the British did not come into the region in the traditional fashion of invading from the north-west via Afghanistan. Instead, they gradually made way into the country from their modest beginnings as traders in Bengal. The Sikhs had an established army, whose strength was clearly visible during the two Sikh wars with the British.[24] The Battle of Chillianwala (district Mandi Bahauddin in Pakistan) was fought during the Second Anglo-Sikh War and proved to be one of the bloodiest. The British East India Company suffered a considerable blow, both in numbers and in the long term to its prestige as a superior force. At the time, both armies claimed victory but ultimately the British army reigned over Punjab. Shortly afterwards, the Sikh army was utilised when irregular Muslim and Sikh forces assisted the British in suppressing the uprising in 1857, when the *sepoys* of Bengal army revolted. After the mutiny, the British government

---

21 In 1801, Ranjit Singh was formally proclaimed Maharaja in Lahore. He continued to expand his kingdom beyond the borders of the Punjab and in 1809, he signed a treaty of friendship with the British representative Charles Metcalfe.

22 This is the collective term for the Sikh community. During the festival of Baisaki 1699, Guru Gobind Singh inaugurated the *Khalsa*. The *Panj pyare* (five men representing the pure, casteless community) put themselves forward for sacrifice and were in turn baptised, then the Guru was baptised by them.

23 To read further on Ranjit Singh, see J. S. Grewal, *The Sikhs of the Punjab* (New Delhi: Foundation Books, 1999), 99–127.

24 For further details on the role of the Indian Army and Punjab, see Rajit Mazumder, *The Indian Army and the Making of Punjab* (Delhi: Permanent Black, 2003).

assumed direct control of India from the East India Company; it was to mark a new stage in formal empire in India.

The mutiny was a watershed in many respects; and for the Punjabis, this meant a greater role in the British administration and significantly, in the British Indian Army. Punjab was important not just because it was a frontier state, adjoining Afghanistan, but also due to the potential economic benefits that it presented. The heavy investment in building up the infrastructure, such as roads, rail links and the postal and telegraph system, was vital for linking markets, transport and communications, which eventually led Punjab to become the 'granary of India' during colonial rule. We can see from Table 2.1 the developments in infrastructure and the fiscal benefits of that investment. Beginning in the 1870s right through to the 1930, Punjab underwent vast socio-economic change, made possible largely due to this investment in the infrastructure.

Table 2.1: Development of Punjab during British Colonisation

Year	Railway Mileage	Canal Mileage	Miles of Metalled roads	Cultivated Area (millions of acres)	Land Revenue (Rs., in lakhs)
1872–73	410	2,744	1,036	18.8	201
1882–83	600	4,583	1,467	23.4	206
1892–93	1,725	12,368	2,142	26.7	223
1912–13	4,000	16,935	2,614	29	360
1932–33	5,500	19,601	3,904	30.9	428

Source: M. S. Randhawa, *Out of the Ashes – An Account of the Rehabilitation of Refugees from West Pakistan in Rural Areas of East Punjab* (Chandigarh, 1954), 35.

The Grand Trunk Road, as the main artery, continued to play an important part in this process of making India British. The colonial power was now in control of the majority of the road, which stretched from Calcutta to Khyber Pass; the construction of Garrison towns along the road is intrinsically linked to the securing of the empire in the wake of the mutiny. This is also the route of recruiting soldiers for the British Indian Army. Muslim *Rajputs*, along with Sikh *Jats*, had also aptly demonstrated their loyalty to the British by supporting them during the mutiny and were also rewarded for this loyalty.[25] Consequently, army recruitment became a significant feature of Punjab under the British. This was enshrined in what became known as the martial races ideology.[26] On

---

25 Talbot, *Khizr Tiwana*, 28.
26 See further, Heather Streets, *Martial Races: The Military, Races and Masculinity in British Imperial Culture 1857-1914* (Manchester: Manchester University Press, 2004).

the eve of World War One, Punjabi martial races formed 54 per cent of the entire British Indian Army. Though the Sikhs were a minority community, they featured prominently in the Indian Army;[27] most were *Jat* Sikhs who belonged to the *Manjha* areas of Punjab.[28] The *Jat* Sikhs were traditionally agriculturalists, but due to the unreliable income from agriculture, the army increasingly became an attractive profession into which they could venture. This trend, to some extent, had already started under Maharaja Ranjit Singh; due to the liquidation of the Khalsa Army, unemployment was rife, and 'the only alternative left to them was to exchange the sword for plough'.[29] Punjabi Muslims from the agriculturally poor areas of Rawalpindi, Jhelum and Shahpur also featured heavily in the Indian Army. They traditionally came from *Rajput* families. Tan Tai Yong also makes the point that recruitment in Punjab was based not on just class but also on locality. The most prominent areas for recruitment were Amritsar and Lahore for *Jat* Sikhs; the Salt Range, mainly Jhelum and Rawalpindi, for aristocratic Muslim tribes; a smaller number of Hindu and Muslim *Jats* from south-eastern districts of Rohtak and Hissar; and from Kangra mostly *Dogras*.[30]

From the mid-1880s, the Punjab province experienced rapid growth on the back of an elaborate irrigation project which saw the development of the canal colonies. Vast areas of uncultivated lands in the *doabs* of south-west Punjab were transformed into the richest farming tracts in British India. This included places like Lyallpur, Montgomery and Jhang, which are now in West Punjab. Malcolm Darling, a retired British official, writing about his travels on the eve of independence notes:

> I hate plains, as I hate bores – one cannot get away from either. But the Punjab plain is not boring. It has the most virile peasantry in India, and perhaps the most prosperous in Asia, and it has the finest irrigation system in the world, fed by its five rivers. Fifty years ago this end of the plain was a semi-dessert...[31]

---

27 See further, Rajit K. Mazumder, *The Indian Army and the Making of Punjab* (Delhi: Permanent Black, 2003).

28 This is the region in central Punjab between Beas and Ravi Rivers, covering the region roughly from Amritsar to Kasur and from Lahore to Bhairowal.

29 Prem Vati Ghai, *The Partition of the Punjab, 1849–1947* (New Delhi: Munshiram Manoharlal Publishers, 1986), 18.

30 See further, Tan Tai Yong, *The Garrison State* (New Delhi: Sage, 2005), 74–5.

31 Darling, *At Freedom's Door*, 59.

Map 2.3: The Canal Colonies (now in West Punjab)

By the time the British had finished with this semi-dessert wasteland, the canal colonies made up about one-third of the Punjab region. Irrigation projects that were completed between 1860 and 1920 brought close to ten million acres of land under cultivation.[32] These developments in the province turned it into a major exporter of grains and cotton, confirming the emphasis by the colonial power on agricultural rather than industrial growth;[33] however, the project was also seen as a form of 'social engineering' and an artificial construct that lacked homogeneity in terms of language, geography and economy.

---

32 Grewal, *Sikhs of the Punjab*, 128.
33 Talbot, *Khizr Tiwana*, 4.

Seeds of Nationalism

Although the Indian mutiny of 1857 never reached deep into Indian society, it was one of the strongest challenges to the British presence in India. Nationalist writers, such as Vinayak Damodar Savarkar, like to view it as the 'first war of independence,'[34] but the official view portrayed by the colonial power was more dismissive and viewed it as a mere revolt by disgruntled *sepoys*. Changes in style and emphasis followed. First, the British crown assumed direct control. There was also a growing realisation that the transformation of Indian society, which was desired by Evangelicals and Utilitarians alike, was politically dangerous. The colonial state sought to strengthen its hold in the strategically important Punjab region by establishing 'collaborative' links with the dominant castes and representatives of the landholding communities. Nevertheless, earlier Christian missionary activity in the region, along with the wider modernising influences of colonial rule, had created a religious ferment in the towns. As elsewhere in India, these also were the focus of the growth in associational life that culminated in the emergence of the Indian National Congress (INC) in 1885. Early Congress delegates, however, generally welcomed colonial rule and the enlightenment that it brought. Their criticism was centred more on the lack of professional opportunities they possessed in comparison with their British counterparts.

It was only by the 1920s that the mass of the Indian population was being drawn towards what became the nationalist struggle. Mahatma Gandhi[35] led the Congress into a new era, giving it the national cohesion required to form a credible challenge. Punjab, for its part, played an important role in the nationalist struggle. The Jallianwala Bagh massacre in Amritsar in 1919 raised the stakes by providing Gandhi with the moral authority and a national platform through which a truly nationalist struggle could emerge. It produced many opponents of colonial rule in India, including Lala Lajpat Rai, Saifuddin Kitchlew, Bhagat Singh and Udham Singh.

---

34 Vinayak Damodar Savarkar, *The Indian War of Independence, 1857* (New Delhi: Rajdhani Granthnagar, 1970) [first published 1908]. Savarkar is also considered the ideological inspiration for right-wing organisations in India such as the Bharatiya Janata Party and Rashtriya Swayamsevak Sangh.

35 Under Gandhi, the INC in 1920 adopted a new Constitution that enabled the INC to reach rural areas. By expanding its base into village India and reducing membership fees, the INC increased its membership from two million in 1921 to nearly five million in 1942. Francis Robinson, 'The Indian National Congress,' *History Today*, no. 32 (1982): 32–40.

The Namdhari sect,[36] located in Baini Sahib near Ludhiana, viewed themselves as the first group to challenge British presence in Punjab. They claim to be the torchbearers of India's freedom struggle in challenging the British and evoking nationalist feeling among ordinary people at the end of the nineteenth century. They used methods of non-cooperation and boycott of British goods to challenge British legitimacy while encouraging social reform to rid society of inequality, especially towards women. They often raided butcher shops, slaughterhouses and liquor stores in their efforts to cleanse the faith but the colonial authorities were alarmed at their activities and deemed them as anti-British rebels. Consequently, their leader Ram Singh was exiled to Rangoon in March 1872.

While the nationalist struggle took shape and turned into a formidable challenge, the relationship between Hindus and Muslims began to deteriorate. The increasing divergence in politics was both a representation and a result of communalised identities. The foundation of the Hindu Mahasabha in 1915, and its precursors like the Hindu Sabha that existed in Lahore since 1882, was a testament to growing disparity in communal politics. Furthermore, the communal representation in the form of separate electorates was embedded and institutionalised in 1909 following the Morley–Minto reforms. The creation of a separate Muslim state based on the 'two-nation theory' was not, however, an inevitable outcome following the formation of the All-India Muslim League in 1906.[37] Support for the Muslim League was largely concentrated in the United Provinces, where the famous Aligarh University provided its ideological heartland, but in Punjab, it was relatively weak and had little impact. The Muslim League's marginalisation in Punjab is evident in the 1937 provincial elections,[38]

---

36   The Namdhari sect was founded by Baba Balak Singh's disciple Ram Singh in 1857. Popularly known as Kukas, they are particularly noticeable due to their uniform white clothes and round turbans, similar to Guru Nanak. Although they are considered as unorthodox by the mainstream Sikh bodies, they view themselves as reviving Sikh orthodoxy. John Bowker, ed., *The Oxford Dictionary of World Religions* (Oxford: Oxford University Press, 1997), 679; Namdhari pamphlet, *Namdharis The Freedom Fighter* (Sri Bhaini Sahib, Ludhiana: Kuku Martyrs Memorial Trust, N.D.).

37   The AIML has over the years been shortened and referred to often as the Muslim League. However, there is an important and political distinction between the two. The AIML does significantly imply that this was a party representing Muslims all over India and not just in the Muslim heartland. To read further on the AIML see, *The Sole Spokesman*.

38   Following the Government of India Act 1935, provincial elections were held in the Punjab in 1937. This gave the INC a chance of governing at the provincial level.

in which it captured just two seats. The results confirmed the dominance of the INC nationally, but in Punjab it was the Unionist Party that prospered. The Muslim League, with the exception of Bengal, performed poorly in the other major Muslim centres. It is, therefore, remarkable that within ten years the call for a separate Muslim state became a realistic possibility.

The Unionist Party[39] ruled in Punjab under Sikander Hayat Khan[40] and then under the leadership of Khizr Tiwana.[41] By the time Khizr had taken over in 1942 the Muslim League was beginning to make an impact nationally. In Punjab, the League confirmed its strength in the 1946 election results when it won 74 out of 175 seats, making it the single largest party.[42] This was a crucial victory as the electoral success in Punjab made the idea of a separate homeland a reality and provided the legitimacy needed by the Muslim League; Jinnah termed Punjab as the 'cornerstone' of Pakistan. Neeti Nair argues that contrary to popular perception, some high-profile Hindus also preferred the partition option in the decades preceding independence. There is, she argues, a convergence taking place of communalised politics and anti-colonialism in Punjab during this period.[43] Khizr's Unionist Party, in coalition with other parties, still held the balance of power but was under immense pressure from the League, which felt cheated, as it was the single biggest party. Khizr had previously been successful in countering the influence of the League and its demand for a Pakistan; he had managed to put forward his own vision of a united Punjab within a federal India.[44] However, Khizr found the pressure of public disorder arising from the League's direct action campaign overbearing and was forced to resign on 3 March 1947. The Unionist Party, which had dominated Punjabi politics for the past twenty years, managed to block the League's attempts to form a ministry due to the fragile balance of votes. But tensions were mounting outside the legislature as communal organisations in the region all laid claim to the historic land. This eventually led to governor's rule in the province at arguably the most crucial time in its history.

---

39 The Unionist Party first emerged in 1923 under the leadership of Fazl-i-Hussain. The party drew support from all three communities in the Punjab and its support base cut across class differences, drawing support from both landowners and peasant proprietors. Talbot, *Khizr Tiwana*, 51.

40 See further Iftikar H. Malik, *Sikander Hayat Khan (1892–1942): A Political Biography* (Islamabad: National Institute of Historical and Cultural Research, 1985).

41 See further political biography of Khizr Tiwana by Talbot.

42 Grewal, *Sikhs of the Punjab*, 175.

43 Neeti Nair, *Changing Homelands* (Cambridge, MA: Harvard University Press, 2011), 257.

44 Talbot, *Khizr Tiwana*, 1.

W. H. Auden

Partition, 1966[1]

Unbiased at least he was when he arrived on his mission,
Having never set eyes on this land he was called to partition
Between two peoples fanatically at odds,
With their different diets and incompatible gods.
'Time,' they had briefed him in London, 'is short. It's too late
For mutual reconciliation or rational debate:
The only solution now lies in separation.
The Viceroy thinks, as you will see from his letter,
That the less you are seen in his company the better,
So we've arranged to provide you with other accommodation.
We can give you four judges, two Moslem and two Hindu,
To consult with, but the final decision must rest with you.'

Shut up in a lonely mansion, with police night and day
Patrolling the gardens to keep assassins away,
He got down to work, to the task of settling the fate
Of millions. The maps at his disposal were out of date
And the Census Returns almost certainly incorrect,
But there was no time to check them, no time to inspect
Contested areas. The weather was frightfully hot,
And a bout of dysentery kept him constantly on the trot,
But in seven weeks it was done, the frontiers decided,
A continent for better or worse divided.

The next day he sailed for England, where he quickly forgot
The case, as a good lawyer must. Return he would not,
Afraid, as he told his Club, that he might get shot.

---

1   Anon, 'W.H. Auden's unsparing poem on the partition of India,' accessed 13
     February 2017, https://scroll.in/article/674238/wh-audens-unsparing-poem-on-
     the-partition-of-india.

3

Handing Over the Reigns

The transfer of power in India was hastily planned; however, in the closing days there was a collapse of law and order, especially in the province of Punjab. This highly militarised area responded with some of the worst violence seen in the history of the subcontinent. And so, the smooth transfer of power and the creation of two states were forever tainted with the blood of civilians. Tracing this extraordinary period through personal experiences of violence, forced migration, and finally, rebuilding torn lives highlights the fact that this was not just a moment in history but instead, it was a decision which impacted millions of lives and lasted for many years; and some are still wandering around in the streets of their childhoods. Although lives were rebuilt, the memory of ancestral homelands and lost childhoods remained with the people. The fractures caused by imperial collapse and the partition became permanent and so for many refugees their former homes remained with them only in memory. It is perhaps for this reason why some people, especially in Punjab, have not reconciled to the idea of partition; the lack of closure is equally evident in the response of the two new states and their inability to have any form of an open post-conflict reconciliation.

When the British decided to hand over the reins of power in India, the result was not a seamless transition of power from colonial rule to two independent countries of India and Pakistan. The reality was much more chaotic, with widespread lawlessness creating the space for unprecedented levels of communal violence. With the toxic mix of large numbers of demilitarised personnel and weaponry following World War Two, the militarised Punjab (*Sikh*) states and law and disorder as the British exit, at stake for the average masses was their livelihoods, their homelands and their lives. Most were taken by surprise at the levels of violence, chaos and mass forced migration that followed.

The question of dividing the country was itself a consideration that only surfaced in 1940 with the Lahore Resolution. Several mistakes by the INC led to the rise of the League during this period. Its refusal to share power with the League in the United Provinces, following the 1937 provincial elections, is regarded as a major turning point. Furthermore, during World War Two the

League shrewdly supported the colonial power, while the INC leadership was in jail for opposing the decision by Britain to declare war on India's behalf. During the war years, Jinnah secured a much stronger position than before and could begin bargaining for a separate homeland.[1]

It was only in the wake of the Unionist government's resignation that Punjab slid into communal violence. Until this time, the province had escaped the communal violence that had earlier engulfed other areas in India such as Calcutta and Noakhali in East Bengal and then spread to Bihar.[2] The disturbances in Lahore and Amritsar and in the Rawalpindi division of the province in the wake of Khizr's resignation marked a trend towards increased levels of violence and it being viewed as a legitimate political tool. The demarcation of territory in response to the impending British departure, combined with the highly militarised nature of Punjabi society, made the situation significantly different from previous 'communal riots'.[3] In the lead-up to the violence in March 1947, the League had been pursuing a campaign, 'Direct Action Day', against the incumbent Khizr ministry in Punjab. When the ministry resigned on 2 March, it was amid growing unrest in the district. In Rawalpindi and Lahore, there were some serious disturbances, which resulted in the estimated death of 3,000. Swarna Aiyar suggests that the March violence showed signs of a move towards organised violence and the emergence of 'private armies' in carrying out formulated plans.[4] Crucially, the March violence set the benchmark for further and more gruesome reprisal hostility in August 1947.

The Punjab violence is also seen as a major factor in Mountbatten's decision to bring forward the date of departure from India. Initially planned for June 1948, the date changed to August 1947, which effectively left no time to prepare a smooth transfer of power and even less time to consider

---

1   For further information read Ian Talbot, 'The Growth of the Muslim League in the Punjab, 1937-46,' in *India's Partition: Process, Strategy, Mobilisation*, ed. Mushirul Hasan (New Delhi: Oxford University Press, 1993); Francis Robinson, *Separatism among Indian Muslims* (London: Cambridge University Press, 1974).

2   J. Nanda, *Punjab Uprooted: A Survey of the Punjab Riots and Rehabilitation Problems* (Bombay: Hind Kitab, 1948), 16.

3   Swarna Aiyar, '"August Anarchy": The Partition Massacre in Punjab 1947,' *South Asia* XVIII (1995): 13–36.

4   See further, Aiyar and Anders Bjørn Hanson, 'The Punjab 1937-47 – A Case of Genocide?,' *International Journal of Punjab Studies* 9, no. 1 (January–June 2002): 9–12.

how the country would be divided. The violence in the Punjab, and elsewhere in India, had ended the hopes of restoring the May 1946 Cabinet Mission's proposals for a united India. The British administration was keen to exit as soon as possible to avoid being embroiled in a prolonged civil conflict, while the embryonic states of India and Pakistan were too focused on the end game to foresee the repercussions of partition, especially in terms of the forced migration, but also the longer-term economic and psychological consequences of this division.

The British Government put forward the 3 June Plan (Indian Independence Act, 1947) that accepted the partition of Punjab in favour of a two-state solution to independence. Punjab was unusual because it comprised three main communities: Hindus, Sikhs and Muslims. Even Viceroy Mountbatten acknowledged that some special consideration was necessary for the Sikhs.[5] Table 3.1 provides an overview of the religious composition in pre- and post-partition Punjab. While the 1941 census shows that Muslims were the majority community, in reality this varied across the province, and areas in central Punjab were the most mixed. For example, areas like Gurdaspur, Nakodar, Phillaur, Jullundur and Una, all had majority Muslim populations but went to East Punjab. Similarly, Nankana Sahib, Mandi Bahauddin, Sargodha, Rawalpindi, Lyallpur and so on, were all non-Muslim majority areas but ultimately went to West Punjab. Moreover, the 1941 census is largely considered to be unreliable because it was done under wartime conditions, and it became a source of tension when minorities put forward their claims to the Boundary Commission.[6] Historically, Punjab had a strong pluralist and composite cultural tradition that statistical data and simple religious categorisation do not reveal.[7] It was also, importantly, the spiritual homeland of the small but significant Sikh community, which added further complexity at the time of partition. The princely states remained excluded from the Radcliffe Boundary Commission discussions; yet they were to form an integral part of the new nation-states and had to accede their autonomy.

---

5   Satya Rai, *Partition of the Punjab: A Study of Its Effects on the Politics and Administration of the Punjab 1947-56* (Bombay: Asia Publishing House, 1965), 50.

6   Lucy Chester, *Borders and Conflict in South Asia: The Radcliffe Boundary Commission and the Partition of Punjab* (Manchester: Manchester University Press, 2009).

7   Meeto (Kamaljit Bhasin-Malik), *In the Making: Identity Formation in South Asia* (Gurgaon: Three Essays Collective, 2007).

Table 3.1: Religious Composition of Population in East and
West Punjab 1941–51

	1941 United Punjab	1951 West Punjab[a]	1951 East Punjab[b]
Total population	34,309,861	20,651,140	17,244,356
Hindus	29.1%	0	66%
Muslim	53.2%	98%	2%
Sikhs	14.9%	0	30%
Christians	1.5%	0	1%
Others	1.3%	2%	0

Source: Census of India 1941 and 1951; Census of Pakistan, 1951.
[a]According to the 1951 Census of Pakistan, there were 33,052 Hindus, and 402,856 others; no Sikhs and Christians were recorded.
[b]68,712 others were recorded but the percentages are rounded off and are represented by 0 per cent.

Drawing Up the Border

The 3 June Plan, or more popularly known as the Mountbatten Plan, was accepted by the main leaders Nehru and Jinnah and the Sikh leader Sardar Baldev Singh. According to the plan, the areas of Bengal and Punjab would be divided between Muslim and non-Muslim districts. The Boundary Commission was set up on 30 June 1947 with a mandate to 'demarcate the boundaries of the two parts of the Punjab [and Bengal] on the basis of ascertaining the contiguous majority area of Muslims and non-Muslims. In doing so, it will also take into account other factors'.[8] The commission consisted of four judges: Justice Din Muhammad and Justice Muhammad Munir (both Muslims),[9] Justice Mehr Chand Mahajan (Hindu)[10] and Justice Teja Singh

---

8   Kirpal Singh, ed., *Select Documents on Partition of Punjab–1947: India and Pakistan* (Delhi: National Book Shop, 1991), xxxiii.

9   Munir was an alumnus of the prestigious Government College, Lahore, and served as the Chief Justice of Pakistan from 1954 to 1960. He has written several books including *From Jinnah to Zia* (Lahore: Vanguard Books, 1960) and *Highways and Bye-ways of Life* (Lahore: Law Publishing Company, 1978).

10   Mehr Chand Mahajan, like Munir, was also an alumnus of Government College, Lahore; Mahajan also served as the first Prime Minister of Jammu and Kashmir in October 1947 and played a significant role in the state acceding to India. He then became the third Chief Justice of India in January 1954 until his retirement at the end of the year. *Looking Back: The Autobiography* (Bombay: Asia Publishing House, 1963).

(Sikh). The commission chairman was the British barrister Sir Cyril Radcliffe. During the public sittings, all the parties were allowed to present their cases to the commission. The Muslim case largely rested on the basis that their population majority in contested areas should be considered mainly in the demarcation of the boundary line. The non-Muslim case rested on economic conditions, as they contributed significantly to the economy of central Punjab. The Sikhs also tried to claim 'a special position', since this was their spiritual homeland.[11] It was of course the 'other factors' in the mandate that raised much controversy: To what extent would 'other factors' trump the population majority of the Muslims?[12] Significantly, there were differences of opinion between the different counsels regarding the other factors and what exactly these entailed.[13]

It is worth understanding some of the challenges and dilemmas that the commission had to deal with when sifting through the complexity of the lived realities of places. Mahajan, in his report, makes an interesting point about the city of Lahore, which historically and at the time of partition was claimed by all communities. The city has a rich history and was once the seat of power under Ranjit Singh. The Justice says:

> The town of Lahore in my view stands on a special footing. It has been metropolis of the Punjab for several hundred years. Both east and west have contributed to its prosperity. Its economic life has mainly been developed by the enterprise of the non-Muslims.... In truth both the Muslims and non-Muslims can legitimately claim Lahore as their own town though on different grounds.... If I could, I would have suggested that this town should be left in the joint management of both the communities as a free city, its freedom being guaranteed by the two Dominions with a suitable constitution in which one community may not dominate over the other.[14]

He then goes on to deliberate about the city, weighing the different arguments that have been presented, but it can be clearly seen how difficult it was, to be carving out spaces that had been previously shared by all communities. How do you divide a shared past? There is no objective

---

11 Singh, *Select Documents*, Report of Mr Justice Teja Singh, 4 August 1947, 353.

12 Singh, *Select Documents*, xxiv.

13 Singh, *Select Documents*, Report of Mr Justice Teja Singh, 4 August 1947, 347.

14 Singh, *Select Documents*, Report of Mr Justice Mehr Chand Mahajan, 3 August 1947, 333–4.

formula for this; it can only work arbitrarily while leaving a trail of the disgruntled and displaced behind.

The Sikhs, on the other hand, were the only community who claimed the land on the basis that it was linked integrally to their faith and therefore the very basis of their identity. The issue of Sikh shrines is an interesting one, especially when we read into the discussions and different arguments presented by the commission judges. Justice Teja Singh, himself a Sikh, argued that the ten Sikh Gurus were the equivalent to Christ for Christians and Hazrat Mohammad for the Muslims. United Punjab was naturally abundant with historic gurdwaras that are associated with the life and times of the ten gurus. Teja Singh goes on to state that conversely, 'There is not a single shrine of the Muslims in India that is founded by their prophet or which was built to commemorate any incident in his life, for the simple reason that he lived, worked for his whole life and died in Arabia'.[15] However, Justice Din Muhammad's argument is worth quoting here in detail:

> ...Even the Muslims have their shrines in all the districts claimed by the Sikhs and they are as much sacred to the Muslims as the Sikh shrines to the Sikhs. Secondly, Sikh shrines will be as much needed for the Sikhs residing in West Punjab as for those residing in East Punjab. But what is most important to consider is that how can lifeless structures of bricks and mortar or mud be taken into consideration as against the interests of millions living creatures of God whose culture, whose religion and whose very existence is jeopardised by placing them under foreign domination and this aspect of the case gains all the more importance in view of the present attitude of mind displayed by both the Hindus and Sikhs against the Muslims. [16]

There is then a fundamental disagreement over the importance of Sikh shrines; for the Sikhs, these are not just shrines but associated with the formation of the faith and the life and times of its founders. Interestingly though, Din Muhammad envisages a future in which Sikhs would be residing on both sides of the border, and therefore, it would fundamentally not be a problem, being quite dismissive of the Sikh shrines and reducing their importance to bricks and mortar. Justice Teja Singh, in his assessment, is critical of this viewpoint and

---

15 Singh, *Select Documents*, Report of Mr Justice Teja Singh, 4 August 1947, 358.

16 Singh, *Select Documents*, Report of Mr Justice Din Muhammad, 5 August 1947, 390.

argues that this is either deliberate or a failure to appreciate the significance of these shrines. In his report, he states that 'I am afraid the Muslim League has either not cared to understand the sacred character of the Sikh Gurdwaras or it has deliberately ignored it with a view to place them on the same footing as their religious places situated in different parts of India. In ordinary parlance, the term "Gurdwara" means any place used by the Sikhs for worship'.[17]

Yet, regardless of how one views the shrines, there is an incredibly difficult decision to be made about partitioning these sacred spaces. Justice Muhammad Munir, in his report, points out the likely impact of prioritising shrines: 'It is obvious to any one who gives any importance to the Sikh shrines that demarcation of the boundary on this principle would lead to anomalous results'.[18] More derisively, he goes on to argue that if this argument was applied consistently, the Sikhs would not only claim the whole of Punjab but also lay claim to the province of Bihar and dominions of the Nizam. Thus:

> The claim of the Sikhs therefore, on the ground of the location of their shrines is wholly untenable, and we would be flagrantly departing from our terms of reference if we attached any importance to it. As already pointed out, if the Sikh shrines could be considered as a factor in favour of the non-Muslim case, the claim of the Muslims on this ground could not be ignored and would almost extend to every part of the country over which they ruled for several centuries and which contains the shrines of many renowned Muslim saints who spread Islam to this country where that faith still claims ten millions of followers.[19]

In addition to these deliberations of communal shrines, there were also many flaws in the process. The commission was provided with outdated maps and census material. Radcliffe had no previous experience of South Asia or cartography but was given the responsibility for drawing the partition line in six weeks. Radcliffe himself only arrived in India in July 1947, and although he complained of the short timeframe, the Boundary Commission nevertheless reached their decision just days before independence, and determined the fate of millions of people. There was of course more controversy to follow,

---

17 Singh, *Select Documents*, Report of Mr Justice Teja Singh, 4 August 1947, 357.
18 Singh, *Select Documents*, Report by Mr Justice Muhammad Munir, 6 August 1947, 424.
19 Singh, *Select Documents*, Report by Mr Justice Muhammad Munir, 6 August 1947, 424.

particularly surrounding the level of influence Viceroy Mountbatten had on the final line. The main misunderstanding rests on the following letter dated 8 August 1947, from George Abell (private secretary to Mountbatten) to Stuart Abbott (private secretary to Evan Jenkins):

> I enclose a map showing roughly the boundary which Sir Cyril Radcliffe proposes to demarcate in his award, and a note by Christopher Beaumont describing it. There will not be any great changes from this boundary, but it will have to be accurately defined with reference to village and zail boundaries in Lahore district. The award itself is expected within the next 48 hours, and I will let you know later about the probable time of announcement. Perhaps you would ring me up if H.E. the Governor has any views on this point.[20]

The problem was that Sir Francis Mudie, who succeeded Jenkins as governor of West Punjab, shared this earlier version of the map with Jinnah and 'wanted to prove that the original award has been changed by Lord Mountbatten and that was the cause of the delayed announcement'.[21] This has prompted many to comment on the level of influence Mountbatten had on the boundary. However, in a personal letter dated 2 April 1948, Lord Mountbatten wrote to Lord Ismay:

> I shall always be grateful to you for having cautioned me not to try and bring any direct influence to bear on Radcliffe concerning the actual award beyond expressing the following general view. So far as I remember I said to him that Sikh attitude had become rather worse than we had anticipated and when he was balancing the boundaries of East and West Pakistan I sincerely hoped that he would bear the Sikh problem in mind. I think I went so far as to say that if he was really satisfied that overall decision both East and West was absolutely fair to both the communities then I trusted that any generosity to Pakistan should be more in Bengal than in Punjab since there was no Sikh problem in Bengal.[22]

To make matters worse, Pakistan was created on 14 August 1947, and at midnight, on 15 August, India gained independence but the actual boundary between the countries was not announced until after independence. While

---

20   Singh, *Select Documents*, 456.
21   Singh, *Select Documents*, xxv.
22   Singh, *Select Documents*, xxvi.

the boundary awards for Bengal and Assam were announced earlier, the award for Punjab was delayed until the afternoon of 16 August. A number of factors led to this decision to delay the announcement in Punjab. The timing of the announcement was discussed with the staff and it was remarked by Mountbatten that he would prefer to postpone its appearance until after independence celebrations, 'feeling that the problem of its timing was really one of psychology and that the controversy and the grief that are bound to arouse on both sides should not be allowed to mar Independence Day itself'.[23] Furthermore, this was advisable due to the fact that 'subsequent communal riots may be dealt with by the successor Governments and responsibility for the bloodshed should not rest with the British Government'.[24] Indeed, Lord Mountbatten said in the staff meeting on 9 August, 'Without question, the earlier it was published, more the British would have to bear the responsibility for the disturbances which would undoubtedly result'.[25] The British view was clearly to exit India as soon as possible to avoid being embroiled in further conflict and to leave with the least amount of blood on their hands.

As an individual, even Sir Cyril Radcliffe is not without controversy. One of Radcliffe's virtues was apparently his lack of any familiarity of Indian politics and more importantly, any previous knowledge of the region that he was going to divide.[26] This was supposed to ensure that he dealt even-handedly with the conflicting territorial claims. Although, Lucy Chester questions the perceived notions that Radcliffe was ignorant about India prior to his arrival as the chair of the boundary commission. Radcliffe, an establishment figure, would have had some insider knowledge due to his role as director general in the Ministry of Information during the World War Two. He also had some personal connections via his brother who died in India in 1938. So despite being seen as an impartial figure, he would have had some conception of the political landscape in India, though this is not the same as actual lived experience of the land and its people. What is interesting in Chester's analysis is that Radcliffe was very much an establishment figure, committed to his

---

23 Singh, *Select Documents*, xxv.

24 Singh, *Select Documents*, xxv.

25 Singh, *Select Documents*, xxv.

26 Tan Tai Yong, '"Sir Cyril Goes to India": Partition Boundary-Making and Disruptions in the Punjab,' *International Journal of Punjab Studies* 4, no. 1 (1997): 7.

sense of duty to the British government and that brings into question his role as an impartial arbiter with regard to the boundary-making process.[27]

Curiously, Radcliffe's relationship with Mountbatten also continues to raise questions over the extent to which Mountbatten influenced the boundary award. Mountbatten allegedly influenced the boundary lines in Gurdaspur and Ferozepur, despite some of the *tehsils* having Muslim majority populations, but it is difficult to weigh the exact level of 'influence' Mountbatten had on the outcomes of the boundary commission.[28] Arguably, this is one of the bitterest legacies of the boundary, which is intertwined with the Kashmir issue as it provides a corridor into India.[29] While the controversies surrounding Mountbatten's role will continue, Chester does offer an interesting insight into how Radcliffe felt when leaving India:

> I station myself firmly on the Delhi airport until an aeroplane from England comes along. Nobody in India will love me for my award about the Punjab and Bengal and there will be roughly 80 million with a grievance who will begin looking for me. I do not want them to find me. I have worked and travelled and sweated – oh I have sweated the whole time.[30]

This is a rare insight, because the enigmatic Radcliffe was obsessive about destroying his personal papers. Apparently, when asked by Z. H. Zaidi, the editor-in-chief of the *Quaid-i-Azam* Paper Project in 1967 about his personal papers, Radcliffe responded by suggesting that he 'had destroyed his papers because he wanted to maintain the validity of the Awards'.[31] And so his role is left mostly to speculation and conjecture; however, it does show his own awareness of the repercussions in drawing the lines and perhaps he also sensed that he would be blamed for this unpopular award. It would be impossible to divide and create new boundaries without also creating enmities along the

---

27 Chester, *Borders and Conflict.*
28 Tahir Kamran, 'The Unfolding Crisis in Punjab, March-August 1947: Key Turning Points and British Responses,' *Journal of Punjab Studies* 14, no. 2 (2007): 203.
29 Q. Abid and M. Abid, 'Boundary Commission Tilting in Favour of "Other Factors",' *Pakistan Vision* 12, no. 2 (2011): 36–65.
30 Chester, *Borders and Conflict*, 100.
31 Farooq Ahmad Dar, 'Boundary Commission Award: The Muslim League Response,' *Pakistan Journal of History and Culture* XXXIII, no. 1 (2012): 24.

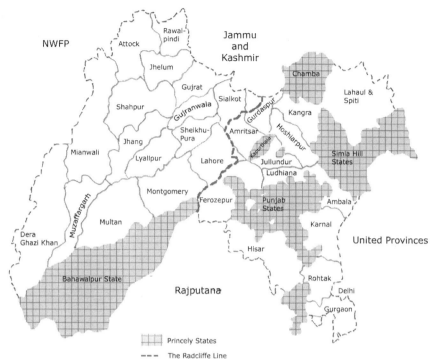

Map 3.1: The Radcliffe Line

way; Radcliffe's saving grace is that the majority of those people would remain ignorant of his existence yet their future citizenship and nationality was being drawn by him.

The Unmixing of People

And so the Radcliffe Line was eventually drawn and the fate of millions of people was decided. No prior notice was provided to the people who were still uncertain about which side of the border they would be on. The majority of people remained oblivious to the political wrangling over the boundaries and most, until the violence and chaos spread, remained in their homes regardless of the new international boundaries reluctant to leave (and abandon) their homes. During the months of August to December 1947, almost all the Sikhs and Hindus of West Punjab left Pakistan, and similarly nearly all the Muslims of East Punjab and many from adjoining areas left to create new homes in the Dominion of Pakistan.

Even though some non-Muslims started to migrate in the wake of riots and violence in Rawalpindi in March 1947, neither the Indian nor the Pakistani governments really anticipated the mass migration. Little attention was paid to any form of a planned exchange of population, the Government of India felt it was inconceivable that people would just leave their ancestral lands and property and migrate.[32] Jinnah, on the other hand, had also envisaged a Pakistan that included other religious minorities as is evident in his presidential address to the Constituent Assembly of Pakistan on 11 August 1947. Indeed, the Muslim League leadership vowed to protect the minorities in Pakistan and thus prevent a mass exodus.[33] Jinnah famously iterated:

> You are free; you are free to go to your temples, you are free to go to your mosques or to any other place or worship in this State of Pakistan. You may belong to any religion or caste or creed that has nothing to do with the business of the State.[34]

Similarly, Liaquat Ali Khan as Prime Minister of Pakistan 'considered it his duty to stand up for the rights of the Sikhs in West Punjab as much as the Indian leaders stood up for their rights in East Punjab. He emphasised that complete religious freedom would be allowed'.[35] Despite these reassurances, during the Constituent Assembly of Pakistan debates, Mr. Kiran Sankar Roy, a representative from East Bengal, makes clear his views regarding the division:

> Frankly, Sir, we are not very happy. We are unhappy because of this division of India. We are unhappy because of the partition of Punjab. We are also unhappy because of the partition of Bengal. But as this arrangement has been agreed upon by the two great parties, we accept it loyally, and shall work for it loyally. (*Cheers*). We shall accept the citizenship of Pakistan with all its implications. (*Cheers*)... And in

---

32 Rai, *Partition of the Punjab*, 72.

33 Brigadier Rajendra Singh, *The Military Evacuation Organisation 1947–48* (New Delhi: Government of India, 1962), 9.

34 Jinnah's presidential address, 11 August 1947, Constituent Assembly of Pakistan Debates, vol. 1, no. 2, accessed 14 February 2017, www.na.gov.pk/uploads/documents/1434523779_849.pdf.

35 Minutes of a meeting held at Government House, New Delhi, 16 August 1947, to receive the awards of the Boundary Commissions which demarcated the boundaries between India and Pakistan in Bengal and the Punjab. IOR: L/P&J/10/117, accessed 6 March 2017, www.bl.uk/reshelp/findhelpregion/asia/india/indianindependence/indiapakistan/partition9/.

return, Sir, we shall expect the rights and privileges of the minority guaranteed in the constitution, guaranteed not only in the Constitution but actually respected in the day to day working of the Government.[36]

Yet the idea was not completely inconceivable, because Jinnah had also suggested an exchange of population as early as 10 December 1945 and Ghazanfar Ali Khan, who was one of Jinnah's close aides, considered an 'exchange of population a necessary corollary' to the establishment of a Muslim state.[37] Upon hearing the results of the award, Sardar Baldev Singh felt that the only solution would be large-scale population transfers.[38] While the secular orientated Indian National Congress could accept a territorial division, a division of peoples would totally negate its ideology and force it to accept that India was indeed made up of 'two nations' with irreconcilable differences.[39] The colonial government alternatively was completely focused on leaving India at this point and had neither anticipated nor planned for a mass transfer of population as a result of its policies. Yet, the idea of planned exchanges of populations and the so-called 'unmixing' of ethnic communities was something used extensively following World War Two in Europe, so it is surprising that it does not feature in the discussions in the exit plan for India.[40]

The engulfing violence in the province that forced many people to flee their homes in turn meant more people were forced out to make space for the incoming refugees. It was clear to the leadership that events had spiralled out of control and it forced the leaders of India and Pakistan, Jawaharlal Nehru and Liaquat Ali Khan, to issue a joint statement at the end of August 1947:

The Punjab was peaceful and prosperous only a short while ago. It is now witnessing scenes of horror and destruction and men have become worse

---

36 11 August 1947, Constituent Assembly of Pakistan Debates, vol. 1, no. 2, accessed 14 February 2017, www.na.gov.pk/uploads/documents/1434523779_849.pdf.

37 Quote from *Dawn* in Rai, *Partition of the Punjab*, 72.

38 Minutes, 16 August 1947, IOR: L/P&J/10/117.

39 Address by *Quaid-i-Azam* Mohammad Ali Jinnah at Lahore Session of Muslim League, March 1940 (Islamabad, 1983), 5–23. This may have been motivated by the fact that non-Muslims contributed significantly to the economic vitality of the regions that became Pakistan.

40 Matthew Frank, 'Fantasies of Ethnic Unmixing: "Population Transfer" and the End of Empire in Europe,' in *Refugees and the End of Empire: Imperial Collapse and Forced Migration during the Twentieth Century*, eds. Panikos Panayi and Pippa Virdee (Hampshire: Palgrave Macmillan, 2011).

than beasts. They have murdered their fellow beings with savage brutality and have spared neither women nor children. They have burnt houses and looted property. Even people fleeing in terror have been butchered. Both Government (*sic*) are thus devoting all their energies to the task of restoring peaceful conditions and protecting the life, honour and property of the people. They are determined to rid the Punjab of the present nightmare and make it at (*sic*) once again the peaceful and happy land it was.[41]

The full statement is aimed at restoring order and giving the impression that the respective governments are in control of the situation. However, the newly formed governments of India and Pakistan had also, once they realised the scale of the migration, set up organisations like the Military Evacuation Organisation and the Liaison Agency to deal with the movement of people across the borders. The problem of course was that although the decision-makers had prepared themselves for the establishment of two new states and subsequently the division, no one had prepared themselves for the ensuing violence and mass migration that followed this event. What followed was a response to events that were largely out of their control. And so, when the independence celebrations were taking place in August 1947 in New Delhi and Karachi, the regions of Punjab and Bengal were the scenes of massive murder and uprooting.

While it is easy to scapegoat and blame Radcliffe, the man-in-charge of drawing up the fate of millions of people, he is not himself singularly responsible for the debacle that followed the departure of Britain from India. The responsibility must lie with all those who at the time were in positions of leadership. Certainly, the colonial power must accept that the speed with which it decided to 'divide and quit' India appears miscalculated. Yet, would a delay have made things any better? Were the Indian politicians too eager to assume power at almost any cost? Moreover, how much was their use of communalism for political purposes responsible for the violence in the first place? And among all these questions, no one actually asked the people of Punjab and Bengal whether they wanted to be divided and if so, which country would they like to accede to? And it was perhaps the Sikhs who were the most bewildered by the outcome. Though the Sikh leaders had accepted the 3 June Plan, they realised that they might now have to part with not only the Sikh shrines, but also the canal colonies in West Punjab, which they had contributed so much

---

41   Singh, *Select Documents*, Joint Statement of Pandit Jawahar Lal Nehru and Liaquat Ali Khan to the people of East and West Punjab, 508.

into making them fertile. This was a small, compact but significant community in undivided Punjab, which now saw its homeland split.[42]

The demise of the British Empire in India is a turning point not just in British colonial history but also in understanding the post-colonial states of India and Pakistan. The lingering legacy of partition had enormous repercussions for these fragile nascent nations; the long nationalist struggle gave way to divided, fragmented but nevertheless jubilant nations. The joy of independence for many was overshadowed by the partition of India to create the new state of Pakistan. The process of dividing and partitioning territories was much easier for Radcliffe on paper than it was in practice. This was not just a physical separation but a division of people, emotions, ancestral lands and properties; it was a partitioning of people whose primary identifier now was their religious identity, while their caste, class, linguistic or ethnic identity had receded, albeit temporarily.

The longer-term repercussions of this violent beginning for India and Pakistan have overshadowed the trauma and dislocation felt by millions of innocent people who were forced to flee their homes. Yet, only days before in the Constituent Assembly of Pakistan Mr. M. A. Khuhro, representing Sind, proudly asserted, 'Within these 6 or 7 years, as my Honourable friend, Nawabzada Liaquat Ali Khan, rightly said, without any bloody war and without any serious sacrifice of that kind, you have been able to get this Pakistan for the Mussalmans of this part of the country'.[43]

A bloodless war, it saw the realisation of Jinnah's dream and Gandhi's vision of *Swaraj* but the reality was somewhat different. So, while the process of carving up India was pre-planned, the exchange of population was not; though disruption and violence was expected, the ability to deal with this was inadequate and while New Delhi and Karachi celebrated their new existence, neither thought this would be the source of such hostility between the two countries. Within Punjab, it was clear for the politicians that placating the Sikhs would be difficult. Nehru was aware of the bad effects the boundary award could have on the Sikhs.[44] The legacy of decolonisation in India has therefore had ramifications far beyond merely transferring power. While the people were divided up, no one thought through the impact of their decisions *on the* people.

---

42 V. P. Menon, *The Story of the Integration of the Indian States* (Calcutta: Orient Longmans, 1956).

43 11 August 1947, Constituent Assembly Debates.

44 Minutes, 16 August 1947, IOR: L/P&J/10/117.

Ahmad Rahi

For Balraj Sahni[1]

For you, *my* country is a foreign-country
For me, *your* country is a foreign-country
O fellow yogi, dressed in white – Live on!
Your camp here, my camp there

The World saw tears spilling by the millions
I saw those ones that did not spill
Though of these no one took account
The white pearls of eyes were no less precious

Those who were locked in a prison of their memories,
Prisoners of the heart, have never been released
The times that flown away with the winds
We were unable to forget despite our attempts

Have you gone *to* your land or *from* your land?
Ever since you've gone, this thought haunts me
A thought that has robbed me of sleep
How could that thought let you live?

Our boat sank in midstream
Some drowned; others, too, failed to swim.
O eternal partner in pain!
Your wounds remain fresh; mine, too, have not healed.

Residing in my land, O foreign friend
The pain of mine is the same as yours
You left this place with a wailing soul
From there I came with a crying heart.

Could there be any more sorrow than this?
You think of here, I think of there.
All the broken hearts – How could we reckon them!
Millions here, millions there.

---

1   Balraj Sahni, 'Mera Pakistani Safarnama' (1963), Trans. by Gibb Schreffler, *Journal of Punjab Studies* 13, nos. 1 and 2 (2006): 93.

How they've ravaged the nest!
A twig here, a sprig there.

Even as we arrived, we arrived nowhere
Each place cries to us.
God willing, on these paths
May there be no other traveler.[2]

---

2   Here the word for 'traveler' (*rahi*) doubles as the poet's name, effectively
highlighting the poet's own experiences because of the partition.

4

Violence, Migration and the Making of the Refugee

Sitting in his office, Khawaja Muhammad Zakariya thinks back to a tumultuous time decades ago when his country was violently split in two. His father hurried home one day, telling his young son they had to gather up their money and jewelry and leave their Muslim neighborhood immediately for an uncle's house across town. "The day we moved…that area was attacked, and many were killed and injured but we had left about two hours before," Zakariya said, recalling the violence-plagued months leading up to partition. The family later left Amritsar for good, taking only the valuables they could carry, joining other families on packed trains to Lahore.[1]

Many like Zakariya were forced to flee their homes, desperately clinging onto any valuables they could and escape towards an unknown future. There was chaos, a lack of control by the authorities, and general fear – a fear of an uncertain future, a fear that threatened the safety of their lives and their families and daughters. While the Boundary Commission had decided on the line that created India and Pakistan, the people on the ground were uncertain of the complete ramifications that the drawing of the line would have on their lives. The violence unleashed the mass forced migrations of millions, overnight turning them homeless and into state refugees. They had not chosen this path, the politicians had. Yet they were paying the price, with their lives shattered and livelihoods lost. The overriding narrative of partition is the accompanying violence; it is difficult to discuss this period without mentioning the senseless, and indeed, the intended violence that engulfed the region. It did not matter whether or not you were directly affected by the violence because most people will have experienced the repercussions of it, like Zakariya who fled before

---

1 'The retired professor of Urdu literature in his mid-70s spoke from his office at Punjab University in Lahore, just 50 kilometres (30 miles) from the Indian city of Amritsar. He was relaying his life history to a volunteer from The 1947 Partition Archive.' Anon., 'Murder, Rape and Shattered Families: 1947 Partition Archive Effort Underway,' accessed 8 May 2016, www.dawn.com/news/1169309.

the violence claimed the lives of the people he grew up with. They witnessed the mass movement of people, which saw the demographic transformation of their neighbourhoods. They saw neighbours fleeing, either from the violence or from the ensuing violence that was spreading and engulfing everyone. It is difficult to fully understand how this region succumbed to the frenzy of violence in August 1947.

Making Sense of the Violence

There are a number of problems associated with the study of partition-related violence. These concern the extent to which it was spontaneous or planned, the degree to which any localised case studies can form part of a broader historical narrative and the extent to which partition violence differed from 'traditional' communal violence.[2] These issues also raise the question of the extent to which the concepts of 'ethnic cleansing' and 'genocide' are useful in understanding the events in Punjab. These concepts are still relatively new in the study of partition but they are important in the wider historiographical context. In more recent research, writers such as Talbot, Anders B. Hansen and Paul Brass have attempted to bring the Punjab experience into the main literature on genocide, which has been largely dominated by the Holocaust perhaps because the contemporaneous events in Europe overshadowed those in Asia.[3] More controversially, it could be argued that there is even a 'hierarchy of suffering' especially when we consider the vision of 'the emaciated women and men liberated from concentration camps';[4] anything else would become invisible in comparison with these shocking and disturbing images. The

---

2   Veena Das and Ashis Nandy, 'Violence, Victimhood and the Language of Silence,' in *The Word and the World: Fantasy, Symbol and Record*, ed. Veena Das (New Delhi: Oxford University Press, 1983).

3   Ian Talbot, ed., *The Deadly Embrace: Religion, Violence and Politics in India and Pakistan 1947–2002* (Karachi: Oxford University Press, 2007); Anders B. Hansen, *Partition and Genocide: Manifestation of Violence in Punjab 1937–1947* (New Delhi: India Research Press, 2002); Paul Brass, *The Production of Hindu-Muslim Violence in Contemporary India* (Seattle: University of Washington Press, 2003); and Ishtiaq Ahmed, *The Punjab Bloodied, Partitioned and Cleansed* (Karachi: Oxford University Press, 2012).

4   Vinay Lal, 'Partitioned Selves, Partitioned Pasts: A Commentary on Ashis Nandy's, "The Death of an Empire,"' accessed 17 July 2013, www.sscnet.ucla.edu/southasia/History/Independent/deathofempire.html.

photographs used to depict partition by Margaret Bourke-White are equally disturbing: charred bodies and skeleton valleys, where vultures await to fill their bellies.[5] These were the realities for millions of people.

At the most basic level, there is a dispute concerning the number of casualties arising from the partition-related violence; estimations vary considerably. It is in reality an impossible task to ascertain precise figures, and hence numbers have varied to suit political objectives. Indian nationalist writers have tended to lean towards the higher end of the spectrum and British writers have tilted towards the lower end, while in Pakistan the casualties represent the price of demanding a separate state from the domineering Hindu majority. This is hardly surprising as successive governments in both India and Pakistan have emphasised the problems the new states were able to surmount, while British governments have wished to preserve a legacy not marred by scenes of disorder. Veena Das also alludes to the fact that, in the process of naming the violence, the language falters due to the complexity of what is at stake. She argues, 'several kinds of social actors in any event of collective violence make it difficult to determine whether the event should be named as an instance of "sectarian," "communal," or "state-sponsored" violence. Is it described appropriately in the framework of "riots," "pogroms," "civil disturbances," "genocide," or a combination of these?'[6] This vernacular does not even begin to understand the other complex layers present, where the victim and the perpetrator can be the same

The debate surrounding the number of casualties is long-standing. It was still a concern to Lord Mountbatten, even years after he relinquished the office of Viceroy of India. In a letter to Penderel Moon (a British civil servant), written 2 March 1962, he declared that he was 'keen that an authoritative record should be left for the historians long after I am dead...' though he was not particularly eager to defend himself at this stage, 'nor joining in the argument'.[7] The inconsistency surrounding the casualties is obvious from the following extract in the letter by Mountbatten to Moon:

---

5   Khushwant Singh, *Train to Pakistan* (New Delhi: Lotus Collection, Roli Books, 2006), Photographs by Margaret Bourke-White, Time Life 1947.

6   Veena Das, *Life and Words: Violence and the Descent into the Ordinary*. (Berkeley, CA: University of California Press, 2006). E-book version.

7   *Letters on Divide and Quit*. Letter from Mountbatten of Burma, 2 March 1962. Mss Eur F230/34, India Office Records and Private Papers, British Library.

My estimate has always been not more than 250,000 dead; and the fact that your [Moon] estimate is not more than 200,000 is the first realistic estimate I have seen. I have often wondered how the greatly inflated figures which one still hears were first arrived at, and I think that they were due largely to the wild guesses which were made in those emotional days after the transfer of power. That they still persist is very clear; for example, Mr Leonard Mosley's latest book gives, I understand, the figure of 600,000, and only the other day a backbench conservative MP told one of my staff that the figures were three million![8]

In 1948, G. D. Khosla, who became Chief Justice of East Punjab High Court in 1959, led the Fact-Finding Commission by the Government of India to refute the Pakistani charge of genocide against Muslims emerging from United Nations debates over the Kashmir conflict.[9] Although the reports were not made public, shortly after this, Khosla wrote *Stern Reckoning*. In this book he estimates the number of casualties to be around 200,000 to 250,000 non-Muslims and probably an equal number of Muslims, bringing the total to nearly 500,000.[10] The historian Patrick French contends that deaths numbered closer to one million.[11] In a recent interview, the Indo-Canadian writer Shauna Singh Baldwin suggested the figure of five million.[12] Many of the police records were destroyed during the disturbances and due to the lawlessness of the state at the time; the records that do exist are unreliable in providing a comprehensive picture. Furthermore, it is difficult to calculate and differentiate between those that died directly due to the violence and those that died during the mass exodus through starvation, disease and other secondary factors. The truth in reality will never be known because it is an impossible task and, as Pandey suggests, casualty numbers are based on rumour and repetition, which continue to reverberate.[13]

---

8   *Letters on Divide and Quit.*
9   Tan Tai Yong and Gyanesh Kudaisya, *The Aftermath of Partition in South Asia* (London: Routledge, 2000), 253.
10 G. D. Khosla, *Stern Reckoning: A Survey of Events Leading Up to and Following the Partition of India* (New Delhi: Oxford University Press, 1949, reprint 1989), 299.
11 Patrick French, *Liberty or Death: India's Journey to Independence and Division* (London: Harper Collins, 1997).
12 Anjana Rajan, 'Memory's Harvest,' *The Hindu*, 14 May 2011.
13 Gyanendra Pandey, *Remembering Partition: Violence, Nationalism and History in India* (Cambridge: Cambridge University Press, 2001).

Most understandings of communal violence in India have focused on post-independence Hindu–Muslim clashes. These are regarded as different from the partition violence, which arose in exceptional circumstances, sometimes seen as resulting from a temporary 'madness'. The 1947 partition riots are also often depicted as being different from 'traditional' communal clashes of the colonial era. Suranjan Das has produced the most comprehensive analysis of riots in colonial Bengal. He sees the 1941 Dacca Riots as marking a turning point in violence.[14] Earlier riots were spontaneous and displayed a strong class orientation. The later violence was communally inspired and well organised. Das and Ashis Nandy see 'traditional' violence in terms of a feud in which communities continue to live together afterwards.[15] Shail Mayaram terms this type of violence as 'consensual'. These were about 'renegotiating' local hierarchies of power, not about 'purifying' localities of a rival 'other'. Partition violence, however, was different in character; it was more intensive and moved beyond an exchange of violence in the public arenas to engulf the private arenas. An integral part of the violence was what might be termed 'power rape'. Such violence terminated community interaction.[16]

Studies that emphasise the 'spontaneous mob' features of the 1947 violence look back to writers such as Gustave Le Bon for inspiration. Collective crowd behaviour really emerges from the writings of Le Bon. In *The Crowd: A Study of the Popular Mind*, he suggests that all individual responses were lost in crowds. What emerged was a 'collective mind', which made people 'feel, think, and act in a manner quite different from that in which each individual of them would'.[17] This would provide the anonymity needed to take away the personal responsibility of the participants. Emile Durkheim's ideas certainly resonant with Gustave Le Bon's, suggesting that crowd members are capable of conduct of which individually they are incapable and that the passions that

---

14　Suranjan Das, *Communal Riots in Bengal 1905–1947* (Delhi: Oxford University Press, 1991).

15　Das and Nandy, 'Violence, Victimhood,' 177–90.

16　Shail Mayaram, 'Speech, Silence and the Making of Partition Violence in Mewat,' in *Subaltern Studies IX: Writings on South Asian History and Society*, eds. Shahid Amin and Dipesh Chakrabarty (New Delhi: Oxford University Press, 1996).

17　Gordon Marshall, ed., *A Dictionary of Sociology* (Oxford: Oxford University Press, 1998), 88. See further, Gustave Le Bon, *The Crowd: A Study of the Popular Mind* (New York: The Viking Press, 1960), with a new introduction by Robert K. Merton.

seize crowds can produce action which is either heroic or barbaric.[18] Paul Brass, on the other hand, refutes this idea as blame displacement, suggesting that crowds cannot be viewed differently as Durkheim suggests.[19] Donald Horowitz, in his extensive study, *The Deadly Ethnic Riot*, is also critical of Durkheim's understanding of crowd behaviour, but suggests that crowds can draw support from social approval.[20] In this respect, the collective behaviour of crowds may differ significantly from individual responses.

Given that some responses by individuals may be irrational, and while not trying to displace the blame as Brass suggests, it is possible that individuals whether in crowds or otherwise may be fuelled by their more 'primordial passions'. This 'mob mentality' may be influenced by their primordial instincts rather than compelled by any broader political aims. Sudhir Kakar also acknowledges that some change has to occur for the outbreak of violence; in this case, the 'communal identity has to swamp personal identity in a large number of people, reviving the feelings of love connected with early identifications with one's own group members and the hate toward the out-group'.[21] The 1947 violence in Punjab was marked by atrocities that Horowitz sees as evidence of the 'spontaneous quality of riot behaviour'.[22] Many of the massacres were carried out by mobs in murderous frenzy.[23] Horowitz does go so far as to see some planning involved in the attacks, for example, on the refugee trains. But others like Javeed Alam argue that there was 'no involvement of large organisations or the state as the instrument of mass killings'.[24]

Anders Bjorn Hansen though is more critical and argues that the intentions, intensity and degree of organisation of the violence by communal groupings warrant the violence in Punjab to be understood as a manifestation

---

18 Donald Horowitz, *The Deadly Ethnic Riot* (Berkeley: University of California Press, 2001), 35. See further, Emile Durkheim, *The Elementary Forms of Religious Life* (New York: Free Press, 1995).

19 Brass, *Production of Hindu–Muslim*.

20 Horowitz, *Deadly Ethnic*, 35, 344.

21 Sudhir Kakar, *The Colours of Violence: Cultural Identities, Religion and Conflict* (Chicago: University of Chicago Press, 1996), 192.

22 Horowitz, *Deadly Ethnic*, 13.

23 Leo Kuper, 'Genocide and the Plural Society', in *Ethnicity*, eds. John Hutchinson and Anthony D. Smith (Oxford: Oxford University Press, 1996), 270.

24 Cited in Pandey, *Remembering Partition*, 58.

of genocide.[25] Interestingly, partition violence has not traditionally been incorporated into broader accounts of genocide or ethnic cleansing, as we understand these terms today. Recent literature such as *Centuries of Genocide*,[26] continues to overlook the massacres that took place in Punjab 1947, as does Mann's analysis of ethnic cleansing.[27] Some new studies are beginning to examine this period as it provides a useful comparative dimension.[28] One explanation for this omission is that the term has been deployed in relation to the Holocaust and the post-Cold War violence in the Balkans and Rwanda. This raises the question whether it is appropriate to apply this retrospectively to events in Punjab. However, individual case studies do point to organised and systematic acts. For example, Ian Copland refers to the Muslim expulsion in 1947 from Alwar and Bharatpur as not just a communal episode, but also a case of systematic 'ethnic cleansing', frequently a precursor to genocide.[29]

The 1948 United Nations Convention on the Prevention and Punishment of the Crime of Genocide defines genocide as, 'acts committed with intent to destroy, in whole or in part, a national, ethnical, racial or religious group'.[30] Not all scholars though subscribe to this view, partly due to the omission of other persecuted groups within this limited definition. Hansen interestingly points out that during the partition of Punjab, there was no well-defined category of victim and perpetrator; in fact there was a civil war-like conflict escalating during the handover of power. Furthermore, there were primarily three groups (Muslims, Hindus and Sikhs) and each group was 'capable of being the perpetrator and the victims depending on their power and influence in given areas'.[31] One of the other problems is that genocide is itself associated, and sometimes used synonymously, with the term 'ethnic cleansing'. Ishtiaq

---

25 Hansen, *Partition and Genocide*.

26 Samuel Totten and William S. Parsons, eds., *Centuries of Genocide: Essays and Eyewitness Accounts* (Abingdon: Routledge, 2013).

27 Michael Mann, *The Dark Side of Democracy: Explaining Ethnic Cleansing* (Cambridge: Cambridge University Press, 2005).

28 Pippa Virdee, '"No-man's Land" and the Creation of Partitioned Histories in India/Pakistan,' in *Remembering Genocide*, eds. Nigel Eltringham and Pam Mclean (Abingdon: Routledge, 2014).

29 Ian Copland, 'The Further Shores of Partition: Ethnic Cleansing in Rajasthan in 1947,' *Past and Present* 160 (1998): 216.

30 1948 United Nations Convention for the Prevention and Punishment of Genocide (Art. 2).

31 Hansen, *Partition and Genocide*, 3.

Ahmed, who has been considering this dilemma vis-à-vis partition violence, suggests that 'Ethnic cleansing is a generic term that covers removal of a distinct population — on the basis of ethnic, religious, sectarian and other such factors from a specific territory'. Ahmed argues that while genocide results in the destruction of a nation or people in part or whole, ethnic cleansing can lead to the same but using less severe methods. There is, however, a distinction in 'whether the intention was to rid unwanted people from a territory or to destroy them physically'.[32] The former was certainly evident in Punjab, which was further exacerbated by the refugees fleeing from the fear of reprisal killings.

Regardless of whether the terms 'genocide' and 'ethnic cleansing' are deployed, a debate still rages regarding the 'spontaneity' or 'planning' of the violence. The role of the local state is important here. For such writers as Brass who see links between partition and post-independence communal violence, the complicity of the local law enforcement agencies and the political motivations of the 'producers' of violence are crucial factors.[33] Brass has nevertheless termed the Punjab violence as 'retributive genocide' which becomes enveloped in a 'cycle of revenge and retribution',[34] and the boundaries between victim and perpetrator become completely blurred. Other scholars have suggested that this could be seen as a form of fratricide. This could include not only assaults on the 'other', but also the murder of women of one's own family to spare them from the 'dishonour' associated with rape and abduction. Jason Francisco shares this view and argues that 'the partition stands as the archetype of what I would call nationalist fratricide, the conflict between people of a common cultural heritage'.[35] He contends that this is distinct from ethnic conflict, or nationalist genocide, which is characterised by state-sponsored persecution or slaughter of cultural or religious minorities, such as the European Jews. Even Khosla's book, which was first published in 1949, describes the magnitude of horrors of 1947 with the comment that 'history has not known a fratricidal war of such dimensions'.[36] But it was women who bore the brunt of the most

---

32   Ahmed, *The Punjab Bloodied*, 6.
33   Paul Brass, 'The Partition of India and Retributive Genocide in the Punjab 1946–47: Means, Methods and Purposes,' *Journal of Genocide Research* 5 (2003): 71–101.
34   Brass, 'Partition of India,' 72.
35   Jason Francisco, 'In the Heat of Fratricide: The Literature of India's Partition Burning Freshly,' in *Inventing Boundaries: Gender, Politics and the Partition of India*, ed. Mushirul Hasan (New Delhi: Oxford University Press, 2000), 372.
36   Khosla, *Stern Reckoning*, 4.

horrific crimes, leading to what could be described as forms of femicide.[37] There are first-hand accounts of abductions, mass honour killings, women's bodies being mutilated and violated, indescribable crimes aimed at inflicting pain on the 'other'. These accounts have largely remained buried under the burden of prioritising the immediate needs of the nation and to recover the so-called *izzat* of the nation.

Furthermore, the notion of a hierarchy of suffering can also be applied to the partition violence itself. Leaving aside the global perspective, one only has to look to the 'chief sufferers' of partition violence and migration.[38] The plight of the women, low castes and children has only recently begun to be addressed by scholars, with a new generation of writers willing to tackle and challenge taboo subjects such as violence, rape and the abduction of women allowing some barriers to be broken.[39] It is estimated that 75,000 women were raped and abducted during this time on both sides of the border, although Khosla estimates the number of abducted women at 200,000 or more. Women were brutalised and dishonoured to inflict collective wounds on the 'other'. This also triggered 'pre-emptive' sacrifices by women to prevent 'dishonour' in the family. The most quoted episode is of the Sikh women in Thoha Khalsa (in Rawalpindi district, Pakistan), which has been immortalised since Butalia recovered this account in *The Other Side of Silence* during the March 1947 massacres in Rawalpindi.[40] The account begins with Sant Raja Singh who took the life of his daughter and martyred her after praying and asking for forgiveness. This is then followed by Sardarni Gulab Kaur, who plunged into the well and committed suicide rather than be dishonoured. In total around ninety women, all of one lineage, perished. The account has been used to show the bravery and courage of the women. Further, Rameshwari Nehru (who was a social worker and head of the Women's Section in the Ministry of Relief and Rehabilitation) likened the 'pre-emptive' sacrifices to the old Rajput

---

37   This concept has its roots in feminist discourse, where violence is viewed as a tool of repression and male dominance. For a discussion on this, see Jill Radford and Diana E. H. Russell, eds., *Femicide: The Politics of Woman Killing* (Buckingham: Open University Press, 1992).

38   Andrew Major, 'The Chief Sufferers: The Abduction of Women during the Partition of the Punjab,' *South Asia* XVIII (1995): 57–72.

39   Urvashi Butalia, *The Other Side of Silence: Voices from the Partition of India* (New Delhi: Penguin, 1998); and Ritu Menon and Kamla Bhasin, *Borders and Boundaries: Women in India's Partition* (New Jersey: Rutger University Press, 1998).

40   Butalia, *The Other Side*.

tradition of self-immolation in which women sacrificed themselves on the funeral pyres of their husband.[41] Shauna Singh Baldwin, however, questions the patriarchal discourse associated with this, which she terms as 'bravery', 'duty' and 'martyrdom'.[42] By doing so, the violent act performed by the male head is justified. The fact that some women did not die and others were not so forthcoming for this 'sacrifice' is less visible and what is remembered is the 'heroic' act. Crucially writers such as Veena Das refute this, and argue that these women have simply become objects of national honour and serve only to promote the interests of the newly created nation-states.[43]

Those who regard the violence as unplanned either ignore the role of the state or maintain that its collapse in 1947 was a crucial factor in explaining the outbreaks. The main difference between the violence in the years preceding partition and the partition violence itself is that in the former there was still a functioning government, admittedly a weak one, on occasions. The collapse of state authority during the transitory period of transferring power is probably one reason why the violence was so widespread and horrific during the months following partition. As is discussed later in chapter five, during my research on Malerkotla, a small Muslim princely state in the Indian Punjab, the role of the state was crucial in maintaining law and order; consequently Malerkotla remained a haven of peace for Muslims while surrounded by the partition violence in neighbouring British India.[44] Conversely the riots that occurred in Rawalpindi in March 1947 followed the resignation of the minority government formed after the election of 1946 by Unionist Khizr Hayat Tiwana.[45] Arguably then, the vacuum created by the absence of a functioning authority was a prerequisite for violence to occur in Rawalpindi and was certainly prevented in Malerkotla.

The State and the Making of a Refugee

At the end of August, two weeks after partition had taken place, there was, however, still some hope that the law and order situation would improve.

---

41   Pandey, *Remembering Partition*, 88.

42   Shauna Singh Baldwin, *What the Body Remembers* (London: Anchor, 2000).

43   Veena Das, *Critical Events: An Anthropological Perspective on Contemporary India* (Delhi: Oxford University Press, 1995), 70.

44   Pippa Virdee, 'Partition and the Absence of Communal Violence in Malerkotla,' in Talbot, *The Deadly Embrace*.

45   Tahir Kamran, 'The Unfolding Crisis in Punjab, March-August 1947: Key Turning Points and British Responses,' *Journal of Punjab Studies* 14 (2007): 187–210.

Indeed, 'the Prime Minister of Pakistan expressed the hope that, as the general situation improved, those gathered in refugee camps would return to their homes'.[46] Many of the refugees that I have interviewed, and discussed later in this chapter, have frequently said that once the troubles settled down, they had hoped to return to their ancestral homes.

However, it was also beginning to dawn on the authorities that some movement of peoples was inevitable due to the uncontrollable levels of violence. The Defence Minister of Pakistan, Liaquat Ali Khan, wrote to the Governor-General of India, Mountbatten, on 28 August 1947:

> From all reports conditions in Eastern Punjab are far worse than could have been imagined. In Amritsar, Hoshiarpur, Jullundur districts and parts of Gurdaspur, Ludhiana and Ferozepore districts complete breakdown of administration. Thousands of men, women and children massacred and large proportion of Muslim villages burnt. Abduction on a large scale. Reign of terror in these districts has driven hundreds of thousands to West Punjab. Number of Muslim refugees may run upto a million or more.[47]

In the telegram, the minister notes that the refugees may run into a million or more, and of course this number escalated into many millions by the end of 1947. He goes on to say that it appears the Sikh objective is to 'exterminate or drive out entire Muslim population from this area'.[48] One of the bloodiest massacres was in Sheikhupura. G. D. Khosla terms the district as a 'by-word',[49] for murder, loot, arson and rape that took place between 17 and 31 August.[50] In a statement sent to Rameshwari Nehru, the extent of the partition violence becomes clear. The statement notes that in the space of 24 hours, 10,000 people were killed in Sheikhupura by the 'Muslim military and police or were burnt

---

46 Minutes of the sixth meeting of the Joint Defence Council held at Government House, Lahore, 29 August 1947, in Singh, *Select Documents*, 505.

47 Defence minister, Pakistan, to governor-general, India, 27 August 1947. National Documentation Centre (NDC), *Disturbances in the Punjab, 1947: A Compilation of Official Documents* (Islamabad: Government of Pakistan, 1995), 365.

48 Defence minister, Pakistan, to governor-general, India, 27 August 1947. NDC, *Disturbances in the Punjab*, 365.

49 Khosla, *Stern Reckoning*, 126–40.

50 Menon and Bhasin, *Borders and Boundaries*, recount the story of Dr. Virsa Singh, who says that he personally killed fifty women in Sheikhupura to save their honour.

alive in the houses'. In this case it appears that the Baloch soldiers and the local leadership were culpable for the massacre but the statement also notes how some people, regardless of the dangers, were compelled to save and protect the lives of the 'other' community. For example, 'the local president of the league, Mr. Anwar had given shelter to about 65 members of the families of his friends. One Mrs. Rafi, a wife of a police inspector saved about 70 lives',[51] highlighting that even in this extreme situation not all humanity had vanished.

Sheikhupura district included Nankana Sahib and thus was the spiritual homeland of the Sikh community, as it is the birthplace of the founder of Sikhism and for this reason alone many Sikhs found it difficult to believe that it would now be in Pakistan. But like the rest of central Punjab, the district was an amalgam of different religious communities who came to co-exist over generations.[52] Yet, now nearly 150,000 Sikhs were gathered for the mass exodus.[53] They took refuge in local schools and gurdwaras and the Sacha Sauda camp alone had over hundred thousand people as refugees from neighbouring areas all gathered.[54] The creation of refugees by these acts of violence left people helpless in their loss of family members and property. Some wrote to religious organisations such as the Hindu Mahasabha in desperate pleas of help:

> I am refugee from Sheikhupura proper which has been a scene of total mascure [sic] and I have lost six members of my own family including brother, his wife two daughters one son and my own wife. Now I have to look after two families myself alone. I, therefore request that a suitable quarter for ten members may kindly be allotted to me to live in…At present, I am staying in a refugee camp in New Delhi. I beg to point out that we had at Sheikhupura three houses and 50 bighas [1 *bigha* is roughly equivalent to 1/3 of an acre] of cultivated land and all our houses and property has been looted by the rioters. Now I am absolutely penyless [sic][55]

---

51 Rameshwari Nehru Papers, no. 25, four-page statement about Sheikhupura sent from Lahore, 28 August 1947. NMML, New Delhi.

52 See the chapter on 'Composite Culture in Pre-Partition Punjab.' Meeto (Kamaljit Bhasin-Malik), *In the Making: Identity Formation in South Asia* (Gurgaon: Three Essays Collective, 2007).

53 Sir Francis Mudie to Mr Jinnah, 5 September 1947, in Singh, *Select Documents*, 511.

54 Menon and Bhasin, *Borders and Boundaries*, 49.

55 Letter sent to the Magistrate, 17 September 1947, by Prem Nath. Hindu Mahasabha, File C-168. NMML, New Delhi.

Until September 1947, the governments were unable to accept the reality that a mass transfer of population was necessary. Once the violence reached uncontrollable levels and chaos engulfed the Punjab region, the two new dominions had to accept that the exchange of populations was an inevitable outcome of partition. There were fears that the 'holocaust at Sheikhupura will probably be repeated in many other mofussil areas in West Punjab and that 40,000 lives are in danger during next 48 hours'. It was therefore recommended that a 'transfer of population should take place'.[56] But the nature of that exchange was not clear. Would the exchange involve repatriation or resettlement? Mahatma Gandhi's view on this was that 'the migrants must eventually return to their homes and lands that the two Dominion Governments must extend the fullest protection of their minorities'.[57] In many ways, the refugees themselves were of the same opinion. The interview below with a migrant from Sialkot, which resonates in many other oral accounts of refugees' experiences, illustrates the hope that uprooting would only be temporary. Sarwan recollects:

> People just tied locks to their houses in our village. We told our neighbours that we would be back soon. Some people who were our sympathisers said not to go. People lost a lot, most left everything there. We had one horse and brought along as much as we could. We didn't know that we would not return. We just went until things calmed down.[58]

Similarly, in Manto's *The Assignment,* there is quiet optimism about the communal violence, 'two weeks or so of unrest and then business as usual'. It was seen as 'temporary inflamed political passions',[59] which would soon subside. And so people began to move but only temporarily. These views were reiterated in an interview with Rana, who migrated from Ludhiana. Like many others, he thought that eventually there would be an opportunity to go back to their ancestral lands but even with this hope in mind, it was still an emotional and painful process.

> When we migrated from India, many Muslims thought that they would come back after two to three months. It was stupidity, I think. Even

---

56 Letter to Nehru from High Commissioner for India Camp, Lahore, 27 August 1947, in Singh, *Select Documents*, 502.

57 *After Partition* (Delhi: Publications Division, Government of India, 1948), 59.

58 Interview with Sarwan Singh, Lal Bazaar, Malerkotla, August 2001.

59 Saadat Hasan Manto and Introduction by Daniyal Mueenuddin, *Mottled Dawn: Fifty Sketches and Stories of Partition* (India: Penguin, 2011), 11.

feeling all this, we were not sure about migration...The riots kept on gaining strength and ferocity and only two options were left with us to die or to migrate. Some Muslims wanted to stay in their homeland and die there while the rest thought about the other option because the army of the [Sikh] States had surrounded them and they didn't have weapons to defend themselves. Some of our Sikh friends waited for us on the way. At the sight of my maternal uncle, they started crying and embraced him. They gave us some bread and few other items of necessity. They loaded those items on a horse and handed the reins to us.[60]

It was first noted on 7 September 1947 at the Emergency Committee meeting between India and Pakistan that the movement of people was their first priority.[61] Conceived as an afterthought, the ineffectual Punjab Boundary Force,[62] which comprised of Indian and Pakistani troops under a British commander, Major General Thomas Wynford Rees, was wound up. Rather than protecting everyone, the Punjab Boundary Force was seen to be taking sides and communally divided.[63] Both governments had vowed to cooperate and to use all resources available to them to provide safety for migrants.[64] The Punjab governments set up the Liaison Agency, to oversee the evacuation of refugees, which was headed jointly by two chief liaison officers (CLOs) based in Lahore and Amritsar. Each district also had a district liaison officer (DLO) who relayed information to the CLO about ground activities regarding the status of refugees and evacuation plans. This agency along with the Military Evacuation Organisation (MEO) was responsible for the movement of people across the borders of Punjab. They determined the priorities for the movement of evacuees based on the reports provided by the district officers and in consultation with a priority board.[65]

---

60   Interview with Rana, Chiniot Bazaar, Faisalabad, February 2003.

61   Brigadier Rajendra Singh, *The Military Evacuation Organisation 1947–48* (New Delhi: Government of India, 1962), 11–12.

62   See further Robin Jeffrey, 'The Punjab Boundary Force and the Problem of Order, August 1947,' *Modern Asian Studies* 8, no. 4 (1974): 491–520.

63   Defence minister, Pakistan, to governor-general, India, 27 August 1947. NDC, *Disturbances in the Punjab*, 365.

64   Pippa Virdee, 'Partition in Transition: Comparative Analysis of Migration in Ludhiana and Lyallpur,' in *Partitioned Lives: Narratives of Home, Displacement and Re-settlement*, eds. Anjali Gera Roy and Nandi Bhatia (New Delhi: Pearson, 2007).

65   Satya Rai, *Partition of the Punjab: A Study of Its effects on the Politics and Administration of the Punjab 1947-56* (Bombay: Asia Publishing House, 1965), 78.

In the immediate aftermath of partition, the Indian government was on average shifting 50,000 Hindus and Sikhs a day.[66] All modes of transport were used – railways, motor trucks, foot convoys and aircraft. Generally, large foot convoys were utilised by rural migrants as they could transport their cattle and bullock carts, whereas trains were easier for evacuating urban migrants. Compelling images of partition remain the foot convoys, *kafilas*,[67] which stretched over many miles and the trains with their compartments and roof spaces packed with refugees.[68] The *kafilas* like the trains were the target of attacks by Muslims and non-Muslims alike, even though they were assisted by the military. From Table 4.1, we can see that the MEO managed to assist the evacuation of the majority of people by the end of November. The figures in the table are not the final totals as there were still pockets of people who were stranded. In addition to the modes of transport listed, there were about 30,000 people who were evacuated by air from West Punjab.[69] By 26 November 1947, the MEO's task of evacuating people was nearly complete, with the exception of some pockets of people in remote areas, abducted women, converted people, and scheduled caste[70] refugees who still required their assistance.[71]

Table 4.1: Evacuation Figures - Total upto 22 November 1947

	Non-Muslims	Muslims	Total
By motor transport	349,834	215,690	565,524
By rail	849,500	943,720	1,793,220
By foot	1,014,000	2,385,165	3,399,165
Total	2,213,334	3,544,575	5,757,909

Source: Weekly Reports on Refugees, 23 November 1947, Liaison Agency Files, LVII/26/45, PSA.

The vast majority of people crossed the newly created border on foot, forming snake-like *kafilas* which, though protected by the army, were still attacked by the opposing communities who were themselves going in the

---

66 *After Partition*, 52.

67 See further, Margaret Bourke-White, *Halfway to Freedom: A Report on the New India in the Words and Photos of Margaret Bourke-White* (New York: Simon & Schuster, 1949).

68 Khushwant Singh's fictional novel has most poignantly captured the emotion and fear of these train journeys experienced by some two million people. See further, *Train to Pakistan* (London: Chatto & Windus, 1956).

69 Singh, *Military Evacuation Organisation*, 108.

70 Official term for untouchables.

71 Singh, *Military Evacuation Organisation*, 109.

opposite direction. For others, the exhaustion of travelling was too much; the weak were simply left to perish, while the dead were abandoned without any burial rites. Foot convoys regardless of these problems remained the most practical method of transport for the largely agricultural Punjabi community, who could at least take some essential foodstuff, equipment and cattle with them. The trains were the second most popular form for transporting the refugees, yet the history of partition is replete with horrific stories of pre-planned attacks on trains, trains filled with corpses denuded of all identity and of burning trains arriving at platforms and motivating further reprisal killings. Some were lucky enough to survive:

> They [Sikhs] blocked the way of our train – halting our journey for three days. It seemed that the Sikhs were preparing for a big attack. There were four to five military men of Baloch regiment with us. With great effort of these soldiers our train set off again. Going on a little ahead, we found scores of Sikhs lying on the ground, who were ready to attack our train. Our military men opened fire on them and the entrenchments of Sikhs became their graves.[72]

Khushwant Singh's fictional account is perhaps the most widely quoted reference which captures all the absurdities of partition and is set in the background of trains travelling between new borders.[73] It portrays Mano Majra, once a sleepy village but now on the newly created border between India and Pakistan. The book poignantly ends with the dilemma facing the main protagonist over what action they, as individuals, should take regarding a planned attack on a train headed for Pakistan with Muslim refugees. *Train to Pakistan*, written in 1956, was an important piece of fictional writing because it brought out the human dimension of partition. Rather than focusing on the 'great men', Singh was telling the story of how the decisions taken by them affected ordinary villages like Mano Majra and how their lives are thrown into turmoil by these decisions made faraway.

A refugee recalls the moment when Muslim and non-Muslim *kafilas* crossed each other near Wagah, which poignantly illustrates that sometimes the refugees' shared suffering was able to overcome hostility.

---

72 Interview with Saleem, Faisalabad, December 2002. Saleem migrated from Ludhiana.

73 Singh, *Train to Pakistan*.

They stopped where they were, and we stopped where we were. They were Muslim and we were non-Muslims. And no one spoke. We went on looking at each other. They had left their homes and friends behind, and so had we. But there was a strange kind of kinship, this kinship of sorrow. We were all refugees. We both had been broken on the wreck of history.[74]

The sentiments echo those of the poet Daman, when he says, 'that you have lost, as we too have lost in this divide'. In the end, approximately 7.3 million people crossed into India, 6.5 million into Pakistan, and 0.7 million into Bangladesh. The same figures taken as a percentage present a different story, 2.04, 20.9 and 1.66 per cent, respectively; the task for Pakistan is proportionally much more significant.[75]

Upon arrival, the refugees sought refuge in any makeshift accommodation that was available to them. Schools and colleges were closed until the end of February 1948 so that the buildings could be used as temporary shelter. Students were enlisted to assist the running of the camps. Other temporary camps had to be erected to cope with the masses of refugees. While there were camps dotted all over the Punjab, there were also so-called 'concentration camps', like the Walton Camp in Lahore and the Kurukshetra Camp in present-day Haryana, which were focal points for the movement of people. Such camps were responsible for housing as many as 300,000 people at any one time.[76] These facilities had to be improvised rapidly to accommodate the unanticipated tide of refugees.

Despite being in refugee camps and being stateless, the journey across the new border marked a sense of relief for many refugees – Stephen Keller makes the analogy with the feeling of having reached the 'promised land'.[77] In an interview with Kabir, he also recalled the sense of relief felt by everyone upon reaching Atari, comparing it to a religious shrine which they had finally

---

74 Andrew Whitehead, 'Refugees from Partition,' in *India Disasters Report: Towards a Policy Initiative*, eds. S. Parsuraman and P. V. Unnikrishnan (New York: Oxford University Press, 2000).

75 Prashant Bharadwaj, Asim Ijaz Khwaja and Atif Mian, 'The Big March: Migratory Flows after the Partition of India,' *HKS Faculty Research Working Paper Series* RWP08-029, June 2008, 7, accessed 21 May 2017, www.hks.harvard.edu.

76 *After Partition*, 56.

77 Stephen Keller, *Uprooting and Social Change: The Role of Refugees in Development* (New Delhi: Manohar, 1975), 59.

reached.[78] But this jubilation was short-lived. Makeshift refugee camps accommodated the millions who were uprooted, homeless and destitute and by the end of December 1947, there were more than 160 refugee camps all over India and 85 of those were in East Punjab.[79] August and September were still part of the monsoon season and this hampered the logistics of the evacuation process even further. It was noted that 'floods washed away roads and railway tracks and bridges, broke up transport and communications...mercilessly washed away the evacuees who were encamping in low-lying areas between Amritsar and Jullundur'.[80] Refugees themselves vividly recount stories of the floods sweeping in swollen bodies and blood-flowing rivers, images they are unable to confine to the past. Khurshid recounts her experiences:

> We witnessed atrocities of Hindus and Sikhs towards Muslims. They murdered Muslims brutally and shattered their bodies to pieces with spears. Displayed the corpses in the air on their blades and threw them on the earth afterwards. Those were the rainy days and water became red with blood of the corpses lying unattended on the ground. When we started from there, our feet got red with the bloody water.[81]

Khaira's account in Talbot and Tatla's *Epicentre of Violence* highlights the extent to which people became quite immune to otherwise disturbing and horrific accounts, which was for many the only way to survive the experience.

> During the movement of the convoy we used to drink water from a small stream which ran parallel to the passage. I remember, many times when we drank water from the stream, there were dead bodies flowing through it, one bloated body passing, then another one coming from the distance. This chain of dead bodies hardly stopped. People would just wait to let the body pass before filling their glasses of water.[82]

The impending winter presented further problems, with provision of warm clothing and blankets becoming a priority for the Governments of India

---

78 Interview with Kabir, Jhang Bazaar, Faisalabad, February 2003.
79 Department of Relief and Rehabilitation, Punjab, *Millions Live Again: A Survey of Refugee Relief in East Punjab* (not dated).
80 *Millions Live Again*, 4.
81 Interview with Khurshid, Raza Abad, Faisalabad, February 2002.
82 Interview with Sardar Bhaqwant Singh Khaira in Ian Talbot and Darshan Singh Tatla, eds., *Epicentre of Violence* (Delhi: Seagull, 2006), 53.

and Pakistan. While the provision of clothing, food and housing was at least something which could be calculated and catered for, the psychological impact of this trauma is something which has received little attention. One of the earliest studies was by Stephen Keller who spent time with Sikh and Hindu Punjabi refugees and tried to examine the social impact of this displacement. In his study, Keller identifies three stages in the refugee experience. The first one, which is relatively short, is the point of arrival in which the refugee is numbed by the experience and often overcome by grief. The second stage is survivor's guilt. Keller recounts a story of a man who became separated from his mother and came to Amritsar. There was a sense of guilt because his mother had been left behind, while he had survived. As a result of these feelings, he became restless, anxious and incapable of settling down. The continued inability to reconcile to this separation and the associated guilt eventually led him to Pakistan, to search for his mother, and although he was not able to locate her, there was at last some sort of closure for him.[83] This sense of restlessness felt by refugees and the inability to settle down resonates in many accounts provided by refugees. The final stage, according to Keller, is marked by aggression, not necessarily physical aggression but a stage in which the refugee feels invincible enough to take risks; this could be risks in business or even in the political sphere. As one of the refugees says, 'we have gone through so much; what more can happen to us? No one can do anything to us that can be more terrible than has already occurred. Why should we be afraid?'[84]

Rehabilitation of Bodies and Minds

One area where we witness women's agency at work is through the women who were assisting in the refugee camps and the rehabilitation of refugees. While reading the reports in *The Pakistan Times* it is obvious that the task of refugee rehabilitation was too great for the newly established Government of Pakistan and the Muslim League to handle alone; it required combined efforts. Consequently, groups that were the most capable, such as local students, were enlisted to assist with the unfolding human tragedy. Women were also taking the initiative themselves and organising and mobilising other women to work and contribute in refugee camps. Indeed, this was a crucial time for Muslim women to come out of seclusion (*purdah*) and assist in the rehabilitation process. It was an appeal to their maternal instincts, but moreover, it was also

---

83   Keller, *Uprooting and Social*, 62–3.
84   Keller, *Uprooting and Social*, 116.

an opportunity for women to improve and educate themselves. As these reports from *The Pakistan Times* show, girls were encouraged to aid in the relief and rehabilitation of women and as a result the students of Islamia College for Women, Lahore, organised themselves into groups. They made trips to the Mayo Hospital daily for distribution of clothes to sick refugees and were also involved in writing letters or broadcasting messages for the illiterate. In a press note released by the Ministry of Refugees and Rehabilitation, it was noted that 'so far they have delivered 1,200 clothes to the refugees in the hospital and written hundreds of messages'.[85] In addition to this, the college also opened classes for knitting and sewing, with all members of staff and students involved in voluntary work; this was in the form of contributing forty minutes of their time every day which was spent knitting jerseys and sweaters. The college, in a further effort to aid the rehabilitation of girls, decided to admit refugee students free of tuition fees and also provided free board in their hostel.[86]

The partition violence left the medical services stretched to the limit in dealing with the wounded and maimed women and children. In addition, the lack of fully trained support further hindered this desperate situation. Soon after partition there was an appeal by Fatima Jinnah, who had formed the Women's Relief Committee, '…to Muslim nurses and Muslim girls and women trained in first aid to offer their services for the noble cause of saving the lives of hundreds of their unfortunate sisters'.[87] Those willing to do this work were instructed to contact the women's section of the Muslim League. Interestingly, some of the initiatives took place before the official response by the state authorities, again emphasising the importance of how people often used their own networks and initiatives to mobilise support and provide aid for refugees.

One of the earliest initiatives was the establishment in 1948 of the Pakistan Voluntary Service (PVS) in Lahore, formed under the guidance of Begum Liaquat Ali Khan,[88] Miss Macqueen, Begum Shah Nawaz,[89] and Fatima

---

85   *The Pakistan Times*, 30 October 1947.
86   *The Pakistan Times*, 30 October 1947.
87   *The Pakistan Times*, 7 September 1947.
88   In 1949, Begum Ra'ana arranged a conference with women from all over Pakistan; this resulted in the creation of the All Pakistan Women's Association. This was a voluntary and non-political organisation designed to support and strengthen women socially, culturally and through improved provision of education.
89   Begum Shah Nawaz and Begum Shaista Ikramullah were the only two women in the Pakistan Constituent Assembly and Central Legislature in 1947. Shah Nawaz was also one of the founding members of the All Pakistan Women's Association.

Jinnah.[90] Begum Ra'ana Liaquat Ali Khan was the wife of the first Prime Minister of Pakistan and assumed a leading role in the women's voluntary service. The organisation encouraged women to take up responsibilities such as the administration of first aid, distribution of food and clothing, dealing with health problems and epidemics but voluntary help also took the form of providing the refugees with the much needed moral and emotional support. Begum Shah Nawaz, a leading Muslim League figure and a member of the Constituent Assembly, made an appeal to women in West Punjab to come forward and work for the noble cause as she saw it. In a statement on 23 September 1947, she said:

> …Their mangled bodies, their tear-filled eyes and their trembling hands await whatever succour and hope we can give them. At this hour, it is the duty of every Pakistani man, woman and child to do his or her duty. My sisters, you have never failed your nation. When patriotism called, you came forth in thousands and did not hesitate to face lathi, tear-gas and bullets and some of you went to jail. Today your country needs you as never before…You are the real soldiers of Pakistan. Your motherland needs you. Your helpless sisters await your aid. You have never failed your nation before I know that you will not fail now.[91]

Initially, there was a good response to this appeal and hundreds of women had offered their voluntary services to PVS regardless of the problems with transport and logistics which hampered the relief process. Begum Shah Nawaz, who was a special assistant in Rehabilitation and Employment, was keen to maintain the momentum and appealed to every woman to register her name in the women voluntary service's register.[92] However, a week later, there was a report in the newspaper again noting the lack of women who were willing to come forward and volunteer:

> Many women who stayed back from enrolling their names did so because they felt they were not sufficiently educated. It will surprise them to find that the kind of help needed in the refugee camps and hospitals is what

---

90　Fatima Jinnah is referred to as Madr-e-Millat, mother of the nation. She played a leading role in the resettlement of refugees and was proponent of women's emancipation, encouraging their participation in the creation of the Pakistan state.

91　*The Pakistan Times*, 23 September 1947.

92　*The Pakistan Times*, 1 October 1947.

most of us are competent to render. To comb a dusty head with wounds and blood clots, to wash faces smeared with dirt and tears, to soothe the nerves of an old woman broken in body and spirit both – to comfort a young mother who has been tossed off this side of the shore to face an uncertain destiny at the hands of the strangers – these are activities for which any woman is trained, and while rendering them, she will be educating herself further.[93]

There are many accounts and reports of Fatima Jinnah visiting camps, not only to boost morale but also to highlight the important work being done by individuals on a daily basis. This served as a further incentive for more women to become involved in the rehabilitation of refugees. On one such visit, *The Pakistan Times* on 30 October 1947 reports:

Miss Jinnah, who was shown round a number of refugees, in particular to stranded women and girls recovered from non-Muslims. She expressed her deep sympathy with them in their suffering. There were a number of lady volunteer workers busy helping the refugees in the camps. Miss Jinnah appreciated their work. Begum Azin Ullah is in charge of these workers. She explained that there is a batch of 60 workers who work in two shifts.[94]

In October 1947, the West Punjab government also opened an 'Industrial Home for Mohajir widows and destitute women of middle classes to give them industrial training, which would enable them to earn independent living in due course'.[95] The training provided not only ranged from work skills such as tailoring, embroidery work, spinning and weaving of tape, to the more immediate concerns of the nation like elementary nursing and first aid, but also provided for religious instruction.[96] Trainees were provided with free boarding and lodging but with the hope that they would eventually become self-sufficient once they started earning money. Employment exchanges were set up in order to find suitable positions for women. Other social services were also available, notably, marriage bureaus were set up where names of girls and boys of marriageable age were entered in order

---

93 *The Pakistan Times*, 7 October 1947.
94 *The Pakistan Times*, 30 October 1947.
95 *The Pakistan Times*, 15 October 1947.
96 *The Pakistan Times*, 15 October 1947.

to find them suitable partners.[97] Lahore was the main hub of activities where homes for destitute women such as the Sir Ganga Ram Widows' Home and also a Girls Training College were established. Women who were rescued from East Punjab were brought to homes such as these if no relatives were traced.

The women who were at the forefront of these activities were predominantly from elite backgrounds; they were articulate and able to organise and generate support for assisting refugees. We, therefore, repeatedly see the names of women like Fatima Jinnah, Begum Liaquat Ali Khan, Miss Macqueen and Begum Mumtaz Shah Nawaz being reported as taking a leading role in organising these activities. While it was essential to have this strong female leadership, more practical and urgent assistance was also required in the form of collecting bedding, blankets and warm clothing due to the onset of winter. On 20 December, there was yet another public appeal: 'Help is required from every one especially women. I mention women, because after all they are the managers of the household. Winter clothes help should primarily be their concern. Let the women of Pakistan prove that they are good managers'.[98] There were also recommendations for 'every housewife' to follow which would greatly benefit the 'cause of humanity'. The advice is simple:

> Why not organise a knitting competition in your *mohalla* or your town. Young girls would love to show their prowess, and every week there would be a fair collection of knitted garments to send to the refugee relief centres. These are some of the things which women can do to help in this great task before the country. Remember, each garment you give will save a human life.[99]

What these newspaper reports show is the active role of women in the rehabilitation of refugees in Pakistan. They were integral to the needs of ensuring that the refugees had some support and assistance when they arrived in camps. Women helped in camps, provided medical care, domestic help and education or even just merely donated warm clothing for the refugees. It enabled women to become active agents in the creation of the new state and saw an increasing number of women come out of seclusion to assume a greater role in society.

---

97   *The Pakistan Times*, 11 October 1947.
98   *The Pakistan Times*, 20 December 1947.
99   *The Pakistan Times*, 20 December 1947.

Evidently both the governments of India and Pakistan were surprised, and unprepared for the movement of people; many of the people themselves had no plans to move either. As refugees, some found acceptance, others moved around until they settled, and the rest found the promised land did not welcome them. Tatla depicts the experience of one family from the Sandal Bar:

> Yes, we were taunted by the term, sometimes called *panahgir*, more often, refugees. Someone will say, look, 'a refugee is here'. We would try to divert the conversation by saying, 'we are your brothers' and sometimes argue 'we are not refugees, and we have come back to our native lands', did not we have everything here? [sic] Some did help us, others were hostile. 'Refugee' was a shameful term, a tag we carried for year, [sic] whenever the term was mentioned, we felt ashamed. It still does.[100]

Their common religious identity was not always enough for them to be assimilated easily into the new landscape but they were stuck with the language of religious labels such as *panahgirs* or *muhajirs*[101] for Muslim refugees and *sharanarthis* for Hindu and Sikh.[102] The term *muhajir* has largely become an important source of identity for Urdu-speaking partition-related migrants and their descendants from the United Provinces living particularly in Karachi. It is therefore mostly associated with the Urdu-speaking people, rather than the Punjabi migrants. The terms themselves also disguised the fact that they were now aliens in their own lands. The label of 'refugee' was etched upon them permanently, a term to be associated with the destitute, helpless, and homeless. But over time, this temporary dislocation turned into a fragile permanence and with that a new identity emerged. They had not chosen this necessarily at the point of departure but there was little chance of now returning to what they had known before their lives were ruptured.

---

100 Darshan Singh Tatla, 'The Sandal Bar: Memoirs of a Jat Sikh Farmer,' *The Panjab Past and Present* 29, nos. 1 and 2 (1995): 173.

101 The word, however, had very different connotations because *mohajir* is an Arabic word meaning immigrant or emigrant and is associated with the migration of the prophet Muhammad and his companions when they left Mecca for Medina.

102 Vazira Fazila-Yacoobali Zamindar, *The Long Partition and the Making of Modern South Asia: Refugees, Boundaries, Histories* (India: Penguin, 2007), 8.

Khwaja Fariduddin Masud Ganjshakar, popularly known as Baba Farid[1]

Farid, if you are maltreated
Do not react with violence and projection
Visit the Other
And kiss his feet in humility and affection!

Farid, do not belittle the dust
The living march on its bed
The dead are buried under its crust

Farid, meet evil with good
Show no hatred or revenge
Your being will stay away from vanity
Healthy and pure in serenity

Mian Muhammad Baksh

Saif-ul-Malook[2]

Dushman marey tey khushee na karey, sajnaa wee mar janaa,
Deegar tey din gayaa Mohammad, orrak noon dub jana.

Do not rejoice at the death of your enemy because your friends too have to die,
The afternoon sun is soon going to set.

---

1   Harjeet Singh Gill, *Sufi Rhythms: Interpreted in Free Verse* (Patiala: Punjabi University, 2007), 5, 7 and 14.

2   *Sufi Poetry*, accessed 8 October 2016, https://sufipoetry.wordpress.com/category/mian-muhammad-baksh/.

5

Sacred Malerkotla

The partition-related violence adds to what is undoubtedly one of the most violent centuries, characterised by conflict, genocide and persecution at a truly global level.[1] The birth of India and Pakistan was therefore completely over-shadowed with communal violence, particularly in Punjab. Since independence, India has continued to experience numerous violent episodes of communal violence and so it seems remarkable to find places like Malerkotla that defy this prevailing perception. This is even more remarkable given that in 1947, when the province of Punjab was being carved up to create the new states of India and Pakistan, Malerkotla remained a safe haven for people while the rest of the surrounding districts were engulfed in some of the most horrific violence recorded. Among this picture of chaos, indiscriminate violence and brutality, there is another history of partition, that of the harmony and friendship shown by communities towards each other. This is often overlooked by the studies of partition, which tend to focus on the destruction and disruption caused by the partitioning of the Punjab province. Much more has been written about Malerkotla in recent years, as a model of tolerance, inter-communal relations, inter-religious harmony and so on. The town is a powerful reminder of what is possible if the prevailing political and social forces desire peace and harmony.

Malerkotla's experience in 1947 also sheds light on a number of wider issues and complexities behind the breakdown in law and order. Within Partition Studies little is written about the absence of violence in 1947, partly because it questions the received histories of the East Punjab Muslims' sacrifices in the achievement of a Pakistan homeland, and within 'Sikh' East Punjab discourse it is an unfortunate reminder of a different and more tolerant plural history. By focusing on the violent nature of communalised histories, both nations can be justified in promoting and maintaining the current stance which continues to endorse division rather than reconciliation. Yet, if for a moment more accounts of cross-communal collaboration were recognised more widely, it would challenge the often jingoist state discourse. In essence,

---

1   See further, Michael Mann, *The Dark Side of Democracy: Explaining Ethnic Cleansing* (Cambridge: Cambridge University Press, 2005).

it would help build bridges across those international boundaries and so accounts of inter-faith dialogue in colonial Punjab remain peripheral to the wider 'high politics' which continue to dominate today, as they have previously.

In Malerkotla, the popular myth that its peace rested on the blessing of Guru Gobind Singh on the town raises the question of the extent to which traditional notions of the sacred and of *izzat* may have prevented violence rather than promoted it. This stands in sharp contrast to debates already discussed in the previous chapter of how religiosity and *izzat* also prompted acts of violence. The differential experience of violence in the state and in the neighbouring areas raises the question of the extent to which communalism and communal violence differed in princely India to that in British India. Moreover, Malerkotla provides us with how conflict management and inter-faith dialogue can aid communal harmony. For these reasons, Malerkotla serves as an important area for understanding the endurance of peace when surrounded by violence.

Princely Malerkotla and British Rule

In contemporary India, Malerkotla is perhaps one of the few places where one can truly get a flavour of pre-partitioned Punjab; it is a town in which Muslims, Sikhs and Hindus reside, and interestingly in East Punjab, a town where the Persian script is still publicly and widely visible.[2] In 1947, Malerkotla was one of a handful of small princely states ruled by Muslims in the East Punjab region. The walled town of Malerkotla was the heart of a small Muslim kingdom and unlike the much larger neighbouring Sikh princely states and the British-administered districts, it largely escaped the violence of 1947. Today the former princely state is a *tehsil* of Sangrur district in the Indian Punjab.

What is unique about Malerkotla town is that it stands as the only place in East Punjab that possesses a majority Muslim population, with over 60 per cent belonging to the Muslim community. When the Punjab province was being carved up, the population of Muslims in the Indian Punjab declined from 53 per cent in 1941 to 2 per cent in 1951.[3] Malerkotla, however, has continued to remain an important Muslim centre and, indeed, its Muslim population increased as a result of the partition disturbances. It is this unique

---

2   Asit Jolly, 'Myth of Malerkotla,' *Asian Age*, 11 May 1997.
3   Census of India 1951, vol. 8, Punjab, Pepsu, Himachal Pradesh, Bilaspur and
      Delhi.

demographic feature of Malerkotla that is so fascinating and provides an important case study in understanding inter-faith relationships during the tumultuous period leading up the division of the province. More widely, the case study provides an opportunity to understand how inter-faith dialogue and conflict resolution can be used positively to maintain harmony.

Malerkotla was formerly one of the oldest princely states in the region. The ruling lineage descendants were Sherwani Afghans who came from Kabul in 1467 as officials of the Delhi emperors.[4] Malerkotla, along with Bahawalpur, Loharu, Dujana and Pataudi, formed the only Muslim-ruled states of Punjab. It was also one of the smallest states occupying only 165 square miles of land and a population of 88,000. It was therefore, in comparison, dwarfed by the neighbouring Sikh states of Patiala and Jind, both of which occupied nearly 6,000 square miles; Patiala was one of the most populous with nearly 2 million persons. Territorially, Bahawalpur (now in Pakistan) was the largest of the princely states in Punjab measuring 16,434 square miles.[5]

The population of Malerkotla in 1941 was distributed fairly evenly between the three religious communities; Muslims were the largest group comprising 38 per cent of the population, Sikhs with 34 per cent and Hindus making up 27 per cent. Muslims, however, dominated Malerkotla town. The population of the town in 1941 was 29,321 with the Muslim community comprising 76 per cent of the population (Hindus formed 21 per cent and Sikhs 1.5 per cent); this trend has continued in the post-partition period. Although after partition the population of the Muslim community is much lower, there is still a large concentration in Malerkotla town; comparatively, it has a much higher percentage of Muslims than neighbouring *tehsils*.[6]

In May 1809, Malerkotla along with other *Cis-Sutlej* states came under the protection of the East India Company. The state established close relations with the British and helped them in the Gurkha war, the Bharatpur siege, the Anglo-Sikh wars and in suppressing the revolt in 1857, rendering all possible

---

4   Sir Lepel H. Griffen, *Chiefs and Families of Note in the Punjab* (Lahore: Civil and Military Gazetteer Press, 1940), 530.

5   Data based on Census of India 1941, vol. 9, Punjab.

6   Census of India, Punjab, 1941 and 1961. The 1951 Census does not provide a religious breakdown, thus a comparison is only possible between 1941 and 1961. The figures for 1961 represent only the rural population, but it provides a useful guide as 83 per cent of Sangrur's population was rural.

Map 5.1: Princely India

assistance to the British government.[7] As a state, Malerkotla took its place among the 565 independent princely states that occupied over two-fifths of the subcontinent and one-third of its population.[8] Princely states were the survivors of the traditional Indian political system. The size of these states varied hugely from those comparable in size to France to those that were small enough to be someone's backyard.[9] The princely states are often referred to as a collective body but there are many distinctions between them, apart from their obvious physical variations. The rulers emanated from a diverse ancestral heritage, their cultural backgrounds were as colourful as that of the subcontinent itself and their style of leadership equally varied. However, there was much to unite them, arising from the lifestyle that went with having autocratic power and the mythical status which raised them above the common man.[10]

The British astutely underpinned their rule with the princes' collaboration and thus engaged in formal agreements with some of them, known as Subsidiary Alliances. The princes themselves were fearful of British intrusion into their territory and thus found it more prudent to cooperate and work with the British rather than oppose them, thereby guaranteeing their status. In return, the princes were granted autonomy with respect to their internal affairs. However, they retained a closely connected link to the British empire. This relationship was managed via a network of resident and political agents of the Government of India.[11] The states themselves were pursuing a very different political system to that of the British; they would be best described as 'autocratic dynastic monarchies'.[12] Yet, as Ian Copland argues, '…paradoxically, this unsecular mode of governance proved remarkably effective in keeping the lid on communal violence'.[13]

---

7 Nawab Iftikhar Ali Khan, *History of the Ruling Family of Sheikh Sadruddin Sadar-I-Jahan of Malerkotla* (Patiala: Punjabi University, 2000), 107.

8 Ian Copland, *The Princes of India in the Endgame of Empire 1917-1947* (New Delhi: Cambridge University Press, 1999).

9 Copland, *Princes of India*, 8; and Surjit Mansingh, *Historical Dictionary of India*, (New Delhi, 1998), 332–5. For example, Veja-no-ness in Kathiawar was less than an acre broad and had a population of 184 according to the 1921 census.

10 Copland, *Princes of India*, 12.

11 Ian Copland, 'The Political Geography of Religious Conflict: Towards an Explanation of the Relative Infrequency of Communal Riots in the Indian Princely States,' *International Journal of Punjab Studies* 7, no. 1 (2000): 5.

12 Copland, 'Political Geography,' 1–27.

13 Copland, 'Political Geography,' 5.

An important aspect of this was the fact that the princes unlike the British were not neutral in religious matters. This lessened the scope for disputes in which the adjudication of the rulers was sought over such issues as cow slaughter and the control of sacred space. Copland also suggests that the moral authority of the rulers was a factor; the princes were representatives of an unbroken history that stretched back thousands of years and they had long been recognised as the legitimate rulers and epitomised the tradition of cross-communal support. According to Sir Conrad Corfield (former political advisor to the viceroy), 'personal rule in the States seldom had difficulty in securing this consent [from the people]'.[14] Indeed the rulers, according to him, had no intention of giving up personal rule except under pressure, even though the British progressed with parliamentary democracy in the rest of India. This led to two opposing systems to develop autonomously. By the time independence was looming, it became apparent that the viceroy's policy towards the princes was one of prevarication. Their options for forming states unions were unlikely and the only way they could be admitted to the commonwealth was if they joined up with India or Pakistan. Corfield was critical of this approach which was a 'gross breach of faith'.[15] A new central department was set up in June to deal with matters pertaining to the states, and their relative smooth merger following independence is credited to Sardar Patel who oversaw the Ministry of the States, with V. P. Menon as secretary.[16] Copland has suggested that this was indeed a 'bloodless revolution'.[17] Malerkotla, being a small Muslim state within Punjab, quickly formed alliances after 1947 to become part of the Punjab and East Punjab States Union (PEPSU). This united eight states (Patiala, Jind, Nabha, Faridkot, Malerkotla, Kapurthala and two non-salute

---

14   Sir Conrad Corfield, *The Princely India I Knew: From Reading to Mountbatten* (Madras: Indo British Historical Society, 1975), 175.

15   Memo by Corfield, 29 May 1947, *Transfer of Power*, vol. X, quoted in Copland, *Princes of India*, 255.

16   Read Menon's first-hand account of the integration of the states in India. V. P. Menon, *The Story of the Integration of the Indian States* (Calcutta: Orient Longmans, 1956).

17   Ian Copland, 'The Integration of the Princely States: A "Bloodless Revolution"?' *South Asia* XVIII, Special Issue (1995). Also see Yaqoob Khan Bangash, *A Princely Affair: The Accession and Integration of the Princely States of Pakistan, 1947–1955* (Karachi: Oxford University Press, 2015) to understand the integration of the states in Pakistan. The majority of the 565 princely states were in India with a small number coming under Pakistan.

states, Kalsia and Nalagarh) to form a union until 1956 when it then became absorbed into Punjab State. Interestingly, V. P. Menon notes the lack of interest in political affairs by the Punjab state rulers:

> ...the Maharajah of Jind had no interest in political affairs...the Maharajah of Kapurthala was a very old man... The Maharajah of Nabha has always been dominated by people around him and was mainly concerned with *shikar* and similar pursuits. The Nawab of Malerkotla was a man of undoubtedly pleasant manner; all the same, I could not dispel the feeling that he was one of those whose attitude towards life was governed largely by self-interest. The Maharajah of Patiala was of course the most important of the rulers in this area.[18]

Managing Conflict

Evidently, princely India was not immune from external influences brought about by British rule. It is clear from the British records that there were increased tensions between the communities and signs of the politicisation of communal disputes. However, there was a tradition of cross-communal support in princely India which had developed over many centuries, espousing policies of accommodation towards local minorities. Princes 'used symbolic action to demonstrate the sincerity of their personal commitment to the principle of bi-partisanship'.[19] This was done publicly by attending cross-communal festivals or generally by paying respect at the others' place of worship. There was also a system of 'managed pluralism' whereby issues such as prayer times, routes of religious procession and playing of music were controlled. The most contentious issue, however, was cow slaughter. In most Hindu/Sikh-ruled states this practice was prohibited and the Muslims invariably ended up using alternatives to the cow as a sacrifice on the occasion of *Bak'r 'id*. It is worth noting that under the British administration there were no restrictions on cow slaughter, and that, with the growth of Hindu revivalism in the late nineteenth century, became a major factor in destabilising communal harmony.

In Malerkotla, there were clashes over prayer times during May 1935. These arose due to the recitation of the *katha* in Moti Bazaar, which overlooked the Masjid Loharan, belonging to the more puritanical Ahl-e-Hadith sect. The Ramayan *katha* was being sponsored by Peshawari Mal

---

18 Menon, *Story of the Integration*, 242.
19 Copland 'Political Geography,' 10.

and it continued for days and when it began to interfere with the *isha* (night) prayers of the Muslims, there were protests.[20] Both Hindus and Muslims protested; there were public processions, *hartals* (closures) and unnecessary noise being made during evening prayer times. However, after four nights of continuous tension, the state authorities suspended both the *katha* and *isha* prayers. The tension ultimately though continued and eventually resulted in the attack on Lala Puran Mal, who was vice president of the Malerkotla Hindu Sabha, by four Muslims.[21] The hasty decision by the state to arrest and execute the perpetrators created further tension. Shortly after this event, the body of a young Muslim girl was discovered; she was clutching a copy of the Quran.[22] There was, however, a perception that these cases were being treated differently, with protests being organised by many Muslims at the apparent leniency shown to Hindus.

The issue over the prayer times, however, was finally resolved when the authorities intervened and imposed different prayer times for each community.[23] But there are also signs that the community was becoming more politicised than previously. We can see in the following letter to the Nawab of Malerkotla that there is a perception that issues, which previously had little impact on communal relations, were now being used to exert political pressure on the 'other' community.

> It is a great pity that the feelings between Hindus and Mohammedans should have become strained just as we are on the eve of Provincial autonomy. Twenty years ago, the Muslims were able to carry on their prayers in spite of all disturbances outside of the mosque. The demand that there should be no noise shows that their mental concentration in prayer has become weak. Those who want to pray can carry on their prayers in the midst of all noise.[24]

Second, there is a letter from the All-India Hindu Mahasabha sent to the Nawab of Malerkotla on 2 November 1935. The letter was written in response

---

20 Letter to His Highness from the home minister, Zaman Khan, 19 October 1935. Malerkotla State Records, no. 3, File 74, PSA.

21 Malerkotla Affairs, IOR: L/PS/13/1345.

22 Anna Bigelow, *Sharing the Sacred: Practicing Pluralism in Muslim North India* (USA: Oxford University Press, 2010), 113.

23 Malerkotla Affairs, IOR: L/PS/13/1345.

24 Malerkotla State Records Letter to the Nawab from Prem Bhawan, Solan, 20 August 1935. Malerkotla State Records, no. 3, File 74, PSA.

to allegations that the inspector of police had been siding with Muslims regarding the murder of Puran Mal.

> The Hindu subjects of your Highness have been groaning under various disadvantages, because of their religion and their cup of misery is now full of the brim. It is your highness, who can bring consolation and mitigate their sorrows by acts of justice and fairness, of which Your Highness's subjects are despairing at the hands of your officials.[25]

Again as these documents indicate, there was already a culture of mistrust among the communities, even in Malerkotla. So what is significant in the case of Malerkotla, is that these incidences remained largely confined and did not escalate further into larger communal riots or violent clashes. This is clearly a result of pursuing a more interventionist approach, influencing in the management of temples and shrines, while the administrators in British India maintained distance.

However, the level of communal disturbances in Malerkotla stands in sharp contrast with neighbouring Sikh princely states. Copland recognises that the stability brought by the princely order collapsed in the Punjab region in the 1940s. He links this with the 'breaking down of their constitutional backwardness and relative isolation',[26] and draws attention to the fact that rulers not only 'tolerated', but actually encouraged acts of violence. The level of conflict in such princely states as Patiala and Faridkot contrasts dramatically with the situation in Malerkotla. For example, many Muslims were killed and women abducted when a Sikh *jatha* supported by the Faridkot military attacked the village of Nathu Wala of Faridkot on 18 August 1947.[27]

In Patiala, in a short space of time, around 6,000 Muslims were killed. An indication of the ferocity of this violence is the fact that the authorities

---

25   Letter to Nawab Ahmad Ali Khan from general secretary, AIHM, Padamraj Jain, 2 November 1935. Malerkotla State Records, no. 3, File 74, PSA.

26   Copland, 'Integration of the Princely States,' 42.

27   Situation Reports on Disturbances in East Punjab and Contiguous Areas during and after August 1947, Mudie Papers Mss. Eur. F 164, National Documentation Centre, *Disturbances in the Punjab, 1947: A Compilation of Official Documents* (Islamabad: Government of Pakistan, 1995); Copland, 'The Integration of the Princely States,' 42; and Copland, 2002. Ian Copland builds on the argument which suggests that the Sikh princes colluded with the Akali Dal in hope of establishing a Sikh state after the British departure.

needed four days to clear all the corpses in the city.[28] In *Jat*-dominated rural areas of Patiala, Nabha and Faridkot states, Muslim villages were burned and looted.[29] The authorities in these Sikh states were clearly in collusion with the perpetrators and in some instances sanctioned the violence. There was a similar bloodletting in the West Punjab Muslim-ruled state of Bahawalpur where Sikhs and Hindus were driven out.[30] But, comparatively, Copland has maintained that communal violence was significantly less in the princely states than in the British-administered Punjab by the early twentieth century.[31] He argues that in the 1920s and 1930s the princely states experienced, per head of population, far fewer communal Hindu–Muslim riots than the provinces of British India.[32] At the same time, it is acknowledged that reporting of communal incidences was less common in princely India than British India. But in Punjab, there was considerable violence in the princely states in 1947,[33] some of which was instigated by the rulers themselves.[34]

While there was climate of tolerance in princely India, not all communities were treated equally, the ruling regime's community generally fared much better, securing better employment and educational opportunities. By keeping their heads down the 'other' community managed to co-exist and remained free from harassment, but this did not of course mean that during partition they would remain free from harm.

The Space between Peace and Violence

Amid the accounts of anarchy, brutality and depraved levels of partition-related violence in the Punjab there is this alternative reality. Malerkotla, despite the existence of some tension, seemed to defy the violence enveloping the region at the time.

---

28 Copland, 'The Master and the Maharajas: The Sikh Princes and the East Punjab Massacres of 1947,' *Modern Asian Studies* 36, no. 3 (2002), 686 ff.

29 Copland, 'Master and the Maharaja,' 686.

30 G. D. Khosla, *Stern Reckoning: A Survey of Events Leading Up to and Following the Partition of India* (New Delhi: Oxford University Press, 1949, reprint 1989), 212–16, 288–9.

31 Copland, 'Political Geography,' 1–27.

32 Copland, Political Geography,' 16.

33 Copland, 'Political Geography,' 2–3.

34 Copland, 'Integration of the Princely States'; and 'The Master and the Maharajas'.

On the night of 18 March 1948 Bimal Chand, Pujaeri Jain Sidhu in a public speech dilating upon the disturbances in the Punjab said that Malerkotla State is the only place in the whole province where peace has remained totally undisturbed. Hindus and Muslims are living as brethren. It is due to the efficient management of the Ruler and the Public that such peaceful conditions have prevailed over there. On the morning of 19 March 1948 in the Jain Sathanak Moti Bazaar and at 2–3 pm in village Jamalpura this Jain Sadhu in his public speeches dealt upon the unity amongst people and said that it was because no atrocities were committed in the state that Hindus and Muslims were sitting side by side despite of so grim and awful happenings in East and West Punjab.[35]

There are a number of reasons given for the lack of violence in Malerkotla and one of them perhaps has something to do with the spirit of *ikatth*, which is the unity between different communities.[36] Speaking with the people of Malerkotla, many seemed to suggest that there was something different and unique about the place. This may have something to do with the 500-year-old principality being able to prevent violence engulfing its state during 1947 and also subsequently in independent India, which has seen numerous episodic clashes between Hindus and Muslims. Furthermore, Malerkotla remained peaceful even during the militancy years of the 1980s and 1990s, which gripped much of East Punjab. It was also quite apparent and exceptional that communal harmony was emphasised rather than the usual propaganda of enmity and tension among different communities. In reality, though, it is harder to assess whether this was an image that people wished to project or whether it accurately and genuinely reflected their experiences. Having spent time researching in Malerkotla, some of these personal testimonies provide a glimpse and understanding of amity in Malerkotla.

One of the most compelling interviews conducted in Malerkotla was with Mohammed, a *Kamboj* Muslim. He was born in neighbouring Nabha state and fled to Malerkotla for refuge during the partition violence. He still remembers the events of that period vividly when he was forced to flee his

---

35 Fortnightly Reports to the Regional Commissioner, East Punjab States, 10 April. 1948. Malerkotla State Records, PSA.

36 Anna Bigelow, 'Walking through the Streets of Malerkotla,' *The Tribune*, Chandigarh, 2 December 2000. This was based on research by Bigelow for her doctoral thesis, 'Sharing Saints, Shrines and Stories: Practising Pluralism in Punjab' (University of California Santa Barbara, 2004).

house along with his family. As he narrated his story, tears flowed, evoking the pain and suffering inflicted.

> Well, there was fighting there [ancestral village], it carried on and on, in the end it got too much and we had to go. From Nabha there was this place Nalla, where we stopped. We were all attacked there, everyone got killed. There must have been 400–500 people [mostly from his village]. Yes, they all died… I covered myself within all the dead bodies. They were putting all the bodies into trucks or vehicles… Well, I was still alive, but they were throwing them into the river. Only about 15 people survived this. The river where we were thrown into, there was a bridge near there and I hid. Once they had left the place, we made our way to Nabha city, where we had relatives.[37]

After spending a month in Nabha city, Mohommed came to Malerkotla, where his *bhua* [paternal aunt] lived. Later in the interview, it transpired that in that attack Mohammed had lost all his family, two brothers, grandfather, father and mother. The attackers were apparently a large group of *sardars* [Sikhs], using rifles and other weapons. Interestingly, Mohammed chose to remain in India, even though his *thaya* [paternal uncle] lived in Gujranwala, which became part of Pakistan.

While Mohammed represents the victim of partition violence, Nirmal Singh represents the other darker side, that of the perpetrator. He lived at the time just outside Malerkotla and was involved in the massacres that devastated the area. When the interview was conducted in 2001, Nirmal Singh was 79 years old, frail and blind and possibly living the last days of his life. It seemed incongruous as we sat there chatting about his involvement in the violence surrounded by the beautiful and serene green plains of Punjab while he rocked his young grandson to sleep. He appeared quite passive and unable to commit such a crime, but his past was filled with the dark greyness of partition violence. He talked about a bridge and a train track close to his village where a lot of violence took place. He was involved in some of the conflict along with six other men from the same village. He admitted to killing Muslims and when asked about how many he simply replied, 'What is the use of counting now? In that mayhem, who knows?'[38]

---

37   Interview with Kushi Mohammed, Malerkotla, August 2001.
38   Interview with Nirmal Singh, Malerkotla, August 2001.

When questioned about his motive behind these killings, he responded that 'they assaulted our women and sent them here for us. At that time our blood was boiling. At that time we just wanted to cut them up and eat them'.[39] Nirmal Singh admitted being caught up in the retaliatory violence, recalling:

> Those women who came from the other side [Pakistan], their *gudiya* [daughters] were taken and assaulted, stripped and then taken to Patiala...Then Patiala answered in the same way, the Muslim girls were abused badly and sent to Pakistan in the trains. I have seen with my own eyes and accompanied them. We were present there during the violence, what's the point of lying to you.[40]

What transpired during the interview was the lack of planning in this instance. The following extract highlights how this was clearly also a time of chaos when many of the men decided to take action themselves, which in this case involved revenge attacks and therefore justified in the eyes of the perpetrators.

> We just went around here and there, no one in the village really did any work during that time... We went to their [victims] villages, we'd go and drag them out of their houses. We'd go to one house kill them and then go to another house and so on. Most of this happened because of *izzat*, because of those trains coming here with bodies. If it weren't for that, none of this would have happened. It lasted for one month... it was very intense during that month.[41]

Whether this is a true representation of what actually happened is difficult to say, as Nirmal Singh may have justified his actions by displacing the blame. His excuse for killing were the trains, which came loaded with dead bodies from Pakistan, and thus his anger was justified on the premise that the 'other' community instigated the violence. There are similar accounts in West Punjab too. Yet, had he felt that his actions were defensible, there would have been no reason to conceal all the events. Interviews with other residents confirmed that he was absent from the village for the month after partition was announced. Moreover, he refrained from telling his children and grandchildren about his role during partition. Nirmal Singh's peers were aware of the sudden material

---

39 Interview with Nirmal Singh.
40 Interview with Nirmal Singh.
41 Interview with Nirmal Singh.

wealth he acquired following this period, but his family apparently remained oblivious as to how exactly this had been obtained.

These personal narratives are important in understanding and contextualising that, while popular mythology suggests no violence took place in Malerkotla, this was not the case in its immediate proximity. While Mohammed fled Nabha to seek refuge in Malerkotla, Nirmal Singh, who only lived 18 km away from the princely state, was involved in the violence. The violence engulfed not only neighbouring princely states, but also the adjoining district of Ludhiana, which was formally under British control. The Muslim localities of Fieldgung, Abdullahpura and Kucha Khilijan and Karipura in Ludhiana city, for example, were attacked and looted on 24 August 1947, while outlying villages as Tehera, Modewal and Malian Bajan were raided by Sikh *jathas* with considerable loss of life.[42]

Furthermore, the reality was that the state was 'always a potential source of trouble', it was always feared that agitators from neighbouring Ludhiana would cause trouble but joint police arrangements were in place to keep order.[43] Indeed, it was noted that 'communal rivalries are endemic and almost as explosive as in the Punjab proper…[but] good administration provides the only procurable safeguard'.[44] To suggest that Malerkotla completely escaped communalism in the 1930s and 1940s would be inaccurate, but the administration is key to understanding how the volatile situations were managed effectively to prevent them from escalating. The fragility of the space between peace and violence was always there.

Sacred Malerkotla

Malerkotla, through the ages, has been associated with pluralism and shared religious space; this is most evident in the tomb of Haider Sheikh, the Sufi saint who founded Malerkotla in 1454. A fair is held every Thursday at the *dargah* of Haider Sheikh with offerings being made by devotees spanning across religious boundaries. On the first Thursday of the month, this fair is much larger attracting thousands of people from outside Malerkotla. It is attended by large numbers of Hindus and Sikhs, who make offerings for wishes of a son, wealth, prosperity and so on.[45] Thus, there is certainly an important role

---

42 Mudie Papers in NDC, *Disturbances in the Punjab*, 406–7.
43 Letter to Fitze, 30 January 1942. IOR: L/PS/13/1345 Malerkotla Affairs.
44 Letter to Fitze, 30 January 1942. IOR: L/PS/13/1345 Malerkotla Affairs.
45 *Malerkotla State Gazetteer* (Lahore: The Civil and Military Press, 1904), 44.

played by the presence of shrines which reach out to all communities, which clearly aids in promoting inter-religious relations.

Anna Bigelow has attempted to analyse and contextualise Malerkotla's apparent tranquillity. Her explanations centre on religious and the pluralistic forces that have been influential in Malerkotla.[46] Bigelow has put forward a persuasive argument in her assertions that the positive forces of spirituality and pluralism can prevent or at least inhibit the kind of communal violence seen in 1947 and since. However, while spirituality can act as a form of social disapproval, it cannot explain the decisions made at the state level. The role and behaviour of the state is of vital importance; it is the state after all that is in charge.

Sufi shrines generally in India attract cross-communal devotees and it is not unusual to find Sikhs and Hindus alongside Muslims offering prayers. Denzil Ibbetson,[47] writing in colonial India, notes how shrines such as those of Sakhi Sarwar attracted people from all communities.[48] Ron Geaves and Catherine Geaves also note the eclectic nature of religious life in the region and how the folk traditions within these communities are particularly blurred, especially with respect to tombs and shrines to holy men.[49] Therefore, this explanation of shared sacred space cannot be overplayed. Furthermore, the influence of *dargahs* and their *pirs* elsewhere in North India also did not mitigate communal violence in 1947. A clear case in point of religious sanctity not mitigating partition-related violence concerns Pakpattan. This prosperous town in Montgomery district was the principal crossing point of the Sutlej River. The *dargah* of the famous Chishti Sufi saint Baba Farid (1173–1265) was located at this site.[50] Baba Farid's cross-community religious appeal is

---

46 Anna Bigelow, 'Saved by the Saint: Refusing and Reversing Partition in Muslim North India,' *Journal of Asian Studies* 68 (2009). Anna Bigelow, *Sharing the Sacred: Practicing Pluralism in Muslim North India* (USA: Oxford University Press, 2010).

47 Denzil Ibbetson from the Indian Civil Service carried out the census of the Punjab province in 1881. The Census Report contains rich ethnographic material on the Punjab.

48 Denzil Ibbetson, Edward Maclagan and Horace Arthur Rose, *Glossary of the Tribes and Castes of the Punjab and North West Frontier Province* (Delhi: Asian Educational Services, 1990), 435–7.

49 Ron Geaves and Catherine Geaves, 'The Legitimization of a Regional Folk Cult: The Transmigration of Baba Balaknath from Rural Punjab to Urban Europe,' available online, Centre for Applied South Asian Studies.

50 Chishti is one of the most influential of the Sufi or Islamic mystic orders established in India. It became popular in India through Khwaja Muinuddin Chishti of Ajmer.

evidenced most clearly in the inclusion of his verses in Sikh Holy Scriptures. Yet, Pakpattan was attacked on 23–24 August, the shops and businesses of its Hindu and Sikh population were looted and the non-Muslims were forced to leave the town.[51]

What is unique in Malerkotla is the story of Guru Gobind Singh's blessing of Malerkotla following the ruler of Malerkotla's protest at the execution of his two sons. It still appears to play some part in the minds of people, whether they are Hindu, Sikh or Muslim. It is a fascinating story that seems to have assumed mythical proportions during the passage of time. This myth has travelled beyond the borders of Malerkotla and is now well known in Punjabi folklore. It is worthwhile reciting some of the details of this blessing.

During the Mughal Emperor Aurangzeb's reign (1658–1707), many battles were fought between the Mughal armies and the emerging power of the Sikhs. Prior to the onslaught on Chamkaur in 1705, the Mughal authorities captured Guru Gobind Singh's two younger sons. Betrayed by their Hindu servant, Gangu, the two young boys were asked to accept Islam in exchange for freedom in the court of Nawab Wazir Khan of Sirhind but they refused. The *Qazi* (judge) had told Wazir Khan that under Islamic law the two boys were not guilty of any crime and could not be held responsible for their father's crimes. The *Qazi*, aware that this was against Islamic law, sentenced the two young boys to be bricked up alive; Fateh Singh was less than 6 years old and Zorawar Singh was just over 8 when they were executed. The Nawab of Malerkotla, Sher Mohammad Khan (ruler 1672–1712), wrote a letter of protest to Aurangzeb, arguing that this was in violation of Islamic law, because the enmity was with their father and not with the innocent children.[52] The protest was heard but came to no avail as the boys were bricked up alive and consequently died of suffocation. However, when Guru Gobind Singh came to hear of the Nawab of Malerkotla's appeal, he apparently blessed the house of the Nawab and Malerkotla, declaring that 'his roots shall remain forever green'.[53] The succeeding century witnessed invasions and disturbances in Punjab and a shifting balance of power from the declining Mughal authorities

---

51 Khosla, *Stern Reckoning*, 163.
52 An English translation of an appeal in Persian by Nawab Sher Mohammad Khan of Malerkotla State is available in *The Sikh Review*, January 1967.
53 Khan, *History of the Ruling Family*, 35.

towards the Sikh *misls*,[54] but significantly, Malerkotla remained undisturbed by the Sikh forces.[55]

Over the past 300 years, this protest by Sher Mohammad Khan has continued to be recited and has been popularised in the imagination of both the state and people. It is still cited as one of the most important reasons for Malerkotla's peaceful communal relations. Many of the residents in Malerkotla reiterated this on several occasions during the fieldwork conducted there, citing this as the most plausible explanation for its communal harmony.[56] The people who were interviewed generally felt that the Guru's blessing was still relevant and proudly uphold its symbolic significance for Malerkotla.[57] There were accounts of how Malerkotla was spared in 1947 when surrounding villages witnessed attacks. The following two extracts are examples of the sentiments expressed by the people interviewed in Malerkotla. Both Isher Singh and Ajay Singh explained the apparent lack of communal violence in terms of the Guru's blessing. Isher Singh maintained that

> Malerkotla had a lot of Muslims, considering how much bloodshed was going on here, in Malerkotla by the grace of God this was not the case. There was a blessing by the tenth Guru for the area of Kotla at some time...the Guru's *haa da naara* for Sher Khan, so around 70 villages that existed in the area, there was no violence there.[58]

These sentiments were reinforced by Ajay Singh who declared:

> This protest is in people's minds, of someone standing up for something just and something good. That's the biggest reason, which is what is in people's mind. I don't know what happened but no Muslims were attacked in these villages. No one had any thoughts of attacking them or looting them when they were leaving. Yes, people still believe this, [Guru's

---

54 This was the name of the twelve Sikh armies in the eighteenth century, each led by a chief. The *misls* were associated with the leading Sikh families who controlled specific areas.

55 Khan, *History of the Ruling Family*, 39.

56 This is based on my PhD research, see further unpublished thesis, 'Partition and Locality: Case Studies of the Impact of Partition and Its Aftermath in the Punjab Region 1947–61' (Coventry University, 2005).

57 For a more detailed analysis see Pippa Virdee, 'Partition and the Absence of Violence in Malerkotla,' in *The Deadly Embrace: Religion, Violence and Politics in India and Pakistan 1947-2002*, ed. Ian Talbot (Karachi: Oxford University Press, 2007).

58 Interview with Isher Singh, Ahmedgarh, Malerkotla, August 2001.

blessing] of course it's true. Now even books have been published, about this '*haa da naara*' and Sher Khan.[59]

It is difficult to assess completely how this tale that goes back 300 years is still influencing people but its impact could be attributed to people wanting to believe in something like this. Thus, the stature of the tale is elevated to something far beyond what it means in reality, but people's desire to believe in it suggests that there is also some form of restraint being observed during communal tensions. While historians such as Gyanendra Pandey may dismiss the belief in the Guru's blessing as 'sentimentality',[60] its power lies in the attachment to the notion of *izzat* in Sikh society and in the high status accorded to Guru Gobind Singh, the founder of the Sikh *Khalsa*. The contemporary relevance and impact of this myth is in many respects symbolic. It represents the wanted desire by the people of Malerkotla to believe in its supernatural powers. Residents were proudly stating that the state remained peaceful following the demolition of the Babri Masjid in Ayodhya in 1992. Perhaps due to the small number of Muslims living in Punjab compared to other important centres such as Uttar Pradesh and Gujarat, they pose less of a threat and therefore relative peace is maintained.

Leaders and Leadership

The apparent disparity in communal violence between neighbouring princely states and Malerkotla also brings into the equation the role of the leadership. While the Maharaja of Patiala, Yadavinder Singh, according to some sources,[61] was involved in the conspiracy to purge all the Muslims out of East Punjab in order to create a Sikh state, the Nawab of Malerkotla was being prudent and safeguarded the future well-being of the state in a post-independent India. Although never very competent at managing conflict, the Nawab was able to at least steer the principality away from violent aggression. For these reasons, Nawab Ahmad Ali Khan, who reigned from 1908 to 1947, seems to have a special place in the hearts of the people of Malerkotla and this is certainly noticeable in indigenous written sources. 'He was very much respected and

---

59 Interview with Ajay Singh, Ahmedgarh, Malerkotla, August 2001.

60 See Gyanendra Pandey, *Remembering Partition: Violence, Nationalism and History in India* (Cambridge: Cambridge University Press, 2001).

61 Chaudhri Muhammad Ali, *The Emergence of Pakistan* (Lahore: Research Society of Pakistan, 1973), 254–61 and *Note on the Sikh Plan* (Lahore: Government of Pakistan, 1948).

held in veneration by his subjects and had always evinced a policy free from prejudice… during his rule the State administration had reached a mark of efficiency and the Chief Court was also raised to the status of a High court'.[62] However, the official opinion by the British seems to differ considerably from the above. He is described as a 'charming gentleman of no character or capacity… he is frightened of his own family, and seems constitutionally incapable of understanding finance. The ruling family has an exaggerated sense of its own importance'.[63] Both the Nawab's supporters and detractors obviously wrote with an eye to propaganda and political self-interest. The issue of financial indebtedness though increasingly influenced the discourse regarding his rule.

During World War One, Malerkotla placed all state troops and resources at the disposal of the British government and contributed more than its capacity could sustain. The heavy expenses incurred during this period significantly added to the financial weakness of the state in the post-war period.[64] By the late 1930s, it is clear from the official records that the British had assisted Malerkotla in obtaining substantial loans from Bahawalpur state. Financial indebtedness was, therefore, a major source of tension for the state and became the subject of a campaign by the English newspaper *Muslim Outlook* published in Lahore. The administration was described as being bankrupt ever since the present ruler succeeded to the throne; the result was widespread corruption in the public services and constituted 'gross misrule'.[65] The Nawab's financial irresponsibility was apparently well known: The state had outstanding debts of Rs. 6 lakhs to the Central Bank and Rs. 4.2 lakhs otherwise. The income before World War Two was Rs. 8.5 lakhs and estimates for the post-war period suggest an average income of Rs. 12 lakhs. Campaigns such as those by the *Muslim Outlook* do suggest that some public protest was present in the princely state, although there is little information about its circulation in Malerkotla. Thus, the Nawab was not immune to criticism in the public domain; this is even more significant as it originates from the same community as the Nawab's.

The conduct of Nawab Ahmad Ali Khan, however, stands in marked contrast to that of other rulers of the Punjab princely states in August 1947. The Maharaja of Patiala enforced a curfew on the Muslims of the state on

---

62 Khan, *History of the Ruling Family*, 138–9.
63 Letter to Fitze, 30 January 1942, IOR: L/PS/13/1345 Malerkotla Affairs.
64 Khan, *History of the Ruling Family*, 137–9.
65 Extract from *Muslim Outlook*, Lahore, 19 January 1931, IOR: L/PS/13/1345 Malerkotla Affairs.

31 August. He personally reassured Muslim League workers that the minority community would be safe. Shortly afterwards, a Sikh *jatha* supported by the state military and police attacked the Muslims of Barnala leaving over 3,000 dead. Evidence for the Maharaja's acquiescence in the attacks on Muslims is provided not just by this episode, but by the arming of RSS members and the role of state troops in attacking refugee trains travelling from Delhi to Lahore. At Bathinda, nearly 450 Muslim railway employees and their families were murdered by state troops.[66] The chief minister and heir of the Kapurthala state were seen in a military truck witnessing an attack on a refugee train on 5 September 1947.[67]

Nawab Ahmad Ali Khan in comparison sought to maintain order and to limit the disruption arising from the influx of Muslim refugees. The state of Malerkotla historically attempted to stress and highlight communal harmony in its territory. Indeed, the ruling family's historian and descendant, Nawab Iftikhar Ali Khan, declared that 'due to communal harmony and personal interest taken by the Ruler no disorder took place within Malerkotla State territory and all continued to live in perfect peace and harmony during this period of unrest'.[68] This may appear credulous of the Nawab's role, but he is viewed as a major factor in averting communal carnage in Malerkotla. His personal role, leadership and amicable relations with all communities certainly contributed to the restrained response of the people of Malerkotla. This view was essentially shaped by the political context that was equally important for the maintenance of communal harmony in the state.

The Nawab of a tiny state in an area distant from the Pakistan border, surrounded by Sikh states, had little to gain from stirring communal animosities. This situation did not hold true for the Sikh rulers. The violent attacks on Muslims were not just prompted by revenge, but formed part of ethnic cleansing. Community demarcation and the emptying of the territory of rival religious communities in North India from 1946 onwards display the hallmarks of ethnic cleansing. Ian Copland, for example, refers to the Muslim expulsion in 1947 from Alwar and Bharatpur as not just a communal episode, but a case of systematic 'ethnic cleansing'.[69] This was designed to consolidate a Sikh majority area. The Sikh states gave refuge to *jathas* operating in the

---

66 Mudie Papers in NDC, *Disturbances in the Punjab 1947*, 408–9.
67 Mudie Papers in NDC, *Disturbances in the Punjab 1947*, 404.
68 Khan, *History of the Ruling Family*, 138.
69 Ian Copland, 'The Further Shores of Partition: Ethnic Cleansing in Rajasthan in 1947,' *Past and Present* 160 (1998): 216.

British Punjab and they provided weapons and ammunition for Akali *jathas* in such districts as Jullundur. Attacks on Muslims in the British districts, as in the states, were politically motivated. It was termed by the British CID as the Sikh Plan.[70] This sought to carve out a majority Sikh homeland in central and eastern Punjab by driving out the Muslims. The political motivation of the violence comes out clearly in the demand made to the Muslims of Barra in Patiala to 'leave for Jinnah's Pakistan as Patiala was in India and no Muslim could live there; Khalistan was to be created throughout the East Punjab'.[71] There is also evidence that members from the Nawab's family did not share his enthusiasm for maintaining communal harmony; Ihsan Ali Khan, who was a staunch supporter of the Muslim League, was engaged in illicit activities.[72] It was reported that he 'engaged scores of Muslim ironsmiths to prepare knives, spears and other dangerous weapons openly'.[73] Ihsan Ali Khan had already been under the spotlight even during the prayer time disputes; J. C. Donaldson who was the British investigating officer noted that the Nawab was suspicious of his activities and could potentially stir up further conflict. However, the Nawab was also meddling to thwart any rival branches in the family and as Ihsan was a Shi'a, the Nawab was known to be stirring the Sunnis against Ihsan.[74]

Added to these local tensions were obviously the precarious financial debts, and significantly it had a Muslim population but was surrounded by Sikh majority areas of the Phulkian state and Ludhiana district during a communally charged milieu. This made it a prime target for any attacks by Sikhs and Hindus.[75] The state authorities were apprehensive about trouble

---

70 In *Note on the Sikh Plan*, there are accounts of how the Sikhs were preparing militarily to oust the Muslims from East Punjab and establish Sikh rule in the region after partition. Ian Copland also talks about the 'Sikh Plan' and the plans by the Sikh princes to establish a Sikh state after partition. He argues that the Sikh princes colluded with the Akali Dal in the hope of establishing a Sikh state after the British departure. See further, 'The Master and the Maharajas'.

71 Mudie Papers in NDC, *Disturbances in the Punjab*, 409.

72 Ihsan Ali Khan belonged to the Nawab's family that eventually left Malerkotla and settled in Lahore after partition, where the family had property prior to August 1947. As Ihsan Ali Khan was a supporter of the Muslim League, there were undoubtedly more opportunities in Pakistan than in India.

73 Letter to The Hon. Home, States and Information Minister, 30 August 1947. Malerkotla State, 1947, File no. 2(19) PR/47, NAI.

74 Bigelow, *Sharing the Sacred*, 118.

75 Malerkotla Affairs, IOR.

along its eastern and northern borders. There had been no case of Sikh *jathas* entering the state territory yet but, nonetheless, it was imperative for the swift movement of refugees to Pakistan to avoid the state being a target.[76] It is thus clear that the Nawab of Malerkotla was extremely anxious about the communal situation, especially with reference to the large numbers of Muslims coming into the state, seeking temporary refuge. This would not only burden the state financially, but also threaten the peace by inflaming communal tensions. Brigadier Commander Stuart noted that if trouble was to spread from outside the state, it would '…upset completely the present tranquillity within the state and make its relations with adjoining States difficult'.[77] It is well documented that the arrival of refugees was a major trigger for violence across northern India, even in localities that had previously been unaffected. On 6 September 1947, Nawab Ahmad Ali Khan sent a telegram to Sardar Vallabhbhai Patel, the deputy Prime Minister of India, to request assistance, as the states' resources were inadequately equipped. The state was willing to absorb the cost if the Indian government could render the army.

> There is grave danger of trouble spreading from outside, and though the State Forces are here they are inadequate to meet such a large scale emergency… Thousands of refugees have flocked into the State from the Ludhiana District and Patiala and Nabha States the presence of whom has presented the State with a major problem…Great panic prevails every where in the State.[78]

The role of the state was therefore crucial and this would have been impossible without the use of the army in maintaining control and deterring external attacks. The Nawab used his power to keep the peace in the state especially when it might have been overwhelmed by the refugee influx. On the other hand, the rulers of many of the Punjab princely states turned their armies and influence to the destructive ends of ethnic cleansing. It could also be argued that the absence of a functioning authority was a factor in allowing violence to overwhelm the populace. It is clear from the works of such writers as Ian Talbot that British authority in Punjab was declining from March 1947

---

76 Visit to Malerkotla state by Major Gurbax Singh Gill HQ5 Inf. Bde, Malerkotla Affairs, IOR.

77 Correspondence by Brig. Comd. N. J. B. Stuart re visit to Malerkotla, 25 September 1947, Malerkotla Affairs, IOR.

78 Letter of assistance to Sardar Vallabhbhai Patel from Ahmad Ali Khan, 6 September 1947, Malerkotla State, 1947, File no. 2(19) PR/47, NAI.

onwards.[79] The almost total collapse of authority in East Punjab in August 1947, in part, the result of the withdrawal of the predominantly Muslim police force, created the conditions for the communal holocaust in the region. In such circumstances, a princely state such as Malerkotla in which there was both a functioning government and a ruler committed to maintaining order became a haven of peace.

Malerkotla was peaceful largely because it was not in the interest of its ruling family for violence to break out in the state. The Nawab must have been aware that the future safety of the state lay in maintaining stability and building its relationship with neighbouring Sikh states in the post-independent Indian Union. Any violence against Sikhs and Hindus would have been detrimental to the state's viability in an independent India. The police and the army were thus deployed to prevent rather than abet violence in contrast to what happened in the neighbouring Sikh princely states. In the surrounding former British districts, the instruments of law and order had collapsed because of communal polarisation.

During the partition disturbances, Malerkotla became a 'safe haven' for many Muslims fleeing other surrounding areas. This demonstrates that East Punjab did not overnight become a hostile area, forcing all Muslims to leave. Indeed, what is more astounding is that the influx of Muslim refugees into the town did not result in retaliatory violence. Appeals by the chief minister were made to observe the peace and tranquillity of the town. Combined with the use of the army as deterrence, Malerkotla was able to prevent external aggression in its territory. This would have been ineffectual had the state mechanisms not been in place during the transitional period of the transfer of power.

The differential experience of violence in the state raises the question of the extent to which communalism and communal violence differed in princely India to British India. Malerkotla highlights the importance of a functioning administration that is committed to law and order as a crucial factor in inhibiting partition-related violence. Much of the turmoil in East Punjab arose from the decline of the British administration from the beginning of 1947 onwards, the partisan approach of local officials and the impact on law and order of the disarming and disbanding of the Muslim-dominated police force. What is unique in the case of Malerkotla is that the effectiveness of the army maintaining peace was reinforced by the social disapproval of violence arising from the 'myth' of the Guru's blessing.

---

79   Ian Talbot, *Punjab and the Raj* (New Delhi: Manohar, 1988), Chapter 10.

Ahmad Salim

The Land of Punjab[1]

The Punjab is the land of Dulla.[2]
Here, the brave Mirza[3] was born who spoke of honor.

The land of Bhagat Singh and of the Kharals,[4]
Sacrificing their lives, people follow their destiny.

Though the land of Punjab is very fertile,
Its inhabitants have been reduced to scarcity.

Wells work in communities, but thirst dances upon lips,
Though the harvest prospers, people die of hunger

Again on the land of Punjab has arisen the uproar of hatred,
History has turned a page from the past.[5]

With the ease of cotton flying in the air, people are killed,
In your hands, peace is torn to shreds.

Life is covered with dust at every door,
O Mother, how can I hide this falsehood on your hands.

Your sons are inciting war in far away places,
With great relish they are drinking the blood of others.

Your soil is giving birth to dishonorable ones,
Who watch with pleasure as others' homes burn.

Destroying your honor, they look across the rivers,
In an effort to kill Mirza, they surround him.

---

1   Ahmad Salim from *Kunjan Moian*, translated by Ami P. Shah. *Journal of Punjab Studies* 13, nos. 1 and 2 (1989; trans. 2006): 130–1.
2   Dulla Bhatti is the bandit-hero of a Punjabi legend. See Footnote 11.
3   Hero of the Punjabi story of Mirza-Sahiban.
4   Ahmad Khan Kharal (d. 1857) and Bhagat Singh (1907–31) hailed from the Punjab and were freedom fighters who were executed by the British colonial government.
5   The page from the past alluded to is the horror of the partition which was witnessed again during the partition of West and East Pakistan and the creation of Bangladesh.

Sahiba from the land of Bangla, the life of Mirza,
Her youth has been destroyed, her blooming smiles stolen.

Ranjha[6], the brave lover, has been imprisoned,
His hands are tied, his tongue silenced.

"Chains, chains," everyone screams,
Yet, the people will win this battle of democracy.

Your honor has been debased once again,
Though songs are sung praising you.

Those who honor you deeply, O mother,
Crying they ask you, "are these your sons?"

O Mother who sings lullabies, why is death in your lap?
When will the light of love glimmer in your eyes again?

Let both lands be fragrant, and separated ones re-united,
Tie broken thread, O rider of *Nili*[7].

Let us cross rivers to rejoin the separated.
'Ahmad'[8] says that without Ranjha, Hir is inconsolable.

---

6 Hero of the Punjabi story of *Hir-Ranjha*.
7 Mirza's horse.
8 The insertion of the poet's signature (*takhallas*) is a common feature of Indian poetry.

Migrating to the Promised Land:
A Tale of Two Cities

As people left, abandoning their homes, land and their earthly possessions, they did so in the hope of either returning once the violence had settled down or in the hope of a new 'promised land'. Making that momentous decision to abandon everything they had known previously and leave required courage but many people did so under pressure due to the ensuing violence and not because of choice. Recent research has begun to expose the human tragedy of this migration process and the differential migrant experiences. Moreover, the conflicts between the state and the individuals are clearly visible. Little is known about why urban migrants, who unlike agriculturalists were not directed by the state, settled where they did.[1] Was this because of former business contacts or family connections in a locality? Did they follow the lead of relatives who had already completed their journeys in a kind of chain migration? Was it purely chance, arriving at the 'wrong' railway station that ended their migration? The journey to the 'promised land' was filled with uncertainty and these questions are poorly understood. But individual accounts of migration based on research in Ludhiana and Lyallpur help us in addressing some of the issues raised by these questions.

These two localities provide a comparative dimension to experiences of migration in both East and West Punjab. Both Ludhiana and Lyallpur experienced rapid growth in the post-partition period, which in part can be attributed to the refugee influx and will be examined in greater detail in the next chapter. Historically, there were patterns of migration between Ludhiana and Lyallpur even during the colonial era when the canal colonies were constructed. This pattern of colonial migration has in turn influenced the partition-related movements. When families were fleeing, the state was hardly in control and so people utilised their own pre-existing family and

---

1   For further information on rural resettlement see M. S. Randhawa, *Out of the Ashes – An Account of the Rehabilitation of Refugees from West Pakistan in Rural Areas of East Punjab* (Chandigarh: Public Relations Department Punjab, 1954).

business connections in settling down. This is an area that is hardly explored in Partition Studies. In the vast landscape of Punjab, the story of these two cities is important in trying to understand the transformation of land, space and people from the colonial to the post-colonial. These cities and their people tell a story, which resonates not just within its metropolis boundaries but they speak of the wider transformation of two nation-states. There are things that unite them and there are aspects which divide them, yet their shared past is pivotal in understanding how these cities emerge from the ashes of 1947.

The Sandal Bar and the Land of Dulla Bhatti

Prior to partition, Lyallpur (known as Faisalabad after 1979) was only a small market town, but today it represents Pakistan's main agro-industrial and textile centre. Faisalabad district is located in the heart of the Punjab province in Pakistan. Driving on the Sheikhupura Road to Faisalabad, there are numerous industrial units leading to the city, many of which specialise in textiles. There are high-tech centres specialising in agriculture, textiles and new modern medical centres; however, the trappings of modernity are yet to reach most of the people in Faisalabad district as they live mainly in rural areas. In contemporary Pakistan, Faisalabad is one of the richest areas and the third most populous city. The present-day district of Faisalabad came into being after the development of the elaborate irrigation system introduced by the British in Punjab. The history of Faisalabad is therefore intrinsically linked to the development of the Chenab Colony in West Punjab, and thus most of the history is also that of the agricultural development and colonisation at the close of the nineteenth century. But the land of Dulla Bhatti, the Sandal Bar, has a rich pre-colonial history.[2]

As the impact of the partition was beginning to take shape, conditions in Lyallpur district were relatively peaceful until the end of September. The Sikh

---

2   Dulla Bhatti was born into a family of powerful Rajput *zamindars* and inherited a long tradition of resistance against the Mughal state. Bhatti was also very popular among the lower classes and is seen to play an important role in the history of Punjab's culture. See further Surinder Singh, 'Mughal Centralization and Local Resistance in North-Western India: An Exploration in the Ballard of Dulla Bhatti,' in *Popular Literature and Pre-Modern Societies in South Asia*, eds. Surinder Singh and Ishwar Dayal Gaur (Delhi: Pearson Longman, 2008), 89–112; and Ishwar Dayal Gaur, *Martyr as Bridegroom: A Folk Representation of Bhagat Singh* (New Delhi: Anthem Press, 2008), 33–8.

Picture 6.1: The Clock tower dates back to 1903 and still stands strong and forms the hub of all activities in the city. Eight roads (and eight bazaars) of Lyallpur meet with the Clock Tower at the centre, laid out like a Union Jack

Picture 6.2: Kaiseri Gate, outside Rail Bazaar in Lyallpur. It was built in 1897 to commemorate 60 years since Queen Victoria's coronation

Jat farmers were especially reluctant to abandon their fertile fields; after all they were the very people who had uprooted themselves fifty years ago to transform this waste land. Malcolm Darling, who was in the ICS and posted in Punjab, travelled extensively in the area during the 1920s and thought the Lyallpur Colony was one of the richest tracts of land in India and quite possibly in the whole of Asia.[3] One of the first major incidents in the district was a mass attack on Tandlianwala. On 26 August, a Muslim mob attacked a gurdwara situated just outside the town. The gurdwara was packed with refugees who had sought shelter there. A few days later the town of Tandlianwala was attacked by a large mob. Khosla's findings suggest that over 2,000 people died, with many young girls being kidnapped.[4] Balwant Singh Anand, who was working in

---

3 Malcolm Darling, *The Punjab Peasant in Prosperity and Debt* (Delhi: Manohar, 1977), 132.

4 The figure suggested by Khosla for this incident is alone far more than anything that Lord Mountbatten imagined. According to him, the total number of casualties in Lyallpur was quite low, at 500. Compared to other districts, like Lahore and Sheikhupura where an estimated 10,000 people died, the figure for Lyallpur is quite a conservative estimate. However, it would have been in the

Lyallpur at the time, notes in his recollections that the attack on Tandlianwala really frightened people and made them leave their houses. Anand suggests that this was the beginning of people congregating in groups to seek sanctuary in local gurdwaras and camps in Lyallpur.[5]

The first incident to take place in Lyallpur town was on 3 September during a public meeting at the Clock Tower that had been organised by the deputy commissioner (DC). He began by praising the residents for maintaining peace and goodwill in the town.[6] However, at the meeting, a Sikh was stabbed. The proceedings were immediately suspended, but the incident acted as a catalyst for further stabbings and lootings. This level of violence was relatively mild compared to what was being witnessed elsewhere in Punjab. This also in part explains why the Hindus and Sikhs were reluctant to migrate. Their decision to leave was based on the advice of both the Sikh leader, Master Tara Singh, and the West Punjab governor, Sir Francis Mudie. On 5 September, Mudie wrote to Jinnah, 'I am telling everyone that I do not care how the Sikhs get across the border: the great thing is to get rid of them as soon as possible. There is still little sign of the three *lakh* Sikhs in Lyallpur moving, but in the end they too will have to go.'[7] The following day Mudie came to Lyallpur itself and told the DC that all non-Muslims should be evacuated.

Ratten Singh, who migrated from Lyallpur, recalls Master Tara Singh and Giani Kartar Singh going to Samundri and asking the Sikhs to leave. They felt compelled to follow these instructions. Ratten Singh and his family instinctively knew they were leaving for good and took as many belongings as they could on a *gadha* [horse cart]. While travelling, his niece died as she became ill with a fever. They headed for Balloki Head from where the military

---

    nationalist interest of both Mountbatten and Khosla to present two extreme figures. Letter from Mountbatten of Burma to Penderel Moon, 2 March 1962, Mss Eur. F230/34, IOR; G. D. Khosla, *Stern Reckoning: A Survey of Events Leading Up to and Following the Partition of India* (New Delhi: Oxford University Press, 1989), 166.

5   Balwant Singh Anand, *Cruel Interlude* (Bombay: Asia Publishing House, 1961), 23.

6   Khosla, *Stern Reckoning*, 24–5.

7   Khosla, *Stern Reckoning*, 169. Also see Sir Francis Mudie to Mr Jinnah, 5 September 1947, in Kirpal Singh, ed., *Select Documents on Partition of Punjab-1947: India and Pakistan* (Delhi: National Book Shop, 1991), 511–12.

transported them to Amritsar. After staying in a camp for a week, they came to Ludhiana because of their previous connections there.[8]

Lyallpur district had one of the largest populations of non-Muslim refugees to evacuate from West Punjab. The majority travelled by foot convoys. When the MEO took over the responsibility to evacuate non-Muslim refugees from Western Pakistan, it was estimated that 424,000 non-Muslim people remained in Lyallpur district.[9] Most of the people awaiting evacuation were in Lyallpur itself, with an estimated 175,000 people already been evacuated by 28 September.[10] The majority of the evacuation had taken place by 15 November. The only people remaining were about 17,000, most of whom were scheduled castes,[11] but they were mostly cleared by the end of November 1947.[12] There were also around 5,000 *bazigars*,[13] who had previously refused to migrate but, due to further attacks and looting by local Muslims, had also decided to leave.[14] *Bazigars* are a nomadic tribe that lives off circus-like performances. From the records, it is clear that these *bazigars* were causing some problems for both the East and West Punjab governments. The former was concerned at the way they were treated by local people even though the *bazigars* had embraced Islam. The West Punjab government was also viewed rather cynically by East Punjab, as trying to keep the *bazigars* in West Punjab in order to parade them as evidence of Hindus choosing to remain in Pakistan, even though they had converted. But both governments indulged in these political games where people were often used as pawns. In addition to these, there were also a number of abducted women and girls to be recovered, who numbered around 400.[15] By June 1948, however, it was clear

8   Interview with Ratten Singh, Model Gram, Ludhiana, February 2003.

9   Brigadier Rajendra Singh, *The Military Evacuation Organisation 1947–48* (New Delhi: Government of India, 1962), 83.

10 Weekly and Progressive Refugee State: Non-Muslim, 29 September 1947, Liaison Agency Files, LVII/26/45, PSA.

11 Official term for untouchables.

12 Weekly Reports on Refugees, 23 November 1947, Liaison Agency Files, LVII/26/45, PSA.

13 Letter to DLO, Lyallpur, 18 May 1948. Liaison Agency Files, VIII/21/15-B, PSA.

14 CLO, India to Chief Secretary, East Punjab, 29 April 1948 in Kirpal Singh, ed., *Select Documents on Partition of Punjab-1947: India and Pakistan* (Delhi: National Book Shop, 1991), 612.

15 Singh, *Select Documents*, 614.

that there were still around 3,000 persons and 80 girls, who needed to be evacuated from Lyallpur district.[16] A year on from partition and the official role of the MEO being effectively over, the DLO was still working to recover people from Lyallpur.[17]

In the south and eastern side of Lyallpur city, the Government College became the military headquarters and the Khalsa College had been turned into refugee camps.[18] Ayra High School was also used as a camp, housing around 40,000 people.[19] At Khalsa College, 60,000 people gathered to seek temporary refuge before their departure towards India.[20] Refugees were squatting anywhere they could, in classrooms, on verandas and on playing fields. Anand, who was assisting at the camp, notes that people also started to sort themselves into professional groups. There were doctors, lawyers, engineers, professors, journalists and some government officials,[21] perhaps desperately trying to preserve their professional and class identity in this period of immense uncertainty in which everyone was known primarily by their religious identity. According to the MEO, the camps in Lyallpur were eventually cleared by 5 December.[22]

Khalsa College, like many other camps in the region, was enveloped by a cholera epidemic. Illnesses like dysentery were not the only problem for the occupants. They were also subject to attack, being a sitting target for would-be looters and rapists. On 1 October, a foot convoy of non-Muslims was passing through Lyallpur, when a Muslim mob attacked the convoy near Tarkabad. People nearby at Khalsa College could hear gunshots, which lasted over an hour. The convoy was looted, many bodies were found, others were left for dead and girls were also abducted.[23] As Khalsa College was close by, many of the injured were brought to the camp for medical assistance. However, during the same night, Khalsa camp itself was attacked. The Muslim troops, who were

---

16 Weekly Diary of the Superintendent of Police, East Punjab, on Special Duty in West Punjab for week ending 26 June 1948. Liaison Agency Files, XI/13/32-EV, PSA.

17 Letter to Mehta, CLO, 22 August 1947. Liaison Agency Files, VIII/22/7-EV, PSA.

18 Anand, *Cruel Interlude*, 50.

19 Singh, *Military Evacuation Organisation*, 205.

20 Anand, *Cruel Interlude*, 27.

21 Anand, *Cruel Interlude*, 90.

22 Singh, *Military Evacuation Organisation*, 200.

23 Anand, *Cruel Interlude*, 131–2.

there to protect it, were implicated. The next night, the Arya High School Refugee Camp was attacked. The camp housed mostly Hindus and around 300 casualties were reported with 15 girls being kidnapped.[24] This time the Baluchi soldiers were implicated. When the DC arrived in the morning there were apparently 150 bodies lying in the camp.[25] Designed to provide refuge and shelter, the camps were just as dangerous as the world from which they were trying to escape to seek protection.

One of the largest mass movements to take place during the whole partition process was a convoy that originated from Lyallpur. Hindus and Sikhs numbering 400,000 set off from Lyallpur on 11 September. The first 45,000 people reached Balloki Head, near the border by Ferozepur, a week later and the rest trickled into Indian territories gradually. The Balloki Route was often indiscriminately closed by the Pakistan government and was also prone to occasional Muslim attacks. The convoy was organised by colonists, who came along with their livestock, migrating *en masse* once the decision had been taken to leave Lyallpur. They came from a variety of backgrounds, which included petty shopkeepers, artisans, village menials and once-rich landlords and businessmen and other professionals such as lawyers and doctors. The convoy undertook the journey of 150 miles; most of the people walked, while others who brought their carts or *tongas* used them for transporting goods and the sick and elderly travelling with them.[26] Indian troops provided some protection to the refugees but this was never a guarantee for safety. A sense of normality prevailed in the form of rest breaks, cooking, milking cows, especially for the infants, and tending to the sick. Music and occasional speeches by village leaders helped to raise the refugees' morale. The Indian government assisted by dropping food and drugs by air. Vaccines and doctors were flown in to assist the sick. A field ambulance was sent to Raiwind to inoculate refugees before crossing the border, after which the refugees were taken into reception camps.[27]

Not all the people left Lyallpur by foot convoy. Near Lyallpur at Risalewala there was an airfield which was used to fly people to and from Delhi. Planes were chartered by wealthy individuals; however, as Anand notes, people often

---

24   Ganda Singh, *A Diary of the Partition Days 1947*. Reprinted from *Journal of Indian History* XXXVIII, Part II (August 1960): 243.

25   Khosla, *Stern Reckoning*, 170.

26   *Civil and Military Gazette* (Lahore), 8 October 1947.

27   *Civil and Military Gazette* (Lahore), 8 October 1947.

paid inflated taxi or *tonga* fares to reach the airport and with no guarantee of flights. Anand describes a conversation that took place between the flight attendant and the prospective passengers, each bargaining and willing to pay over inflated prices for tickets like an auction, even though some had booked their tickets in advance.[28] This was clearly a profitable business for the transporters, but the number of people who could access this mode of transport was very few, as noted earlier. Jaswant Singh belonged to a wealthy family; his father owned 12 *marabas* of land in Sargodha. Due to their eminent position as wealthy landlords, they were able to be more flexible about their departure, taking the time to sell their belongings before flying to Amritsar. As Jaswant Singh recalls:

> We stayed in Pakistan until 3rd November. It was only after 15 August that we started selling our belongings, things we could not take with us. No one disturbed us. My father had made arrangements and we flew to Amritsar, where we stayed for some time, then we proceeded to Ludhiana.[29]

Alongside wealth, personal connections were very important in assisting the migration process. The Liaison Agency Records provides evidence of the latter as they contain letters written directly to the MEO requesting assistance. Alongside impassioned and general appeals for help from members of the public, especially with respect to the recovery of abducted women, recorded on pro-formas, there are letters from people that were clearly more likely to succeed because of their influence. For example, Dr Daulat Ram Mediratta of Mani Majra, district Ambala, sent a letter to the Inspector General of Civil Hospital, East Punjab; The Officer Commanding, MEO; CLO, Lahore; and the Deputy High Commissioner for India and Pakistan at Lahore. This was an appeal letter to aid the evacuation of his wife, daughter and personal possessions, all of whom were at the Ayra Refugee Camp in Lyallpur. Dr Daulat Ram was willing to remit any cost incurred in the process.[30] The letter most likely proved successful as added to it is the hand-written response for the attention of the DLO in Lyallpur 'for very early action'.[31] These of course,

---

28   Anand, *Cruel Interlude*, 109–10.
29   Interview with Jaswant Singh, Industrial Area B, Ludhiana, March 2002.
30   Letter to the Inspector General of Civil Hospital, East Punjab, 25 October 1947, Liaison Agency Files, Bundle II + III file 7, PSA.
31   Letter to the Inspector General of Civil Hospital, PSA.

were the desperate pleas of people who could write to people in positions of authority and thereby afford some advantage; others, of course, were less fortunate.

The Land of the Lodhis

Few localities in the Punjab would possess greater strategic interest than Ludhiana. Lying in the primary position of the high road from Central Asia en route to Delhi, it witnessed many successive conquests pass through. Some of the most decisive battles took place in the vicinity, and once across the Sutlej River, there was little to hold back the invaders from assuming control of Delhi.[32] Prior to partition, there was little industry in Ludhiana to really distinguish it from other small provincial towns. It had, however, become the centre of extensive trade in grain, sugar, and cloth. Trade was further boosted along the Grand Trunk Road with the opening of the railway from Delhi to Lahore in 1870.[33] The commercial hub of activity in united Punjab took place, nonetheless, in Amritsar and Lahore. Together, they served the economic and cultural needs of the Punjabi people and beyond. However, in contemporary Punjab, Ludhiana is one of the most important industrial and business centres in India. It is famous for its bicycle industry, hosiery and textile goods, sewing machines and parts, and is often dubbed as the 'Manchester of India'.

Located on the Grand Trunk Road, Ludhiana was a focal transit point for refugees. The city was connected to all the major cities, Delhi, Amritsar and Lahore, and thus was an important stop for refugees who were on the move. Those travelling by foot convoys would have used the Balloki Route, in particular the Ludhiana–Ferozepore–Kasur Road. All refugees from Ludhiana, Ambala, Karnal and Ferozepore districts and from the East Punjab states of Patiala, Jind, Malerkotla and Nabha used this route.[34] Due to the large number of Muslims gathering in Ludhiana, which swelled the local population, the district was prone to attacks by Sikhs and Hindus. There are eyewitness accounts of violence against Muslims in the city itself, particularly in the Muslim-dominated areas of Field Ganj and Chaura Bazaar.[35]

---

32 *Punjab District Gazetteers, Vol XV B. Ludhiana District* (Government of Punjab, 1912), 647.

33 *Punjab District Gazetteers*, 647.

34 Singh, *Military Evacuation Organisation*, 131.

35 Saleem Ullah Khan, *The Journey to Pakistan: A Documentation on Refugees of 1947* (Islamabad: National Documentation Centre, 1993), 183.

Near about the 26th [August, 1947] the shop of S. S. Din, the biggest Muslim merchant in Ludhiana, dealer in arms and ammunition and wine, etc. was looted. Military police stood by. They fired and then the mob looted the shop. Then other shops in Chowra Bazar and other localities were looted. Muslims found there were stabbed. On the next day news was current in the village. 'Deputy Commissioner will get shops looted. So come to the city'. Armed gangs from villages in a radius of 12 to 15 miles were thus mobilised to the city. Looting, arson and massacres started... Some part of this loot was kept in D.A.V. College and distributed amongst those who applied for it (shoes, etc.).[36]

Refugees' desire both for revenge, and to ethnically cleanse local Muslims were factors in the violence in Ludhiana as in other parts of the East Punjab. Another eyewitness account, in *A Journey to Pakistan*, provides an account of Field Ganj, in old Ludhiana. 'On 31st [August] I passed through Ludhiana, stayed there for a short time. I went to Feel [sic.] Ganj, a locality where, on the one side were Muslims and on the other Sikhs. At 3.15 p.m. I saw a dozen policemen leading a mob of about 200 attacking Muslim houses. There was no curfew.'[37] Abdul Rahman, also a refugee from Field Ganj, informed me, 'at the time of partition, the tension was bearable initially. Afterwards, it changed to bloodshed and massacre when the Hindus and Sikhs from the areas of Pakistan went there and told their people about the way they were deserted'. He went on to inform me that the 'bloodshed started on a mass level when Muslims started it in some cities by listening to the stories of Muslim migrants and vice versa'.[38] Sakina Bibi from Saidon da Mohalla, Ludhiana, who is now settled in Faisalabad, expressed similar views.

Actually, the migrants from the areas of Pakistan flared up riots there. While we were in camps, we met some migrants from Lyallpur. They were regretting the loss of their properties and belongings. We were not afraid of Hindus and Sikhs of Ludhiana but feared the migrants from Pakistan who eventually exploited the locals against us. We were afraid of getting killed. They attacked and hewed Muslims, looted their belongings and raped and kidnapped their girls.[39]

---

36   Khan, *The Journey to Pakistan*, 183.
37   Khan, *The Journey to Pakistan*, 183.
38   Interview with Abdul Rahman, Lyallpur Cotton Mills, Faisalabad, February 2003.
39   Interview with Sakina Bibi, Madina Town, Faisalabad, January 2003.

Picture 6.3: The famous Ghanta Ghar, Clock tower in Ludhiana, built to commemorate the silver jubilee of Queen Victoria. Construction begun in 1862 but it was inaugurated later on, in 1906

Mohammad Sadeeq, another refugee from Ludhiana, who also settled in Faisalabad talked about having very good relations in Ludhiana with Hindus and Sikhs before the partition riots. He blamed the extremist organisations, yet maintained that locally things were calm.

> The demand for Pakistan invoked hatred. I don't know who was behind those riots but gradually the enmity increased. We did not fear Hindus at the time of partition but Sikhs. They were up to some mischief. The reason behind the fear was the presence of mischievous organisation amongst Muslims and the other communities. The slogan for Pakistan was the main reason behind tension. No troublesome incidents occurred on local level, neither were there some business quarrel or problem and financial worries. Very few incidents of violence took place in Ludhiana city but the rural areas were under the rage of rioters.[40]

Malik Ludhianvi was a Muslim League activist at the time of partition. He is now settled in the refugee satellite town of Ghulam Mohammad Abad in Faisalabad. His recollections differ from Sadeeq, perhaps because of his political affiliations. His account portrays Ludhiana City as much more violent. His house was close to the famous *Ghanta Ghar* [Clock Tower] in Ludhiana, from where he witnessed the emotional flag raising ceremony on 14 August that marked India's freedom from British rule. It was after this, he recalls, that riots spread in the city.

> Our house was at the dividing line of Madhupuri *mohalla* of Hindus and the *mohalla* of Muslims. So we left before the riots and shifted to Jamalpur at a two miles' distance from our house. Our house was burnt first of all, because we were Muslim League activists and our walls bore the painted slogans of 'Muslim League zindabad' and 'Pakistan zindabad'.[41]

Almost all of the Muslims of pre-partition Ludhiana district migrated. Atiq-ur-Rehman was one of the few who decided to remain. When I interviewed him in 2002, he was the president of the Muslim Council, Punjab, while his brother Maulana Habib-ur-Rehman Ludhianvi was the Shahi Imam of the Jama Masjid in Field Ganj.[42] They are descendants of the Ludhianvi family

---

40 Interview with Mohammad Sadeeq, Katchery Bazaar, Faisalabad, February 2003.
41 Interview with Malik Mohammed Yousaf Ludhianvi, Ghulam Mohammad Abad, Faisalabad, January 2003.
42 Interview with Atiq-ur-Rehman, Jama Masjid, Field Ganj, Ludhiana, March 2002.

that traces back seven generations of their family roots in the city, arriving in 1850. They are also the grandsons of the secular nationalist Maulana Habib-ur-Rehman. As the family was close to the nationalist freedom movement, the question of migration never arose. After partition, the family spent a brief period in Delhi as the mosque in Field Ganj, like many others in the district, was converted into a gurdwara. It was then restored as a mosque in 1956, due to the strong family links with the Indian Prime Minister Pandit Nehru.[43] Bibi Amir Fatima, a spiritual healer from Gill village, just on the outskirts of the city, also remained in India. She experienced no trouble in her village and the family did not feel it was necessary to leave.[44] Her experience of communal harmony remained intact, signified by her continued acceptance by the local community, but this was not the experience for many people.

Like Lyallpur, the process of migration was quite slow in Ludhiana. By 19 October, there were still many Muslims left in refugee camps in the district. MEO figures of camp residents are 120,000 in Ludhiana; Samrala 4,000; Raikot 12,000; Jagraon 10,000; White Bein 40,000; and Sindwan Khas 75,000.[45] Haji Kazim, who was born in Ludhiana, recalls leaving his home and going to the Chhawani Camp in the city.[46] The family stayed there for a day and then left. He said people were desperate to board the trains for Pakistan. In an attempt to get onto a train quickly, their personal belongings were left behind at the station. But they just crammed into the train, which was going to the Indian border city of Amritsar. He recalls their fear at the time. This was only partly reduced by the party of Balochi soldiers who were escorting the train. Everyone felt a huge sense of relief when they reached the border at Wagah. At the same time, however, he remembers being saddened by the sight of some Sikhs who were lying dead at the station and thought to himself that 'the same thing was going on here'.[47]

---

43   'Surviving tension, yet putting up a brave face,' *The Tribune* (Chandigarh), 5 March 2002.

44   Interview with Bibi Amir Fatma, Gill Village, Ludhiana, March 2002. Bibi Fatma has a following among all communities; her devotees also come from the diaspora community in the United Kingdom. Upon entering the simple shrine, there are symbols of all four communities (Christianity, Islam, Hinduism and Sikhism) with all of them leading to the same door.

45   Singh, *Military Evacuation Organisation*, 130.

46   Interview with Haji Kazim, Jhang Bazaar, Faisalabad, February 2003.

47   Interview with Haji Kazim.

Picture 6.4: Shrine at Gill Village

Bashiran Bibi migrated from Saidan da Mohalla in Ludhiana. She remembers having very good relations with the Hindus and Sikhs of the neighbourhood. They received considerable assistance from their friends to aid their departure. Some Hindu friends also maintained contact with them in Pakistan through letters after partition.

It was three months after partition, that we left India. For two months we stayed there and they kept a watch for our safety. The Hindus used to stand guard, protected us while we sold milk. I was married at the age of twelve and gave birth to Hasan at the age of 14. He was born in the camp, during migration. When he was born the Hindus came there to give us *ghee*, rice, clothes and other things. Hindus lived with us in a very friendly manner. We came here on the train, which we took from Ludhiana cantonment station. We stayed for eight days in a camp in Ludhiana cantonment. On the fourth day of our stay in the camp, Hasan was born – so our stay was extended. On the eighth day, we got on the train and came directly to Lyallpur. We came straight to my father-in-law who had reached here eight days prior to our arrival.[48]

Hope and Disappointment

A number of themes emerged from the personal accounts of migration. These contrasted with the 'official' history, which projected a unified and determined effort to assimilate and rehabilitate the refugees in both East and West Punjab. The personal narratives, however, tell a different history of migration. The treacherous journey across the borders, experienced by millions, was often met with disappointment upon arrival. The nepotism and corruption of the bureaucracy was only too visible for the refugees. For many, the upheaval during partition was presumed to be only temporary and thus there seemed little point in making permanent homes when they migrated. Others spent years moving from one place to another in search of resolve and stability. While some used personal relationships and business links to find security in deciding where they would migrate to, others just continued to long for their 'homelands' which with the passage of time just became distant memories.

Abdul Haq migrated from Chaura Bazaar, Ludhiana; he provides a personal account of the adversity and suffering that numerous individuals had to endure. 'Our train took eight days to reach Pakistan from Ludhiana', he declared during the course of an interview in Faisalabad. He goes on to say:

We reached Lahore via Amritsar. There was exchange of fire between the attackers and the military men escorting our train occurred in Amritsar, leaving a lot of people dead. The attackers made every possible attempt

---

48   Interview with Bashiran Bibi, Harcharan Pura, Faisalabad, February 2003.

to kill the people of our train but the military shielded us. The officer was a Muslim, while the soldiers were Dogras. On his orders, the soldiers opened fire on the attackers and forced them to retreat. They ran away leaving behind 20 to 30 corpses. We covered a hundred mile's distance in eight days; it would have taken two and a half hours without the unnecessary delays.[49]

Hindus and Sikhs who crossed the killing fields of the Punjab in the opposite direction, provide similar accounts of torturous terror-filled journeys on trains or gruelling foot convoys across the flooded and bloodied green plains of Punjab. There are accounts of people who were travelling on foot convoys encountering bloated bodies, which had been left behind to rot away. Others lost their loved ones en route, forced to abandon them without any proper burial or cremation.

One of the biggest problems for the large numbers of refugees coming to Ludhiana city was finding suitable accommodation. The number of residential houses and commercial properties available to the incoming Hindus and Sikhs was inadequate. There was not enough Muslim evacuee property to go around. Moreover, some of the abandoned houses were in disrepair because of riot damage. Another problem facing the refugees was that the properties left by the Muslims were inferior to their former houses in Pakistan. Significantly, the Hindus and Sikhs had been largely traders and professionals, while the Ludhiana Muslims were mostly artisans, craftsmen and technical labourers in the industry. Some Muslims were involved in the trade but this was generally as petty traders.

Houses and shops abandoned by Muslims were taken over by the government as evacuee properties under the terms of the Administration of Evacuee Ordinance IV of 1947. This was later amended to the Administration of Evacuee Property Act, 1950. Evacuee property was initially allotted to displaced people on a temporary basis. It was only in 1953–54 that permanent settlement of evacuee properties started. The task was administered by the Ministry of Rehabilitation.[50] In reality though, 'the unauthorised occupation of Muslim evacuee houses by local residents and in many cases, by civil servants meant that the supply of houses for refugees became rapidly diminished'.[51]

---

49   Interview with Abdul Haq, Montgomery Bazaar, Faisalabad, January 2003.

50   V. S. Suri, *Punjab State Gazetteers: Ludhiana* (Chandigarh: Controller of Print and Stationary, 1970), 180.

51   Navtej Purewal, *Living on the Margins: Social Access to Shelter in Urban South Asia* (Aldershot: Ashgate, 2000), 51.

Old Muslim *mohallas* like Field Ganj, Islam Ganj and residential areas around Chaura Bazaar were quickly occupied by Hindu and Sikh refugees coming from West Punjab. This created huge problems when the task of planned permanent resettlement finally commenced.

Refugees from all communities faced similar problems of rehabilitation. Those who had access to influence and money used their connections. People put in claims for compensation, but for some, it often seemed like an arbitrary decision rather than based on verified paperwork. Satya Rai in her work *Partition of the Punjab* notes that nepotism, corruption and bribery were rampant in the administration. Money, power and influence were important factors in the speedy evacuation of friends and family: 'refugees could not get equal justice or attention'.[52] Some individuals took advantage of the chaos and lack of administrative control and used the misery of others to make money: 'one trip with the refugees or with their kit was equal to an ordinary months earnings'[53] for the *riksha wallas*. 'Some people put in claims with much exaggeration', Abdul Rahman told me in an interview in Faisalabad, 'but my father was a religious person', he continued, 'and he actually told the details of his properties and settlement compensated him accordingly'.[54] Refugees frequently had to resort to bribes to get their cases heard. 'We put in claims after migration', Mohammad Sadeeq recalls, 'Our claims were compensated after giving some bribe to the authorities'.[55] Rana further reiterated this point.

> You couldn't get a house without giving a bribe of 20 to 50 rupees to the scouts and clerks of Finance Department etc. I swear nobody was allotted a house without bribe. If we had bribed the authorities, we could have been allotted a huge building. The people who got houses without bribes were either those with relatives in the establishment or those who occupied the houses by force. The people who had relatives amongst government officials, got lands, houses and jobs and the people who were not able to bribe or thought it to be morally wrong could never get settled.[56]

---

52 Satya Rai, *Partition of the Punjab: A Study of Its effects on the Politics and Administration of the Punjab 1947-56* (Bombay: Asia Publishing House, 1965), 87.

53 East Punjab Liaison Agency Records in Rai, *Partition of the Punjab*, 87–8.

54 Interview with Abdul Rahman, Lyallpur Cotton Mills, Faisalabad, February 2003.

55 Interview with Mohammad Sadeeq, Katchery Bazaar, Faisalabad, February 2003.

56 Interview with Rana, Chiniot Bazaar, Faisalabad, February 2003.

Refugees from all communities faced similar problems of rehabilitation and those who had access to influence and money used their connections to ease that process. Corruption and bribery were rampant during this period. Power and influence became important in gaining the spoils of partition.[57] Sardar Ishar Singh Majhail, the East Punjab minister for Refugees and Rehabilitation, was well aware of some of the corruption that was going on. He is reported to have declared in December 1947 that he would take every effort to prevent shops and factories from falling into the hands of rich people.[58] This was in response to reports of members of the Legislative Assembly attempting to acquire factories and workshops in their names or in collusion with other notables.[59] The process of granting loans and allocating evacuee-abandoned property was almost inevitably open to abuse. Bribery, land grabbing and extortion were especially prevalent due to fierce competition for resources coupled with abandoned properties, but Talbot notes that the 'border cities provided additional opportunities for crime'.[60] The legacy of this is also evident in present-day India and Pakistan, where institutionalised corruption is endemic. Ilyas Chattha has recently been unearthing this connection between corruption during the rehabilitation of refugees and its impact on independent India and Pakistan.[61]

People frequently used previous connections in determining their destinations and so the state's role in directing the flow of migration had a limited impact, particularly in urban areas. The situation of the urban refugees interviewed here was of course very different from that of the rural migrants who were directed *en masse* to specific localities and districts. There were also some attempts to redirect skilled urban artisans. But this was far less effective and as is revealed in these interviews, many urban migrants made their own arrangements and used their extended family networks and *biradaris* to get things done. In keeping with the chaos of the situation, there are first-hand accounts that reveal how people just ended up in Ludhiana accidentally. This was because refugees caught the wrong train or just went to the first destination

---

57 Joya Chatterji, *The Spoils of Partition: Bengal and India, 1947–1967* (Cambridge: Cambridge University Press, 2011).

58 *Tribune,* 13 December 1947.

59 *Tribune,* 13 December 1947.

60 Ian Talbot, *Divided Cities: Partition and Its Aftermath in Lahore and Amritsar 1947–57* (Karachi: Oxford University Press, 2006), 68.

61 Ilyas Chattha, 'Competitions for Resources: Partition's Evacuee Property and the Sustenance of Corruption in Pakistan,' *Modern Asian Studies* 46, no. 5 (2012):1182–211.

they could. Bhagwant Kaur and her husband did not know anyone in Ludhiana but made a decision to go there on impulse. She recalls, 'My father-in-law was in government service in Pakistan, he had two options for relocation, Ludhiana or Ambala. We thought about what should we do… we were at the train station and he said we'll go wherever the first train comes to'.[62]

Similarly, Jaswant Singh says, 'we did not have any plans to come here but some of our friends landed here in Ludhiana and we thought why don't we stay here'.[63] Other refugees, however, utilised pre-existing connections to ease the painful process of resettlement. Haji Kazim migrated from Ludhiana to Lyallpur. His *phuphi* [father's sister] was living in Katchery Bazaar, Lyallpur, and that was why he came to Lyallpur.[64] Both Mai Manta and Gurnam Singh also migrated to Ludhiana because of pre-existing family ties.

> When we reached Amritsar we stayed in a gurdwara for three days. Then we told the people there that we want to go to Ludhiana because our relatives have gone there. Then we came to Committee Bagh and stayed there for about seven days. We were provided with food and rations there as well. Then a person from here [Sabzi Mandi] went there and told us to leave because there is house free in Sabzi Mandi. So we left and came here to this gali [narrow lanes]. This whole gali was empty. In our family there are fifteen of us, we all stayed together. We found the rest of them through sending messages and visiting camps.[65]

> The reason we came to Ludhiana was because my *thaya* [paternal uncle] lived here. He was a Reader in the courts with the magistrates, so we all got together.[66]

In addition to family ties, geographic links, business contacts or even the potential for further opportunities were also important factors in determining where people migrated. Ghulam Nadi migrated from Ludhiana. He was aware of Lyallpur's textile background, and because his family worked in this line of business prior to partition, they decided to go to the city.[67] Chaudhari Rehmat

---

62   Interview with Bhagwant Kaur, Sabzi Mandi, Ludhiana, March 2002.

63   Interview with Jaswant Singh, Industrial Area B, Ludhiana, March 2002.

64   Interview with Haji Kazim, Jhang Bazaar, Faisalabad, February 2003.

65   Interview with Mai Manta, Sabzi Mandi, Ludhiana, March 2002.

66   Interview with Gurnam Singh, Sabzi Mandi, Ludhiana, March 2002.

67   Interview with Ghulam Nadi, Gobind Pura, Faisalabad, February 2003.

Ullah migrated from Jullundur. His father was a contractor and had a brick kiln business, which they resumed in Lyallpur. He says:

> Initially, we arrived in Lahore. My cousin received us and accommodated us in the camps near Gurhi Shaho. On the suggestion of some of my friends, I decided to settle in Lyallpur. Baba Ghulam Husain and Karam Ilahi were amongst those friends. I had family terms with Baksh Ilahi, the owner of Crescent Mills [in Lyallpur]. They had businesses spread all over the India. Baksh Ilahi and Gulzaar were in Jullundur [where Chaudhari Ullah lived].[68]

Abdul Rahman, owner of Lyallpur Cotton Mills, highlights the importance of previous connections, and in this case through business links, which greatly helped in the process of resettlement.

> My father and brother purchased shoes for their shops from Agra. The owner of Chief Boot House, Sheikh Bashir Ahmad and his brothers, Sayed also purchased stock from there. That way they became friends of my brother and father. Sheikh Bashir invited my father and brother many times to visit Lyallpur and my brother invited them to Ludhiana. So my brother migrated to Lyallpur to seek help from Sheikh Bashir, who helped him a lot. He was a Councillor of Muslims; told my brother of many houses that were deserted by Hindu and Sikhs and asked him to choose the one of his choice. He also provided us with rations.[69]

Multiple Migrations

Taking a broader look at the Punjab, the residue of colonial legacies permeates everywhere. Particularly pertinent are the connections between the partition migrants and the canal colonies. Both illustrate the long tradition of migration in the region but are also important in understanding the 'side-effects' of colonial rule. Indeed, the Indian government was actively distributing pamphlets in Urdu and Punjabi at non-Muslim relief camps (in both India and Pakistan) that suggested that people who were coming from Sargodha, Rawalpindi, Jhelum, Gujranwala and Lyallpur should settle in Ludhiana

---

68   Interview with Chaudhari Rehmat Ullah, Harcharan Pura, Faisalabad, December 2002.

69   Interview with Abdul Rahman.

district.[70] The consequences of partition for the canal colonies were clearly unforeseen because they were developed in the nineteenth century when the idea of independence, let alone partition, was a remote possibility. Without these earlier migrations and the linkages with the 'motherland', the later population displacement of 1947 would have undoubtedly taken a different form. The personal narratives used here reveal the lack of closure and self-inflicted amnesia about their personal loss, leading to constant shifts and movement in order to reconcile that sudden fracture.

From the mid-1880s, the Punjab province experienced rapid growth and major social engineering based on irrigation projects.[71] In this complex system the colonial power was engaged in maintaining its hold over the frontier Punjab province. Recruitment and retention in the army was a crucial ingredient in colonial policy, in which army personnels were rewarded land in the canal colonies. Agriculturalists from the overpopulated areas of central Punjab migrated westwards to turn this sparsely populated land into what became the 'bread basket' of colonial India. Although migrants to the canal colonies also included Muslims,[72] it was ultimately the Hindus and Sikhs who would be compelled to leave this land in 1947. As Randhawa, in his account of resettlement in India, notes:

> Many of these who came from the canal colonies had their original home in the districts of East Punjab, more especially in the Jullundur Division. These were the colonists who had gone a generation or so ago into the canal colonies and there, with their labour and skill, raised one of the most flourishing systems of agriculture in the world.[73]

While the initial migration to the canal colonies was voluntary and organised, the latter was forced migration often leading to complete abandonment of personal properties. This was obviously the unintended outcome of earlier

---

70 Suri, *Punjab State Gazetteers*, 173.
71 Imran Ali, *The Punjab Under Imperialism, 1885–1947* (Princeton: Princeton University Press, 1988).
72 See further, David Gilmartin, 'Migration and Modernity: The State, the Punjabi Village, and the Settling of the Canal Colonies,' in *People on the Move: Punjabi Colonial and Post-Colonial Migration*, eds. Ian Talbot and Shinder Thandi (Karachi: Oxford University Press, 2004), 3–20.
73 Randhawa, *Out of the Ashes*, 11.

British colonial policies' mixing-up of populations in the nineteenth century giving way to 'unmixing' of communities in 1947.

The transfer of population during this period into the new Lyallpur canal colony has received relatively little attention, given its dramatic impact on the region.[74] Farmers, artisans and even some professionals were drawn by the economic opportunities. Migrants came from throughout East Punjab including Ludhiana. While talking to these residents of Ludhiana it was clear that some individuals re-migrated eastwards to the ancestral homes and quarters in Ludhiana district and Ludhiana city from which their grandparents and parents had earlier departed.[75] Although it is difficult to estimate the exact numbers, many of those who had originally left central Punjab for the canal colonies used their previous family links to return in 1947 in order to re-establish themselves. Pritam Singh's family originally belonged to Dhandhra in Ludhiana district; his grandfather had gone to the Sandal Bar (Lyallpur area) in 1892–93 and Pritam was born in the new colonies. His family, however, still kept links with their ancestral village:

> We still had land in Dhandhra. So we used to return to Dhandhra periodically. We had leased our land to Khem Singh – one of our relatives who used to pay us a bit, you see…Our land amounted to 50 bighas at Dhandhra (10 acres), so we did expect much income from back home. In any case, we visited old village every six months but definitely once a year.[76]

But as he goes on to explain, once rumours started about the creation of Pakistan, the situation became uncertain and they were informed that movement would be necessary. Pritam Singh, in his account, clearly sees the escalating violence as the primary factor in pushing the reluctant Sikhs and Hindus out of the prosperous canal colonies.

> But many people still thought that it is all nonsense. We should not move…Then suddenly everything changed when murders came along. Some Sikh leaders ran through our villages, including Giani Kartar Singh and Udham Singh Nagoke. They told us to get ready for permanent

---

74 See further, Ali, *The Punjab Under Imperialism*; and Gilmartin, 'Migration and Modernity,' 3–20.

75 See further, Darshan Singh Tatla, 'The Sandal Bar: Memoirs of a Jat Sikh Farmer,' *The Panjab Past and Present* 29, nos. 1 and 2 (1995).

76 Tatla, 'Sandal Bar,' 168.

movement back to native lands...As we crossed the border, expressions of happiness, confusion, mixed along with keen discussion about the new border. Where was Hindustan and how did Pakistan begin from this border? We stayed the night just near the new border...Death smelt all around the camps.[77]

During my conversation with Ratten Singh, he told me how his family decided to try their fortunes in Lyallpur following the death of many family members due to a plague epidemic. His father decided to go to Lyallpur as they had heard of the new canal colony. He anticipated the need for a *karyana* (grocers) shop, as they were many farmers and families settled there. Once settled, other family members joined them. Less than forty years later, partition violence forced them to make a return journey to Ludhiana. Ratten Singh's case history is only one example of someone whose family originally migrated to Lyallpur around 1910 and then returned to their ancestral home less than forty years later.[78]

An interview with Malik Ludhianvi suggests that Muslims in Ludhiana had also been influenced by stories from Hindu and Sikh migrants to the canal colonies. Those who had ventured into the canal colonies often maintained links with their ancestral lands (as illustrated by the accounts above) and they often recounted stories to their friends and families of the opportunities in the colonies. These accounts are important because they raise awareness and bring alive places which would otherwise remain remote, distant and unknown; instead the stories bring to life neighbourhoods that people know of, providing a more personalised connection. It was undoubtedly these stories, which in turn influenced Muslims fleeing from the partition violence in places like Ludhiana to seek refuge in Lyallpur, which appeared as attractive destinations. Malik Ludhianvi recalls that there was a rumour, 'that Lyallpur had been allotted to Ludhiana'. He goes on:

> Some people wanted to go to Gujranwala but majority wanted to go to Lyallpur. Because of this we and most of the migrants from Ludhiana reached Lyallpur and started handlooms business. This rumour that Lyallpur would be given to Ludhiana also played its part to attract migrants from Ludhiana. We heard it in the camps and on our way as well. We liked Lyallpur because my father had worked as a driver in Jhang,

---

77   Tatla, 'Sandal Bar,' 170–2.
78   Interview with Ratten Singh, Model Gram, Ludhiana, February 2003.

near Lyallpur. He had seen Lyallpur city and he liked its geographical features and atmosphere very much. It was a new city then. It was famous in Ludhiana that most of the people were migrating from Ludhiana to Lyallpur and Lahore.[79]

The presence of pre-existing business or family links not only influenced the destination of migration, but also assisted in the process of acceptance by the local population. As Sarah Ansari's work has revealed, the migration of refugees into Sind resulted in ethnic tensions with the local population.[80] The conflict between locals and migrants in the Punjab was muted, despite the fact that the migrant population often outnumbered the established population, especially in cities such as Lyallpur and Ludhiana. Even when refugees did not possess pre-existing ties, assimilation was made relatively easier because of a common Punjabi language and cultural values.

Whether people had used their previous connections or whether they just arrived in a new destination, resettlement for refugees was more than just a matter of finding suitable accommodation and employment. For many, it was a long and arduous process involving a number of relocations and taking a number of years before they felt they were 'resettled'. An interview with Puran reveals this problem. When I interviewed Puran, he had his own tailoring business in Ludhiana which he had named after his former home town, *Lyallpur Tailors*. He left Lyallpur like many others in the *kafilas* and arrived initially in Amritsar but, after a few weeks, he decided to go to nearby Gurdaspur. After a few months there, he left for Ropar, near Chandigarh, because he knew some people there. Puran then stayed in Ropar for two years, where he commenced his work in tailoring. He eventually moved to Ludhiana because his in-laws lived there.[81] For Puran and many others like him, it took many years to re-establish everything from scratch and often without state support. For those who lost their businesses in 1947, it took them many years to re-create and re-establish new customers and markets. This was the same for some refugees whether they were in India or Pakistan. Mehr reminisces about his father's reluctance to settle down and start a business because he

---

79   Interview with Malik Mohammed Yousaf Ludhianvi, January 2003.

80   Sarah Ansari, 'The Movement of Indian Muslims to West Pakistan after 1947: Partition-Related Migration and Its Consequences for the Pakistani Province of Sind,' in *Migration: The Asian Experience*, eds. Judith M. Brown and Rosemary Foot (Basingstoke: Macmillan, 1994), 149–68.

81   Interview with Puran, Model Town, Ludhiana, February 2003.

kept thinking about his former home, even though relations between Muslims and non-Muslims became hostile:

> My father lived for 10 years after migration. During that time, he kept on thinking about going back to Jullundur. When it came to purchasing a shop, he hesitated because he thought that we would go back someday. It was God's will, that's what I say; but, no doubt, there was an atmosphere of brotherhood and peace amongst Muslims and other communities before that. Our shop was in the bazaar near the city courts. Our customers, who were very courteous to us and greeted us as 'Mian Ji salam', had swords in their hands during riots.[82]

Similarly, Abdul hesitated before eventually settling down in Lyallpur, while for Jaswant and his family, who resettled in Ludhiana, it was more than a decade before they could establish their businesses:

> It was a struggle of ten to fifteen years before we settled our lives in 1960 or 1965. During the initial two or three years of migration, we thought that we would go back eventually to our homeland; many other people thought likewise, so we didn't show proper interest in setting up businesses. This way some of our time was wasted. Some more of the time was wasted in setting up new businesses.[83]

> It took many years to settle. We started our business in 1957. That was 10 years [after partition]. Before that we did many small jobs, then my elder brothers started a factory. But the status we had there, we could never reproduce here. We had to stand in queues to get rations, flour, sugar etc. We first had to get a ration card and then queue to get our rations. This was at Jawahar Nagar camp [one of the largest camps and located in Ludhiana]. Most of the refugees stayed there but we had a house so we didn't stay there. Our standard of living declined sharply. But once we started working and started our business in 1957, things got better.[84]

At the time of partition, state mechanisms were unprepared for the mass migration that resulted in approximately 14.5 million people being uprooted.

---

82 Interview with Mehr who migrated from Jullundur and was a small vendor at the time of partition, Harcharan Pura, Faisalabad, December 2002.

83 Interview with Abdul Rahman, Lyallpur Cotton Mills, Faisalabad, February 2003.

84 Interview with Jaswant Singh Makkar, Industrial Area B, Ludhiana, March 2002.

Eventually, organisation by the state came into force and a planned evacuation could take place. When we move away from the official response to migration, we begin to see the differential experiences of refugees. Urban refugees were less easy to control and, while the state directed some of the refugees, others made their own plans. Utilising personal networks, refugees were able to migrate to places, which had an element of familiarity, whether this was in the shape of family, friends and business links or, in the case of Ludhiana and Lyallpur, memories and experiences that were shaped by the canal colony migrations between the two localities. Ironically, both Ludhiana and Lyallpur had populations in which 63 per cent belonged to the 'other' community. In Lyallpur, this meant the largest transfer of population in West Punjab. Ironically, some of these were the same people who migrated during the colonial period to ease the tensions of overcrowding in East Punjab and to develop the canal colonies. Without this, the tracts in West Punjab would most definitely have been Muslim-majority areas. In a strange turn of events, it is precisely because this migration had taken place at the close of the nineteenth century that fifty years later these people were forced to make a return journey.

Those with access to information and those who were literate were better prepared. Jaswant Singh's family were able to plan their departure from Sialkot and sell their possessions before leaving, but this was an option open only to the elite. Meanwhile, the majority of the people were forced to abandon their possessions and homes as the only means of safeguarding their lives. Once safely across the border, the full realisation of the upheaval began to sink in. This was only the beginning of that journey, for Muslims and non-Muslims alike. The dislocation of partition lingered on for years to come. The uncertainty of the strange new environment meant that many shifted around two, three or even four times before settling down. This transitory period lasted for years rather than months, and although at the state level refugees were quickly 'processed' and 'rehabilitated', in reality the task was a lot longer and harder.

The personal narratives of migrants in East and West Punjab, Muslims and non-Muslims, highlight the similarities people shared at a human level. The reality was that these people were not that different from each other. They shared the human suffering of partition violence and being uprooted from their homes. They experienced the same trauma related to partition and the dislocation of migration. If there were differences, then they were at the level of class and economic status. While the local population felt some anxiety over the influx of refugees, the refugees themselves found it difficult to forget their home. Memories of homelands are apparent and kept alive in the way

Picture 6.5: Picture taken in Chaura Bazaar, Ludhiana, near the clock tower; a migrant from Lyallpur

Picture 6.6: Picture taken in Lyallpur, near the clock tower; a migrant from Ludhiana

migrants have named their business ventures. Lyallpur Sweet Shop, Lyallpur Tailors, and Lyall Book Depot are all shops run by refugees from Lyallpur in Ludhiana, whereas in Lyallpur you find similar names reflecting the owners' former homes, such as Ludhiana Sweet Shop and Ludhiana di hatti. These are just the small ways in which the refugees have preserved their memories. The reality of the 'promised land' was not completely true and though people reconciled themselves to the new environment, thought of their home was never far away:

> A bit of normalcy had returned and the people were able to forget the past. But where was one to find the wide and fertile fields of Sandal Bar and the canals which supplied them water in abundance! My grandfather and uncle did not like the new land but they had reconciled themselves to their fate. Only my grandmother would spread a carpet beside the decayed wall, mourn over the loss of her middle son, curse Jinnah and Nehru and recalled her innocent grandsons and granddaughters slaughtered by the marauders.[85]

---

85 Sukhwant Kaur Mann's collected short stories published under the title of *Manmattian* (Ludhiana: Chetna Prakashan, 2002). Quoted in Dhanwant Kaur 'Sukhwant Kaur Mann: Preserving Cultural Memory through Fiction,' *Journal of Punjab Studies* 13 (2006): 250.

Saadat Hasan Manto

Invitation to Action[1]

When the neighbourhood was set on fire, everything burned down with the exception of one shop and its sign.

It said: 'All building and construction materials sold here'.

Saadat Hasan Manto

God Is Great[2]

The evening finally came to an end and the singing girl's clients left one by one.

The old man in charge of the arrangements said, 'We came here after having lost everything on the other side, but Allah has showered us with all these riches in a few days.'

---

1   Saadat Hasan Manto and Introduction by Daniyal Mueenuddin, *Mottled Dawn: Fifty Sketches and Stories of Partition* (India: Penguin, 2011), 150.
2   Manto, *Mottled Dawn*, 166.

7

From Refugee to Citizen

There are very few studies which examine the impact of partition on the Punjab's urban and industrial development. Apart from a few key works such as Ian Talbot's work on Lahore and Amritsar,[1] and Tan Tai Yong and Gyanesh Kudaisya's work on urban capital centres in South Asia,[2] a cross-border dimension is almost totally absent. But we can learn a great deal from these comparative approaches. Ludhiana and Lyallpur's growth post-1947 is a story of two towns, separated by an international border but sharing many common features. They provide the background and environment in which refugees emerged as new contributors and citizens to cities' growth. Refugees, contrary to state efforts, migrated to localities that presented them with the most opportunities or where they could utilise their kinship networks. The large volumes of refugees flooding into these two localities fundamentally changed the cities and it is this process that needs to be examined. How did the state, industry and displaced persons respond to this challenge?

These cities, as we have noted earlier, form important case studies because of their economic transformation since 1947. Their growth in recent decades has owed much to the prosperity of the Punjab arising from the Green Revolution, the influx of labour from other parts of the region and the flow of overseas remittances. The foundation of this growth, however, was based on the formative years following partition. This saw a huge influx of refugee labour and capital and also, especially in the case of Lyallpur, witnessed considerable government assistance. Ludhiana was also able to benefit from the decline of its industrial rival Amritsar because of its close proximity to the new international border with Pakistan.[3] So how did these two minor towns, of colonial Punjab, emerge to become the industrial and financial capitals of a divided Punjab?

---

1   Ian Talbot, *Divided Cities: Partition and Its Aftermath in Lahore and Amritsar 1947–1957* (Karachi: Oxford University Press, 2006).

2   Tan Tai Yong and Gyanesh Kudaisya, *The Aftermath of Partition in South Asia* (London: Routledge, 2000).

3   For an early account of the impact of partition on border areas, see K. L. Luthra's work, which examines the impact partition had on the industries of East Punjab.

East and West Punjab's Urban Rehabilitation

> Our story opens with the refugee thronging the province in camps, schools and college buildings, military barracks, temples, inns, and every other conceivable place. The whole land was covered with them. They were frenzied, bleeding, and in great destitution: and their immediate rehabilitation was the most urgent question that faced the country.[4]

The above quotation is from the 1962 Indian publication, *Punjab Industries*, that captures the mood of the subcontinent at the time of partition. It reveals the magnitude of the task of refugee rehabilitation. This was an enormous undertaking for the governments of India and Pakistan, both of which were totally unprepared for this complex challenge that involved almost 15 million people. Of the 5.5 million refugees from West Pakistan, who flooded into India, 3.5 million were from rural areas and 2 million were urban refugees, who had to be accommodated in the existing towns.[5] While there were some *harijans* among the urban migrants along with artisan castes such as *lohars* and *tarkhans*, the bulk of the refugees were from the Hindu commercial castes of *Khatris*, *Aroras* and *Banias*. They ranged from petty shopkeepers to large merchants, bankers and industrialists. It was also from these castes that the bulk of Punjab's professional elite had been drawn from before partition. The urban migrants from West Pakistan were, on the whole, better qualified and possessed higher living standards than the Muslim East Punjab refugees. This created a hugely skewed workforce for Punjab after partition. A considerable part of the Hindu upper caste urban refugees, especially those from Lahore, migrated to Delhi.[6] But a significant number settled in East Punjab. In Ludhiana district, the urban population rose by 29 per cent, while the rural population experienced a decline of 9 per cent between 1941 and 1951.[7]

Impact of Partition on Industries in the Border Areas of East Punjab (Punjab: Board of Economic Enquiry, 1949).

4   R. Dhiman, *Punjab Industries* (Ludhiana: Dhiman Press of India, 1962), 25.

5   Ministry of Information and Broadcasting, *After Partition* (Delhi: Government of India, 1948), 61.

6   See further, Dipankar Gupta, 'The Indian Diaspora of 1947: The Political and Economic Consequences of the Partition with Special reference to Delhi,' in *Communalism in India: History, Politics and Culture*, ed. K. N. Panikkar (New Delhi: People's Publishing House, 1991), 80–108.

7   *Census of India, Punjab District, 1941 and 1951.*

Despite the large numbers of people involved, rural resettlement was less challenging than urban resettlement. Some of these were undoubtedly the same families making a return journey to their ancestral villages, having made the reverse journey some fifty years earlier to the canal colonies. There was the additional problem in East Punjab, unlike in Pakistan West Punjab, that less land was available for the incoming agriculturalists than had been abandoned. This problem was overcome by a scale of 'graded cuts'. In the first instance, West Punjab agriculturalist refugees were temporarily allocated land on the basis of ten acres per family. Refugees who had bullock-carts and cattle with them were moved into areas vacated by Muslims.[8] In time, a permanent system of land allocation was developed and the government published the *Land Resettlement Manual* in 1952 to provide guidance.[9] The existence of extensive land revenue records assisted the 'management' of rural resettlement. In both the Punjabs, rural refugees were settled in districts that were demarcated to receive them. Urban refugees could not be 'managed' in this way and records of property that could be exchanged were less readily available.

Urban resettlement essentially entailed the tasks of addressing the shortage of housing, allocating and matching jobs and stimulating commercial activity again. Although the problems were easy to pinpoint, the solutions were more complicated. Housing in urban areas was very limited and, in East Punjab, a large number of the refugees had to remain in tents and refugee camps until new towns could be developed.[10] The situation was further exacerbated by the fact that many Muslim evacuee houses were damaged during the partition-related rioting and thus had to be repaired before they could be occupied by refugees. There were also some suggestions that the situation was mishandled by officials. A survey of rehabilitation work in East Punjab recorded that 'the housing problem assumed formidable proportions largely due to the mishandling of the situation by the allotment committees and the officials concerned'.[11]

---

8   V. S. Suri, *Punjab State Gazetteers: Ludhiana* (Chandigarh: Controller of Print and Stationary, 1970), 174.

9   Tarlok Singh, *Land Resettlement Manual* (Simla, 1952).

10   *After Partition*, 63.

11   Survey of Rehabilitation Work in East Punjab, 5 January 1951, *Press Clippings of Dr. M. S. Randhawa* (Ludhiana: Punjab Agricultural University Library).

The East Punjab government was provided with Rs. 2.5 crores by New Delhi to develop twelve townships,[12] in the province and was advised to prioritise the management of businesses that were vacated by Muslims in East Punjab.[13] Even by 1950, there were still a large number of displaced persons in East Punjab. Records show that government still had to fulfil the following housing requirements:[14]

a) 20,000 displaced persons without shelter
b) 18,600 displaced persons in tents
c) 25,000 displaced persons occupying places of worship, *dharamshalas* and so on
d) 70,000 displaced persons temporarily housed in mud-huts
e) 260,000 displaced persons living in congested areas for whom alternative accommodation is required

The situation of persons under categories a, b and c was deemed urgent and thus required immediate action. The construction of more mud-huts was approved by the government as a quick and easy solution to the problem of providing accommodation for those living in tents and other temporary dwellings.[15] This was also cheaper than replacing worn-out tents. In addition to this, the East Punjab government developed a cheap housing scheme. Ten thousand houses were to be constructed as part of a long-term strategy, taking

---

12 These houses were part of a wider scheme to construct 4,000 houses in townships of East Punjab; all were situated around half to one mile outside the parent towns. The twelve townships were located at Jullundur, Hoshiarpur, Ludhiana, Khanna, Jagadhri, Karnal, Panipat, Rohtak, Sonepat, Gurgaon, Palwal and Rewari. The scheme consisted of building 4,000 houses in these urban centres, out which 3,873 were actually built. The estimated cost of the scheme was Rs. 23,045,557. Note from P. N. Thapar, Rehabilitation Department, to The Assistant Secretary to the Government of India, New Delhi, Ministry of Rehabilitation, 21 February 1950. *Housing Schemes in East Punjab*, RHB/1(1)/1950, NAI.

13 *After Partition*, 64–5.

14 *Housing Schemes in East Punjab*, NAI.

15 The construction of further 3,500 mud-huts was approved. *Pucca* roofs were added to extend the life of these houses. The mud-huts were intended for displaced persons currently living in tents. A further 9,000 houses were required for those without shelter and those living in other temporary accommodation. *Housing Schemes in East Punjab*, NAI.

into account the growing population.[16] The scheme was designed to meet the needs of 50,000 people on different plots to cater for the differing needs. There was also approval for a further construction of 18,000 mud-huts, which were to cater for 45,000 persons, while 1,000 additional mud-huts were to be utilised for shops, schools, dispensaries, post offices, welfare centres and other amenities.[17]

To facilitate the rehabilitation of urban refugees from Pakistan, the East Punjab government provided loans for those people who wished to pursue their trade and professions. Sardar Ishar Singh Majhail, the East Punjab minister for Refugees and Rehabilitation, had declared as early as December 1947 that a sum of Rs. 50 lakhs would be set aside to help the petty shopkeepers and owners of small-scale industries restart their enterprises.[18] Generally, loans were granted through co-operative societies and in exceptional circumstances directly to individuals.[19] The size of the loan varied according to requirements. For example, traders, merchants and those who were interested in starting a small-scale business could obtain up to Rs. 5,000. Doctors, dentists, radiologists, *vaids*, *hakims* and homeopaths, and lawyers could get up to Rs. 3,000 and for petty shop keepers and all other cases a ceiling of Rs. 500 was set.[20] A Rehabilitation Finance Administration was set up to assist with large-scale industry and business. It could provide loans from Rs. 5,000 to Rs. 10,000 to traders, shopkeepers and those interested in starting a cottage industry.[21]

The East Punjab government had evidently set aside large sums of money to assist the process of urban rehabilitation. The aim, however, was not to breed a culture of dependency, but rather to enable the refugees to become self-sufficient as soon as possible. The process of granting loans and allocating evacuee-abandoned property was almost inevitably open to abuse. Sardar Ishar Singh Majhail was well aware of some of the corruption that was going on. He is reported to have declared in December 1947 that he would take every effort to prevent shops and factories from falling into the hands of rich people.[22] This was in response to reports of members of the Legislative Assembly attempting

16 *Housing Schemes in East Punjab*, NAI.
17 *Housing Schemes in East Punjab*, NAI.
18 *Tribune* (Simla), 13 December 1947.
19 *After Partition*, 64–5.
20 *After Partition*, 64–5.
21 *After Partition*, 65–6. The total budget for the Rehabilitation Finance Administration was Rs. 10 crores.
22 *Tribune* (Simla), 13 December 1947.

to acquire factories and workshops in their names or in collusion with other notables.[23] Interestingly though, even here we see cases in which people use their own personal networks to exchange land and property. For example, the Naulakhiya family was one of the most prominent families in Ludhiana and after migrating to Lahore, they came to know of a Hindu who owned property in Krishan Nagar of 40 marlas; this they felt was comparable to their place in Ludhiana and they went about exchanging their houses.[24]

To assist urban refugees to find suitable employment, the government used employment exchanges. These were already established prior to partition; however, their scope was widened to co-ordinate and match vacancies to the skills of the refugees. In addition, the Ministry of Labour provided technical and vocational training. Some training centres were opened in refugee camps. Refugees could engage in paid work while acquiring new skills such as spinning, weaving and knitting.[25] The rehabilitation of women, especially those who were destitute, widowed or abandoned, was catered for separately under the Women's Section.[26] Commercial opportunities were limited in the aftermath of partition, but it was hoped that the completion of the Bhakra and Nangal dams would greatly boost the economy of the East Punjab.[27]

Ludhiana's Demographic Transformation

While the population of the Ludhiana district declined between 1941 and 1951, the population of Ludhiana city grew by 38 per cent, from 111,639 in 1941 to 153,793 in 1951.[28] This is despite the fact that nearly all of the Muslims

---

23 *Tribune* (Simla), 13 December 1947.
24 Muhammad Aslam, *1947 Mein Ludhiana ke Muslamano par kia guzari?* (Faisalabad: Al-Khair Publishers, 2014). Translation kindly provided by Tohid Chattha.
25 *After Partition*, 66.
26 Destitute widows from West Punjab were assisted by the government. In Punjab four new vocational training centres were set up at Jullundur, Hoshiarpur, Rohtak and Karnal. Only the inmates of the ashrams in these locations were eligible for training. Note from Shrimati Premvati Thapar, Relief and Rehabilitation Department, Women's Section, Jullundur, to L. Jodh Raj, Punjab Riots Sufferers Committee, New Delhi, 4 July 1950. Rameshwari Nehru Papers, NMML.
27 *Press Clippings of Dr. M. S. Randhawa.*
28 The population of Ludhiana district in 1941 was 818,615 and this declined by 1 per cent in 1951 to 808,105. *Census of India, 1941 and 1951.*

migrated. Interestingly, we can see that during the same period the population of Amritsar city declined by 17 per cent, from 391,010 to 325,747. Although the 1951 census does not provide a detailed breakdown of religious composition, by 1961 it is clear that the Muslim community had virtually all migrated to Pakistan. According to 1961 Census of India, only 4,686 Muslims were enumerated in Ludhiana district, compared to 302,482 in 1941. Of the Muslims who remained, only 524 resided in the urban localities of the district.[29] The outgoing Muslims were replaced by Hindus and Sikhs from West Punjab. Prior to partition, Ludhiana was a Muslim-majority locality, making up 63 per cent of the city's 111,639 population. Hindus accounted for 31 per cent, while Sikhs represented only 5 per cent of the population.[30] Post-1947, over 67 per cent of the district's urban population was Hindus and 30 per cent Sikhs.[31] Based on this ratio, it is likely that Ludhiana's population would have been similar to this.

The statistics only illustrate the demographic impact of exchanging populations; they do not reveal that behind these people lay the fabric of Ludhiana city. Muslim workers formed a vital part of the economy. Skilled Muslim workers dominated employment in the flour and rice mills with 83 per cent of workers; in the hosiery sector, Muslims accounted for 61 per cent; and in the textiles industry, they accounted for 78 per cent of the workforce.[32] For many cottage industries, the result was closure; it is estimated that in the towns of Amritsar, Ludhiana and Batala around 40 per cent of the registered factories had to close down as a result.[33] The skills that were lost with the migration of these workers were not, in return, compensated by the new incoming migrants. Instead, there was a mismatch of skills, and pragmatic innovation and reinvention were key to future survival.

To meet the immediate refugee needs, a colony with 1,300 mud-huts was set up called Jawahar Nagar Camp. Mud-huts were cheap and easy to make

---

29 *Census of India*, Punjab District Handbook, 1961.

30 *Census of India*, Punjab District, 1941.

31 *Census of India*, Punjab District Handbook, 1961.

32 These figures are for the district, but most of the industry was located in the city. In Amritsar, Muslim workers accounted for 90 per cent of workers in scientific engineering, 83 per cent of wood workers and 79 per cent in the glass wares sector. In Jullundur, 90 per cent of the workers in the hosiery industry were Muslim, and in Ferozepur 80 per cent of the workers in the textiles industry were Muslims. Luthra, *Impact of Partition*, 32.

33 M. L. Pandit, *Industrial Development in the Punjab and Haryana* (Delhi: B. R. Publishing, 1985), 39.

and were used as a first step to providing suitable housing. However, it was shortly realised that neither 'Jawahar Nagar Camp nor the evacuee houses, vacant sites, shops and industrial establishments would be sufficient to meet the residential requirements of the vast numbers of the displaced persons'.[34] A government report on the relief and rehabilitation of refugees in Punjab shows that in 1950 Jawahar Nagar Camp had 5,570 persons living in mud-huts. More broadly in East Punjab, 95,463 persons were accommodated in this way at the time.[35] In response to the acute housing shortage, a number of new colonies were established around Link Road in Ludhiana to accommodate the large influx of people. In Model Town, 473 houses and 24 shops were constructed, while 685 plots of land were allotted.[36] The cost of the houses constructed was expected to be around Rs. 2,627,611.[37] New roads around the satellite townships were also constructed. In New Model Town Colony a further 290 houses were constructed and 40 shops were built at Jawahar Nagar Camp.[38] At the Old Police Lines, 104 new shops and stalls were constructed to add to 143 shops and stalls already there.[39] From Map 7.1, we can see that much of the development in Ludhiana took place south of the old city, partly due to natural northern boundary caused by Budha Nala (literally means old stream).

These new housing schemes were designed to meet the different needs of the displaced persons coming to Ludhiana. Model Town colony was primarily designed to meet the standards of the rich and upper middle classes, while the cheaper colonies, including the mud-huts, were for those displaced persons who had sought refuge in gurdwaras, *dharamshalas*, homes for abandoned

---

34 Suri, *Punjab State Gazetteers*, 180.

35 *Progress Report on Relief and Rehabilitation in the Punjab*, 20 April 1950. *Housing Schemes in East Punjab*, NAI.

36 Ministry of Rehabilitation, Note from P. N. Thapar, Rehabilitation Department, to The Assistant Secretary to the Government of India, 21 February 1950, *Housing Schemes in East Punjab*, NAI.

37 Four thousand houses were expected to be built under this scheme, out of which 3,873 were completed at an expected cost of Rs. 23,045,557. Out of the 3,873 houses, 2,067 were sold to displaced persons and 334 were kept by the Government of India for sale to displaced military personnel. The houses were sold by auction and the remainder were expected to be sold in April 1950. Note from P. N. Bhalla on behalf of P. N. Thapar, Rehabilitation Dept (Urban), Jullundur. *Housing Schemes in East Punjab*, NAI.

38 Suri, *Punjab State Gazetteers*, 181.

39 Suri, *Punjab State Gazetteers*, 181.

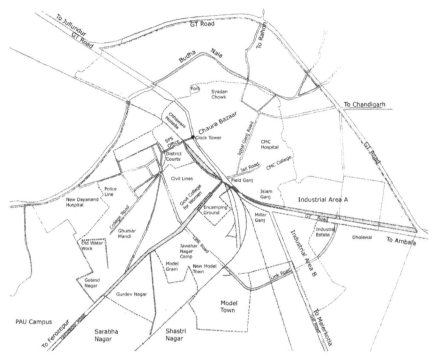

Map 7.1: Townships and Localities in Ludhiana

women and infirmaries.[40] Loans for the construction of houses were provided by the Government of India. These were given on low interest rates and were repayable in 20 years.[41] As part of the industrial development programme, new industrial areas were developed along the GT Road. Labour colonies began to spring up on the outskirts of the industrial areas, which provided the proximity required by labourers to travel to their work place.[42] As the Map above illustrates, the area developed in the post-partition period was in response to the urgent requirements of housing, and the long-term strategic requirements were generally not the priority. Although most of this was done on an ad hoc basis with little planning, some parts were created because of the industrial requirements of the city.[43] Gradually then the foundations were

40   Suri, *Punjab State Gazetteers*, 181.

41   Suri, *Punjab State Gazetteers*, 181.

42   S. V. Auluck, *Intracity Residential Mobility in an Industrial City: A Case Study of Ludhiana* (New Delhi: Concept Publishing, 1980), 28.

43   Auluck, *Intracity Residential Mobility*, 31.

being laid for more specialised areas to emerge, with the industrial area in the east of city leading the way for future development.

Developing Ludhiana

The best way to describe colonial Ludhiana is that it was a small town (with potential) and lagged behind Lahore and Amritsar. Its main economic activity centred around trade and the hosiery industry. Its importance for trade was seen in the number of specialised markets within the old city. There were, for example, Chawal Bazaar (rice), Saban Bazaar (soap), Pansari Bazaar (grocery), Gur Mandi (jaggery), Ghah Mandi (grass), Trunk Bazaar, Lakkar Bazaar (wood),[44] all of which are situated around the hub of the city, Chaura Bazaar (see Picture 7.1). Though the wealth of the city was primarily based on the agricultural well-being of the district, there was also a small presence of hosiery and light engineering industry. In 1947, Ludhiana had 78 registered factories which had increased to 95 by 1952, though this was still considerably less than Amritsar's 235.[45] However, it was the dominance of small-scale industry in Ludhiana, which in 1952 stood at 452 small-scale units compared to Amritsar's 239, that enabled the city to achieve a competitive advantage over its rivals. It is through the dominance of small-scale industry that Ludhiana has emerged as East Punjab's leading industrial centre,[46] surpassing Amritsar and Jullundur. The development of small-scale units was praised by India's first Prime Minister,

---

44 Auluck, *Intracity Residential Mobility*, 25.

45 Of the ninety-five registered factories, eleven were in textiles, thirty-four hosiery, fourteen engineering, thirteen foundry, six metal, four oil and flour, and thirteen miscellaneous. Om Prakash, *An Economic Survey of Industrial Labour in the Punjab, No. 14* (Punjab: The Board of Economic Inquiry, 1952), 3.

46 By the late 1990s, there were about 59 large and medium-sized industries and about 15,000 small-scale registered units flourishing in Ludhiana city, with a combined annual turnover of about Rs. 765 crores. Ludhiana has surpassed all other districts in the Punjab, in small-scale industries, during the last twenty years. This has led to other key centres in Ludhiana district benefiting from the growth in the city. For example, Khanna in particular is a fast-growing centre of small industries such as sewing machines, cycles and cycle parts and woollen hosiery. Samrala and Jagraon towns are also catching up in industry with the establishment of iron re-rolling plants. S. C. Bhatt, *The Encyclopaedic District Gazetteers of India, Northern Zone (Vol. 4)* (New Delhi: Gyan Publishing House, 1998), 671–8.

Picture 7.1: Chaura Bazaar is an old market dating back to the nineteenth century, it literally means 'wide market' and formed the hub of economic and political activity in Ludhiana

Jawaharlal Nehru, who was committed to the country's industrial growth. Nehru though was only too aware of the challenges that lay ahead:

> One of my colleagues had recently made a quick survey of the small-scale industries started in the Punjab since independence and was much impressed with what had been done both by the permanent residents there and those who had come from Pakistan as refugees. I believe he listed 20,000 small enterprises that had grown up in the last few years in the Punjab with a relatively small capital but with a great deal of energy and enterprise. That is the kind of thing which heartens one and increases self confidence... It is the Government's business to create conditions for the rapid spread of medium and small scale industries all over India. The example of Ludhiana, where such industries have thrived shows that this kind of thing could be done everywhere. It would be better for such industries to be started away from big cities.[47]

---

47   Dhiman, *Punjab Industries*, 28.

The expansion of small-scale units, particularly in the hosiery industry, had multiplier effects as it also triggered off-shoot industries in metal-based industries, for example, manufacturing hosiery machines, tools and other equipment.

How can we understand and contextualise the emergence of Ludhiana as a major hub in the East Punjab economy after partition? M. L. Pandit, in *Industrial Development in Punjab and Haryana,* identifies three factors which he maintains were crucial to industrial development in the region as a whole: first, the influx of West Punjab urban-based refugees; second, the presence of *Ramgarhia* craftsmen in large numbers; and finally, the early growth of a number of key industries in East Punjab. Stephen Keller, in *Uprooting Punjab,* offers an additional explanation to this, suggesting that Punjab's business development was rooted in cultural values that encouraged an entrepreneurial outlook and enterprise. However, there is the danger in Keller's and Pandit's work of reproducing cultural stereotypes and of dealing in generalities. More specifically, Ludhiana's post-partition growth can be linked to a number of distinct advantages. Ludhiana's post-partition growth was built on the colonial industrial base in the hosiery industry and the favourable location on the Grand Trunk Road. Refugee entrepreneurs played a leading role as did *Ramgarhia* migrants from elsewhere in the state as well as from Pakistan. Finally, the Indian state itself took a number of measures to encourage industrial growth, although its role was less significant than that of its Pakistan counterpart with respect to Lyallpur's development.

As Ludhiana city expanded, it began to attract entrepreneurs seeking to make their fortunes. They set up their enterprises in a random manner, often choosing any suitable spot. In order to control this unorganised establishment of businesses, the Small Scale Industries Board recommended that industrial estates should be established in areas of East Punjab where this was taking place. As a result of these recommendations, the Punjab government planned five industrial estates in the state. The Ludhiana Industrial Estate was the first to be built in East Punjab and was the largest in India.[48] Its overall management rested with the state government.

The Ludhiana Industrial Estate offered ready-built workshops. It was modern in its outlook and was planned with suitable accessibility for the transportation of goods. There were 224 workshops in all. During the first

---

48   Om Prakash Gupta, 'Ludhiana Industrial Estate,' in Dhiman, *Punjab Industries*, 33. O. P. Gupta was president of the Allottees Association of Industrial Estate.

phase of allocation for the units, fifteen were old businesses that shifted from other congested areas of the city, thirty-one were new businesses and twenty-nine units were allocated to displaced persons from West Punjab.[49] Even though some commercial activity had already started, the Department of Rehabilitation had noted that it was necessary to build additional shops due to the shortages. As a result, 60 shops were planned for Ludhiana; this was part of a wider plan to build a total number of 500 in East Punjab. These shops were generally constructed in what were deemed 'important urban areas in suitable localities'.[50] These were costly ventures, being in prime commercial centres, and Rs. 15 lakhs in all had been diverted for the construction of these shops.

On the Right Track

Part of Ludhiana's success can be explained through its geographical location. An important point made by Luthra in his work, *Impact of Partition on Industries in the Border Districts of East Punjab*, is that, while important commercial centres like Amritsar and Batala declined because of partition, cities located further away from the border such as Ludhiana and Jullundur[51] did not suffer to the same extent. We can see from Table 7.1 that many of the businesses that surveyed in the border areas of Amritsar, Gurdaspur and Ferozepur were keen to relocate elsewhere, either within Punjab or preferably outside Punjab. One of the longer-term consequences of this sentiment has been that Amritsar, which now bordered Pakistan directly, experienced a sharp decline.[52] This was the combined result of the loss of skilled Muslim labourers and the loss of investment in the district. Conversely, though, we

---

49   The units manufactured a variety of goods including power presses, oil engines, cycle and motor spare parts, measuring tapes, conduit pipes, chaff cutter blades, panel pins, nail rivets, nuts and bolts and other consumer goods. Dhiman, *Punjab Industries*, 33.

50   Note from M. S. Randhawa, Department of Rehabilitation, Jullundur, to The Secretary to the Government of India, Ministry of Rehabilitation, 20 December 1950, Ministry of Rehabilitation, NAI.

51   Throughout this book the colonial spelling of Jullundur has been used for consistency. Jalandhar is the contemporary spelling.

52   Gurpreet Maini, *The Giant Awakens: Punjab Industry and Growth* (New Delhi: India Research Press, 2004), 63 ff.

see places like Ludhiana and Jullundur benefiting from this decline in the border areas.

Table 7.1: Number of Factories that Wanted to Relocate Businesses

	Total Surveyed	Relocate Outside East Punjab	Relocate Inside East Punjab	Total Percentage Who Want to Relocate (%)
Amritsar	111	45	25	63
Gurdaspur	21	3	6	43
Ferozepur	7	1	2	43
Jullundur	52	2	3	10
Ludhiana	54	4	1	9

Source: K. L. Luthra, *Impact of Partition on Border Industries* (Board of Economic Enquiry: Government of Punjab, 1949), 71.

Ludhiana's other locational advantage was its position on the GT Road which was the main trade artery of the region. Before partition, the GT Road linked Delhi and Peshawar. It remained after 1947 an important source of access between Punjab and independent India's capital city. Big industrial units are all located along the GT Road, especially major centres like Jullundur and Ludhiana but also feeding into satellite areas and contributing to their growth. A similar situation occurs across the border in Pakistan. A ribbon style of development is visible along the GT road in Lahore. The head offices of leading Ludhiana industries, such as Hero, Avon, G. S. Auto and Ralsons, are located on the GT road. For such industries as the hosiery manufacturers that depend on markets beyond Punjab, good transport linkages are vital. In the woollen hosiery sector, more than 80 per cent of the country's demand is met by Ludhiana alone.[53] In addition to this, woollen hosiery goods are exported to several countries, bringing valuable foreign exchange. Ludhiana has benefited not only from a good road and rail infrastructure, but from the presence of earlier colonial development.

Displacement and Entrepreneurship

The pre-existing industry provided a pool of entrepreneurial talent, technical expertise and capital from which to expand. The colonial period was especially important in increasing the mobility, technical skills and capital of

53 Bhatt, *District Gazetteers of India*, 671–8.

the *Ramgarhia* community, which played a crucial role in the modern growth of Ludhiana's small-scale industry. *Ramgarhia* Sikhs followed the traditional village occupations of carpenters and blacksmiths. They diversified during the colonial era. Many moved out from their central Punjab villages to the canal colonies of West Punjab. A considerable number were employed building the railways in East Africa. The colonial power found it cheaper to recruit artisans such as *Ramgarhias* and *Viswakarmis* to cast and manufacture simple parts and tools rather than import them from England. This gave the community experience of working in a new trade and consequently they were able to diversify further from simple tool making.[54] The work also provided surplus capital that could be used as investment in small-scale enterprises. *Ramgarhias* played a pioneering role in both Ludhiana's famous cycle industries and the machinery sector of the hosiery industry.[55] Management in the hosiery industry has, however, been traditionally the preserve of the trading castes like the *Khatris*, *Aroras*, *Agarwals* and *Oswals*. Indeed, in a mid-1960s' study conducted by UNESCO, it was estimated that in Ludhiana 84 per cent of the textile and hosiery units were managed by members of these castes.[56]

During World War Two the hosiery industry was stimulated by the demands of defence contracts. For Ludhiana, this was a crucial victory, as its manufacturers faced competition from other big groups in Bombay. They were able to produce cheaper goods because work was contracted out to subcontractors who utilised small cottage-style units. In effect, this started the move towards small-scale industry, which has dominated Ludhiana's growth. The hosiery sector did suffer immediately after partition, primarily due to the loss of its skilled Muslim labour force. When Luthra conducted his survey in 1948, he found that 61 per cent of the skilled workers in the hosiery sector in the Ludhiana district were from the Muslim community.[57] This figure represents only the thirty-nine registered factories that were

---

54   To see further about the artisan communities of the Punjab see Harish S. Sharma, *Artisans of the Punjab: A Study of Social Change in Historical Perspective 1849–1947* (New Delhi: Manohar, 1996).

55   *Ramgarhias* along with Dhimans still dominate in this sector. See M. Tewari, 'Successful Adjustment in Indian Industry: The Case of Ludhiana's Woollen Knitwear Cluster,' *World Development* 27, no. 9 (September 1999): 1657.

56   UNESCO, *Small Industries and Social Change, Four Studies in India* (Delhi: United India Press, 1966), 21.

57   Luthra, *Impact of Partition*, 32.

surveyed and out of these thirty-four were in Ludhiana. Loss of trade was another factor; around 30 per cent of woollen hosiery from Ludhiana at the time went to areas that were in Pakistan after partition.[58] It took some time to get things back to normal. Some manufacturers even took the opportunity to change businesses and try other trades and 'hosiery thus remained an industry for those who wanted to sweat and at best earn their humble pie'.[59] The cycle industry has also developed dramatically since independence from its small beginnings during the colonial era. It is thought that a few enterprising *Ramgarhia* artisans from Malerkotla laid the foundations for the bicycle parts industry in Ludhiana.[60] At the time of partition, around twenty-five units existed in Ludhiana that specialised in the production of cycle parts.[61] The industry took off in terms of large-scale production of cycles and related industries after partition.

Can Ludhiana's industrial success be linked to refugees resettling in this locality? Is it possible that the influx of refugees from West Punjab changed the prospects of the local economy? Some research has already looked at this relationship at an all-India and state level. Pandit's field survey of displaced persons showed that half the total number of entrepreneurs in selected industrial centres came from people uprooted from West Punjab.[62] Gurpreet Bal has also maintained that industrial development in East Punjab benefited from the ready supply of displaced persons.[63] To what extent was this a significant factor in Ludhiana? Pandit's figures for the city are illustrated in Table 7.2. We can see from the table that displaced persons formed nearly half of the entrepreneurs surveyed and yet represented only 21 per cent of the district's population, although, given that Muslims represented over 60 per cent of the population in city, the representation of refugees would have been higher in the city than in the district.

---

58 Luthra, *Impact of Partition*, x.

59 Kewal Krishan, 'Woollen Hosiery Industry,' in Dhiman, *Punjab Industries*, 32. Krishan was president of the Hosiery Industry Federation.

60 Manjit Singh, *The Political Economy of the Un-organised Industry: A Study of the Labour Process* (New Delhi: Sage, 1990), 72.

61 Pandit, *Industrial Development*, 120.

62 Pandit, *Industrial Development*.

63 Gurpreet Bal, *Development and Change in Punjab* (New Delhi: National Book Organisation, 1995), 57.

Table 7.2: Background of Entrepreneurs – 1951

Industrial Centre	Number of Entrepreneurs Surveyed	Displaced Persons (%)	Displaced Persons in District (%)
Jullundur	50	88	26
Jagadhri-Yamunagar	48	60.4	20
Ludhiana	74	48.7	21
Gurgaon	51	47.1	8.7
Ambala	30	33.3	20
Batala	33	33.3	35
Patiala-Rajpura	36	30.6	22.8

Source: Based on field investigation by Pandit, except for the last column where percentages are based on data from *Census of India*, Punjab, 1951. M. L. Pandit, *Industrial Development in the Punjab and Haryana* (Delhi: B. R. Publishing, 1985), 39, 126.

Refugees played important roles both as capitalists and as workers in the hosiery and cycle industries. The hosiery trade is in fact concentrated in the small alleys of the old city, where many of the Muslims lived previously and which were then claimed by refugees. Saidan Chowk is one such area; several interviews were conducted in this locality. Nand Lal, for example, migrated from Jhang and is from the *Arora* trading caste.[64] He was allotted a house in Saidan Mohalla and initially started working for Nanda Hosiery in 1948. At the time, he was earning Rs. 10 per month for stitching work. But he gradually increased his skills, learning cutting work, which earned him more money. He even made *toppies* (hats) out of cutting waste. Within four years, he was a master cutter, earning Rs. 300–400 a day. Nand Lal now owns his own hosiery business. Another similar story is that of Gian Chand Ahuja,[65] also an *Arora*, who migrated from Lyallpur. He started off doing a lot of menial jobs and then worked in the hosiery trade, stitching merchandise. In 1953, Ahuja and three other family members started the empty jute bags business. They would collect surplus and waste bags, then recycle and rebrand them into new jute bags. This was an extremely successful trade for the family due to the demand for jute bags for transporting materials at the time. They still operate their jute bag business from the old city.

Some of Ludhiana's most famous refugee entrepreneurs are associated with the cycle industry. Pandit suggests that a major portion of the small proprietors and displaced persons who went into the cycle and cycle parts

---

64   Interview with Nand Lal, Saidan Chowk, Ludhiana, April 2002.
65   Interview with Gian Chand Ahuja, Model Gram, Ludhiana, April 2002.

industry did so with the help of rehabilitation loans and other credit loans from public and private sources.[66] India's biggest bicycle manufacturers, such as Avon, Atlas and Hero, are all Ludhiana businesses started by displaced entrepreneurs. Sohan Lal Pahwa, one of the founders of Avon Cycles,[67] knew about Muslims making cycle parts in Malerkotla. They had a shop in Gill Road, Ludhiana, prior to partition and they also had business links in Malerkotla. This was one of the reasons why the family migrated to Ludhiana from Sialkot in Pakistan in 1947. They started with manufacturing bicycle saddles and brakes in 1948. Soon after the Pahwa brothers started their cycle production business in 1951 as a small-scale industry, rolling off around 250 bicycles. The company has since grown enormously and exports Avon Cycles across the globe.[68]

The *Ramgarhia* community has undoubtedly played a crucial role in Ludhiana's development in the fields of mechanical and electrical engineering. They are dominant in small sector production, which has been the hallmark of Ludhiana's economic development. A parallel in Pakistan is the transformation of the artisan *Lohar*[69] community from blacksmiths to dominant figures in Sialkot's burgeoning surgical instruments industry.[70] During the colonial era, *Ramgarhias* were being drawn to Ludhiana because of the employment opportunities. The first factory for producing sock-knitting machines was started by a *Ramgarhia* migrant from Malerkotla in 1920.[71] Gurmukh Singh, the founder of G. S. Auto, was similarly drawn to the city; the company

---

66 Analysis and Planning Report: Bicycle and Parts (All India), in Pandit, *Industrial Development*, 121.

67 Interview with Sohan Lal Pahwa, managing director, Avon Cycles, Ludhiana, April 2002. The Avon Cycles was founded by Pahwa brothers – Mr Han Raj Pahwa, Mr Jagat Singh Pahwa and Mr Sohan Lal Pahwa.

68 K. N. S. Kang (chief editor), *Business Families of Ludhiana* (Delhi: New Century, 2003), 13–23.

69 For further information on the *Lohar* community see Sharma, *Artisans of the Punjab*.

70 The *Lohars* initiated the industry and continue to dominate it, although other communities have entered it since partition. See K. Nadvi, 'Social Networks in Urban Punjab: A Case Study of the Sialkot Surgical Instrument Cluster,' in *The Post-Colonial State and Social Transformation in India and Pakistan*, eds. K. Nadvi and S. M. Naseem (Oxford: Oxford University Press, 2002), 146–77.

71 Singh, *The Political Economy*, 72.

is one of the leading manufacturer and exporter of auto parts.[72] Gurmukh Singh began his life as an apprentice in a smithy shop in Machiwara, just outside Ludhiana city, and then started working in the bicycle parts industry before moving into automotive parts.[73] Such in-migration by *Ramgarhias* has increased rapidly in the post-independence era, although not always with such spectacular entrepreneurial results. Significantly though, it contributes to the dynamism of the place.

Transforming Lyallpur

As a district, Lyallpur was a very attractive destination for refugee resettlement as it was located in the most fertile area in West Punjab. Until 1947, Lyallpur was mainly a market town and an agro-industry centre with a handful of textile factories. After partition, manufacturing assumed a much greater role in the so-called 'Manchester of Pakistan'. Both the city and the district were demographically transformed as a result of partition. Between 1941 and 1951, Lyallpur city grew in population by 156 per cent, compared to the overall growth of 54 per cent in the district.[74] The population increase can be attributed to the huge influx of refugees into the city, which continued to expand at these phenomenal rates. Between 1951 and 1961, Lyallpur's population grew by 137 per cent. From Table 7.3 we can see how refugee resettlement in Lyallpur district is, compared with other districts in West Punjab. It had one of the highest concentrations of refugees. This proportion increased further in Lyallpur city, where refugees formed 69 per cent of the population in 1951.[75] The West Punjab government in February 1948 had expressed concerns over the large number of people in camps particularly in areas like Lyallpur. It was already a surplus area, but people chose to remain in the camps in the hope that they would eventually be resettled in the locality.[76] Crucially Lyallpur was

---

72   Interview with Jagat Singh, son of Gurmukh Singh, G. S. Auto, Ludhiana, March 2002. The family is very prominent in Ludhiana and are patrons of *Ramgarhia* schools in the community.

73   The company turnover is Rs. 60 crores and over 45 per cent of its products are exported. Kang, *Business Families of Ludhiana*, 70.

74   Government of Pakistan, *Census of Pakistan 1951*. Sargodha during the same period was the second highest; the growth here was 115 per cent and Lahore was 27 per cent.

75   Government of Pakistan, *Census of Pakistan 1951*.

76   Note from Deputy Commissioner, Montgomery, to the Home Secretary to the West Punjab Government, 23 February 1948. Courtesy of SARRC, Islamabad.

considered a 'land of opportunity' especially by those who had come across the canal colony, through previous stories of migration.

Table 7.3: Proportion of Muhajirs in West Punjab

District	Total	Muhajirs	Per cent
Punjab (total)	18,828,000	4,908,000	26
Lyallpur	2,153,000	986,000	46
Lahore	1,895,000	745,000	39
Montgomery	1,816,000	713,000	39
Bahawalpur state	1,823,000	373,000	20
Bahawalpur	970,000	298,000	31

Source: *Census of Pakistan*, 1951

The influx of Muslim refugees completely changed the demographic composition of Lyallpur (see Table 7.4). This was a Hindu–Sikh majority area prior to partition, with non-Muslims constituting 63 per cent of the population. Partition was followed by the total outmigration of Hindus and Sikhs. Incoming East Punjab Muslim refugees settled in such localities as Gobind Pura and Guru Nanak Pura whose names reflected the former Sikh inhabitants. The Hindu and Sikh evacuees had played a dominant role in the city's trade, banking and agro-based industries. They were now replaced by Muslims from the enterprising *Arain* and *Sheikh* communities (especially *Gaubas*, *Chawlas* and *Pirachas*) who had migrated from East Punjab towns such as Jullundur, Ludhiana and Amritsar where they had worked in business and small-scale trading activities.[77] But they were able and willing to fill the niches left by the non-Muslims and so contributed to the city's economic dynamism.

Table 7.4: Composition of Population in Lyallpur Town 1941–61

	1941	1951	1961
Total population	69,930	179,127	425,248
Hindu	47%	–	–
Muslim	33%	97%	97%
Sikh	16%	–	–
Christian	4%	3%	3%

Source: *Census of India*, Punjab district, 1941, and *Census of Pakistan*, 1951 and 1961.

---

77 For further details, see Mohammad Waseem, 'Urban Growth and Political Change at the Local Level: The Case of Faisalabad City, 1947–75', in *Pakistan. The Social Sciences' Perspective*, ed. A. S. Ahmed (Karachi: Oxford University Press, 1990), 207–28.

Picture 7.2: Remnants of the past. Sita Ram Mandir in Rail Bazaar, Lyallpur now converted into a masjid

Housing was an immediate problem because of the huge numbers of migrants. As we can see from Map 7.2, the city is laid out as a square, with eight roads radiating from the central Clock Tower. This area was the hub of

Picture 7.3: Remnants of the past: an abandoned Khasla middle school and gurdwara in Lyallpur, now a Model High School for boys

commercial activity, while residential, religious and other civic activities were also catered for within the bazaar area. The influx of refugees after partition really swamped the commercial and residential area. The development that

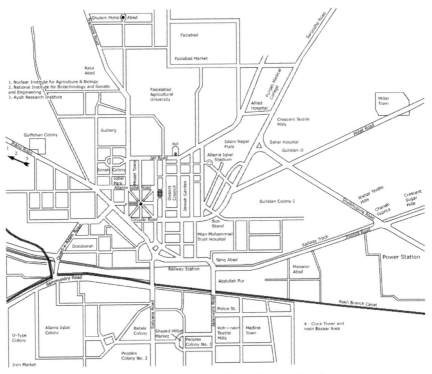

Map 7.2: Townships and Localities in Lyallpur

followed, as in Ludhiana, was ad hoc prompted by the need to immediately house the thousands of refugees. The city developed sprawling slum areas in which there were clusters of *kachi abadies* near factories such as the Lyallpur Cotton Mills.[78]

A number of satellite towns (they included Jinnah Colony, People's Colony, Industrial Labour Colony as well as Model Town) were planned and constructed in Lyallpur to relieve the congestion. These were part of a wider programme of refugee resettlement throughout West Punjab. Similar satellite town schemes were constructed in Multan, Jhang, Montgomery,

---

78 Pasha, based on his own experience of living in Lyallpur since partition and working in the district commissioner's office, argues that the Faisalabad Development Authority, Faisalabad Municipal Corporation and even the government failed to check the uneven growth in Faisalabad, which has led to the planned modern city becoming a big slum. M. Z. Pasha and S. A. Shahid, *From Sand Dunes to Smiling Fields: History of Lyallpur now Faisalabad* (Faisalabad: Kitab Markaz, 1996), 151.

Rawalpindi, Sargodha and Gujranwala;[79] Rs. 8 crores was earmarked for this purpose.[80] The Punjab chief minister, Mian Mumtaz Daultana, was accorded an enthusiastic reception in Lyallpur in late April 1951 when he outlined plans for the construction of 'modern' towns with such amenities as street lighting, underground sewerage and 80 to 40 feet wide roads.[81] A further year elapsed before the completion of the initial scheme on the cattle fair ground at Lyallpur at the cost of Rs. 14 lakhs. This scheme, with its secondary and primary schools, post office, dispensary and recreational open spaces, was designed to provide accommodation for 550 families and included provisions for refugee officers to draw funds of up to Rs. 200 per month for the construction of houses.[82] Early in July 1952, the West Punjab Rehabilitation and Colonies minister, Sheikh Fazal Ilahi, witnessed the public auction of its residential and commercial plots,[83] which had been constructed privately, following government planning support. Daultana was once more in Lyallpur, in September 1952, to open the Rahman Charitable Hospital and Maternity Centre at Ghulam Muhammadabad. He declared that when the satellite towns were completed, they would greatly help in relieving the congestion experienced by people living in Lyallpur.[84]

A further sum of Rs. 20 lakhs was spent by the West Punjab government for the construction of 800 houses. Of this 360 were to be built in the Ghulam Muhammadabad Colony for low-income refugee families, at a cost of Rs. 9 lakhs, 240 in the Industrial Labour Colony costing Rs. 6 lakhs and 200 in the People's Colony at Rs. 5 lakhs.[85] While the city had undergone extensive development to meet the needs of the large number of refugees, it seemed that the provincial government constantly had to make new arrangements. In 1956, the Lyallpur Improvement Trust put forward plans to meet the shortage of housing in the town. It envisaged plans for the construction of 1,500 bungalows and other houses to accommodate 2,000 families in the Civil Lines, Race Course and Jail Road areas,[86] keeping in mind that it was now fast approaching ten years since Pakistan was created, and localities such

---

79 *Dawn* (Karachi), 12 July 1953.
80 *Civil and Military Gazette* (Lahore), 15 May 1951.
81 *Civil and Military Gazette* (Lahore), 26 April 1951.
82 *Civil and Military Gazette* (Lahore), 25 August 1950.
83 *Dawn* (Karachi), 5 July 1952.
84 *Dawn* (Karachi), 21 September 1952.
85 *Dawn* (Karachi), 12 July 1953.
86 *Dawn* (Karachi), 1 September 1956.

as Lyallpur were still struggling with the basic needs of its inhabitants. The challenges were substantial.

Like Ludhiana, many of these new 'model towns' catered for the needs and requirements of the middle class. Working class refugees and labourers lived in the old part of the city, around the Clock Tower. Once industrial activity had taken off in Lyallpur, labourers, again as in Ludhiana, lived close to the industrial area in *kachi abadies* like Mai di Juggi, which were essentially slum areas. These were usually located around the big industrial mills for ease of access.

Prosperity and Growth

At the opening of State Bank of Pakistan in Lyallpur, in December 1956, the Bank's governor, Abdul Qadir, declared that this marked 'not only an important event in the history of the Bank but also symbolised the rapid economic growth that had taken place in Lyallpur after the attainment of independence'.[87] Lyallpur had indeed made such strides that, by the mid-1960s, it ranked second only to Karachi as Pakistan's most industrialised city. In 1965 more than 3,000 industrial units accounted for 20 per cent of the built-up area and employed 75 per cent of the total urban workforce of 65,000.[88] Textiles formed the city's leading industrial sector. The growth and confidence in the textile trade can be seen in the large investments made for setting up the Institute of Textile Technology at Lyallpur.[89] The expected cost of this project was Rs. 50 lakhs, of which Rs. 25 lakhs had been donated by four of the leading textile mills in Punjab, including Koh-i-Noor Textile Mills of Lyallpur.[90] The institute set out to provide technical training, with teachers coming from the United Kingdom to assist in the first five years.[91]

Other important industries included cotton ginning, vegetable oil, fertilisers, rice and grain processing, agricultural implements, jute and sugar mills. In addition to medium and large-sized units, there were numerous small-scale enterprises, as in Ludhiana. These produced items such as coarse

---

87 *Dawn* (Karachi), 7 December 1956.

88 Waseem, 'Urban Growth,' 208.

89 *Dawn* (Karachi), 19 December 1953, and Government of Punjab, *Five-Year Industrial Development Programme for the Punjab, 1951–1956* (Lahore: Government of Punjab, 1952), 43.

90 *Dawn* (Karachi), 18 March 1954.

91 *Dawn* (Karachi), 18 March 1954.

cloth and hosiery. There are similarities in the factors behind Lyallpur's and Ludhiana's post-partition economic growth, namely, colonial infrastructural and economic inheritances and the impact of refugee labour and entrepreneurial enterprise. The main difference is the role of the state as a result of the Pakistan government's much greater commitment to the rapid industrialisation of the locality.

Lyallpur owed its existence to the colonial state's development of the canal colony schemes. It emerged as an administrative centre on the Lower Chenab canal and as a market for the agricultural produce of the region, in particular its cotton and wheat. Lyallpur's planning as a modern city ensured that it was served with good road and rail communications. These have continued to play an important part in its post-independence development. Indeed, much of the city's industrial development has grown up along the link roads to Sheikhupura and Sargodha. The extensive railroad network linking the countryside with Lyallpur led to the emergence of markets for manufactured goods of the local industry.[92]

By the late colonial era, there were the beginnings of industrial development utilising the abundant raw materials of the district's commercialised agricultural produce. Post-partition industrial growth has centred around the processing of these agricultural products such as sugar, vegetable oil, rice and grain. Most importantly locally grown cotton has provided the staple raw material in textile manufacturing. The colonial era's inheritance of agricultural commercialisation and good communications thus forms an important backdrop to the city's post-independence success. Nevertheless, it seems unlikely that it would have experienced its remarkable industrial expansion without the political and demographic changes resulting from partition.

The establishment in 1948 and 1950 of the Koh-i-Noor and Crescent Textile Mills by the Seghal and Chinioti families, respectively, provides the clearest example of refugee involvement in Lyallpur's industrial development. They had developed big export-orientated industrial houses in Delhi and Calcutta before partition, although they both originated from West Punjab.[93] The families competed for political influence in Lyallpur, utilising patron–client networks and the muscle power of their *goondas*.[94] The absence of traditional feudal elites in the city also gave them such opportunities, although

---

92 Waseem, 'Urban Growth,' 208.
93 Waseem, 'Urban Growth,' 210.
94 Waseem, 'Urban Growth,' 210 ff.

the Seghals purchased agricultural land and began to behave in a traditionally 'feudal' manner of coercion and harassment. Apart from the large industrial magnates, there were scores of middle-ranking refugee industrialists. These were members primarily of the *Arain* and *Sheikh biradaris*. They moved from dealing in processed raw materials to production.[95] At the bottom of the industrial ladder were the small-scale operators of hosiery and textile units who were refugees drawn from the former artisan classes. They met the low start-up costs of such cottage industries with either help of government loans or capital they brought from East Punjab.

Refugees also provided much of the labour for the city's industrial expansion. Such workers came from low-income urban refugees and poor peasants who had not been allotted land after migration, but who 'preferred to stay in the city'.[96] Industrial development depended on this cheap labour supply. Refugee workers were later joined by migrants from other parts of the district and elsewhere in West Punjab. Eventually, tensions developed within the city's labour force arising from the area of origin. There was, for example, the conflict between local and non-local workers in the Nishat Mills.[97] Workers from the surrounding villages tended to be less militant than their refugee counterparts.[98]

While Mohammad Waseem has provided an immensely useful overview of the role of refugee labour in Lyallpur's urban and industrial development,[99] until this research was undertaken no first-hand accounts had been collected regarding this process of transforming Lyallpur. A number of interviews were conducted with residents that highlight the way in which refugees from Ludhiana transferred their skills to Lyallpur's textile industry. Previously gained technical and industrial skills and capital acquired in Ludhiana were not only vital for individual refugee rehabilitation in Lyallpur, but were a crucial element in the city's rapid post-independence economic growth. One example of this is a company by the name of Karim Hosiery. The company was founded over 100 years ago at Ludhiana. After partition, the family came to Lyallpur and started their business from scratch. Today the company is the largest socks manufacturer in Pakistan, selling about six million pairs of socks

---

95   Waseem, 'Urban Growth,' 214.
96   Waseem, 'Urban Growth,' 211.
97   Waseem, 'Urban Growth,' 221.
98   Waseem, 'Urban Growth,' 219.
99   Waseem, 'Urban Growth'.

annually.[100] The advantage Lyallpur had was that it was able to tap into the skilled base that migrated *en masse* into the city which led to rapid prosperity; the process would have been slower, had it been dependent on importing the required skills.

Bashiran Bibi spoke of her husband (they were married before partition) setting up one hand loom, and within a year he had progressed to forty hand looms. She talked about how hard they both worked: they washed and dyed the cotton thread themselves as well. With the hard work paying off, they were soon able to purchase a shop of their own. She recalls how they pioneered cotton spinning in the area:

> Yes, we were the pioneers of cotton spinning. Other people also learned it from my husband. He had many trainees. He sold cloth and cotton as far as Dacca, East Pakistan. When East Pakistan was separated, we lost an investment of Rs. 150,000 in that area. He set up a single handloom from the money his father gave him. I brought some money from my father with which cotton thread was purchased. From one handloom, he progressed to forty in a year.[101]

Mohammad Sadeeq initially set up a medical store in a shop allotted to them in Katchery Bazaar, but then went into the handloom industry in 1948. The family settled in Guru Nanak Pura; gradually the handlooms business flourished and they progressed to silk power looms, which turned out to be a big business afterwards.

> I set up silk textile mills in 1953 with the name of Chaudhari Textiles. By God's grace, I prospered to 50 silk looms, 20 towel looms and my export revenue reached millions. I have been an exporter for twenty to twenty-two years and have been to about 8 to 10 countries in this connection. My big brother and I ran a small hosiery factory in Ludhiana and my father just looked after the property. I had experience of hosiery business prior to Partition but loom enterprise was entirely new to me. In the early days of Pakistan, there wasn't much competition and manufacturer could easily get through. Those times, business opportunities were in excess because the country was newly created.[102]

---

100 Karim Hosiery, Ayub Colony, Jhang Road, Faisalabad, accessed 2004, www. golsocks.com/profile.html. The link is no longer available but previously this information was available on their profile.

101 Interview with Bashiran Bibi, Harcharan Pura, Faisalabad, February 2003.

102 Interview with Mohammad Sadeeq, Katchery Bazaar, Faisalabad, February 2003.

Sadeeq had not worked with silk power looms in Ludhiana. But he brought with him the experience of running a factory. It was this background that enabled him to branch out and grasp the new manufacturing opportunities in Lyallpur. The pride in his community's earlier achievements in Ludhiana, revealed in the extract below, was a crucial factor in the enterprise he displayed after migration.

> Ludhiana was called Manchester of hosiery in India and Muslims also had much of the hosiery business of the city – handlooms and small enterprises as well. Our *mohalla* was called Syedon da Mohalla. Syeds were very rich people and had vast properties. Hindus were the richest community. They were the owners of giant mills. Muslims were owners of some good factories of hosiery.[103]

Yousaf Ludhianvi further highlights the role of the Ludhiana hosiery industry. He worked in the handloom business before partition in Ludhiana.

> Ludhiana was famous not only in Punjab but all over the India for its industries. Hosiery and cloth industry of Ludhiana was very famous. *Ansari, Teli, Julahe, Mochi* and nearly all other artisans lived in Ludhiana. The days we started handloom business in Lyallpur, it was difficult to get raw material. I left that business and started working in the cotton mills at the age of 17 to 18 in 1949. I used to operate power loom in the mills of Makhan in Ludhiana so it was easy for me to work in the cotton mills. The handloom business was not a new enterprise for us because we were into same trade before the partition. We knew about *Tarkhans* as they were also present in Ludhiana. We gave 12 to 14 rupees to a *Tarkhan* who made us a handloom. That cloth was not so fine in quality but because of the shortage of cloth, it was sold easily and nobody objected it.[104]

Shafi's interview demonstrates how, when other hosiery/textile factories were established, there were new opportunities for people to get jobs related to the industry. But often it was a difficult period of uncertainty and for the common man, with few benefits.

> My father washed hosiery items for the knitting factories of Hindus and Sikhs. I worked with my father. I was 20 years old at the time. We had

---

103 Interview with Mohammad Sadeeq.
104 Interview with Malik Mohammed Yousaf Ludhianvi, Ghulam Mohammad Abad, Faisalabad, January 2003.

to face many troubles after migration and unemployment was a major problem. Getting a job was very difficult here because of scarcity of industry. Cotton mills were the only option left with people so everyone strived to get a job in them. I adopted many occupations in Pakistan. Initially I purchased a junkyard, afterwards I used to sell *ghee* but eventually I took to the occupation of my father. I started off with washing clothes of people, but when few hosiery factories were established in the area, I switched to washing hosiery items.[105]

The State and Lyallpur

The role played by the Pakistan state in industrial development during President Ayub Khan's so-called 'Golden decade of development' (1958–68) has been commented on widely.[106] Much has been made of the fiscal incentives given to large-scale industrialists in Karachi largely drawn from the Gujarati-speaking *Khoja* and *Memon* refugee communities from Bombay. Mohammad Waseem has, however, also pointed out that powerful bureaucrats gave support at an even earlier stage to East Punjab capitalist migrants from this same background such as Ghulam Muhammad and Chaudhry Muhammad Ali.[107] The downside of state involvement was the scope for bribes provided to officials in charge of the state's 'promotional institutions' and 'regulatory agencies'.[108] Industrial development in Lyallpur was simultaneously an opportunity for graft, a political resource for aspirant parties and individuals and also a means of strengthening the East Punjabi presence in the Pakistan state. Standing behind all of these factors was Pakistan's national interest in rapid industrialisation and the historical and locational advantages of the city as a centre for such development. Muslim refugees themselves pressed Lyallpur's claims for government investment so that it could be turned into 'a big business centre'.[109] These early demands met with success in 1951, when

---

105 Interview with Hajji Mohammad Shafi, Harcharan Bazaar, Faisalabad, December 2002.
106 See, for example, M. Monshipouri and A. Samuel, 'Development and Democracy in Pakistan: Tenuous or Plausible Nexus?,' *Asian Survey* 35, no. 11 (1995): 973–89. Also see Markus Daechsel, *The Politics of Self-Expression: The Urdu Middleclass Milieu in Mid-Twentieth Century India and Pakistan* (London: Routledge, 2006).
107 Waseem, 'Urban Growth,' 211.
108 Waseem, 'Urban Growth,' 212.
109 *Pakistan Times* (Lahore), 12 October 1947.

Lyallpur was declared an industrial zone with attendant incentives for investors. The following year, the Pakistan Industrial Development Corporation was created. This had the responsibility for the development of bigger industries when private capital and enterprise was inadequate.[110]

The Pakistan government took steps to allocate evacuee factories throughout the Lyallpur district. It also allocated business premises within the city. In October 1948, financial support of Rs. 50 lakhs was sanctioned for cotton ginning factories and at the same time plans were approved for a textile handloom weavers' colony.[111] It was hardly surprising that government attention was directed towards the cotton textiles industry. Before independence, the main cotton and textile industries were located in places like Bombay and Allahabad. At the time of partition, there were only four textile mills in West Punjab, and only two of them were in partial working order – Lyallpur Cotton Mills and The Punjab Textile Mills in Lahore. Lala Murli Dhar Shad, the Hindu owner of the Lyallpur factories, stayed on after independence and relocated his family from Delhi.[112] The mills, however, were the scene of a major strike in June 1949 over the issue of the employment of Hindu staff from India to fill technical and non-technical posts.[113] The disjuncture in the available skills base was clearly an issue, which then manifested itself through a communal lens. Due to the disruption caused by partition and the strained relations between India and Pakistan, the import of cloth from these cities was impracticable. The handloom and hosiery factories were unable to resume work because there was a shortage of yarn, which had to be imported from India.[114] The government's Textile Advisory Committee reported in 1951 that Pakistan required an additional 350,000 spindles and 6,562 looms by 1957 to meet demand. It was estimated that 37 crores yards of cloth were needed in the West Punjab alone.[115]

As early as February 1948, the West Punjab government planned the establishment of eight new cotton mills.[116] It simultaneously planned the

---

110 Jafer Mehdi, 'Private Enterprise and Industrial Development,' in Anon, *Industrial Development in Pakistan 1947–1975* (Lahore: Progressive Research Council, 1976), 10.
111 *Pakistan Times* (Lahore), 21 October 1948.
112 *Pakistan Times* (Lahore), 14 June 1949.
113 *Pakistan Times* (Lahore), 21 June 1949.
114 Note by B. A. Kureshi, Rehabilitation Commissioner, Industries, West Punjab. Courtesy of SARRC, Islamabad.
115 Government of Punjab, *Five-Year Industrial Development Programme*, 51.
116 *Civil and Military Gazette* (Lahore), 19 February 1948.

rehabilitation of 40,000 handloom and hosiery workers and their families in the Lyallpur district. The aim was to install 50,000 handlooms and 2,000 indigenously manufactured hosiery machines at a cost of Rs. 1 crore.[117] The degree to which such state action was the result of a visionary understanding that the textile sector would lead industrial 'take-off' in Lyallpur is, however, questioned by the comment of a highly placed official. He declared of the scheme, 'I believe it is the West Punjab Government's first concrete effort to rehabilitate the hordes of refugees, weavers, textile workers and manufacturers who were becoming a menacing state liability'.[118] The founding of the Koh-i-Noor Textile Mills in 1948 marked the first stage in the government's encouragement of the textile industry. It was followed by the starting up of cotton and woollen cloth factories in Multan, Karachi and Lawrencepur.[119] Offshoot industries started to emerge in Lyallpur following the establishment of the Koh-i-Noor and Crescent Textile Mills.

This research in Lyallpur and Ludhiana brings together an important missing element in the study of partition, particularly the cross-border comparative dimension, which has been largely absent. While previous studies have explored the rural rehabilitation of refugees, the urban context has been largely overlooked. The study of Ludhiana and Lyallpur highlights the importance of how urban and industrial development in the Punjab region was manoeuvred both by the state and the people themselves. While both cities possessed locational and institutional inheritances from the colonial area that were prerequisites for growth, Partition provided the circumstances for the 'take-off' of both cities, despite the immediate short-term problems of housing and loss of evacuee skills and experience.

Crucially, refugee entrepreneurs used the opportunities for industrial development to their advantage. While some had relocated strategically to these cities, others were able to take advantage of the new planned growth directed by the state. The patterns of development have been different with the medium-to large-scale cotton textile industry dominating in Lyallpur and small-scale hosiery production leading the way in Ludhiana. The large-scale enterprises in Lyallpur are explained, at least in part, by the greater assistance afforded by the state for industrial development. Although Ludhiana was now located in

---

117 *Civil and Military Gazette* (Lahore), 20 February 1948.

118 *Civil and Military Gazette* (Lahore), 20 February 1948.

119 Shaheen, Javed, 'The Role of Refugees in the Development of Pakistan,' *Nusrat* 5 (July 1959).

the sensitive border state of Punjab in India, it was at a comparative advantage to other areas in the state due to its location on the GT Road, its distance from the border with Pakistan and its proximity to the new state capital, Chandigarh. Thus, unlike Amritsar, Gurdaspur and Ferozepur, Ludhiana could gain comparative advantage. In this respect, Lyallpur also emerged as a new industrial centre because post-1947 there were limited options for Pakistan; the only other big cities were Karachi, Lahore, Dacca and Rawalpindi. India conversely inherited many of the big power houses, so that the challenge for Pakistan was to create new ones from scratch. In this respect, both Ludhiana and Lyallpur benefit from the unique circumstances. Both Ludhiana and Lyallpur were demographically transformed by partition and their capacity to deal with the large numbers of refugees was eased only by the skills and entrepreneurial activity that they could generate in the cities. While this process was not in reality as smooth as it may appear with hindsight, it did provide the foundations through which these two became the power houses in Punjab(s).

Ramanand Sagar

Pimps

She was weaving such apparently unrelated things together as though she was muttering to herself amidst a sweet dream.

Anand could see all these things dancing in her eye – the glistening, shimmering waves of the river, the long row of *sumbul* trees and a small girl swinging like a creeper amidst red, conical flowers. He watched, spellbound, this drama being staged. So much so that the girl became self-conscious and her dream broke abruptly. The string snapped, as it were, and she came out of the romantic trance to the world of bitter reality.[1]

Saadat Hasan Manto

Out of Consideration

'Don't kill my daughter in front of my eyes.'
'All right, all right. Peel her clothes and shoo her aside!'[2]

1   Ramanand Sagar, 'Pimps,' in *India Partitioned: The Other Face of Freedom Vol 1*, ed. Mushirul Hasan (New Delhi: Lotus Collection Roli Books, 1997), 192.

2   Saadat Hasan Manto and Introduction by Daniyal Mueenuddin, *Mottled Dawn: Fifty Sketches and Stories of Partition* (India: Penguin, 2011), 162.

8

Cleansing Hearts and Minds

As part of the Fact-Finding Organisation, G. D. Khosla interviewed 1,500 women. Writing shortly after the incidents, he provides many accounts of women who were subjected to rape, abduction, mutilation and had their bodies completely violated both mentally and physically. Some had to endure public humiliation, others in the presence of their own family members. Khosla states, 'One of the kidnapped girls, relating her experience, said that she had been raped in a most inhuman manner and passed on from man to man till [sic] she completely lost all sense of feeling'.[1] Khosla's objective was to document the violations by Muslims against Hindus and Sikhs, but these crimes did not have a religion. They were crimes against humanity, but society at the same time allowed these to happen as they were happening openly. Indeed, Ayesha Kidwai argues that rather than the perpetrators being rustic simple folk, this was a 'systematic elite patriarchal consensus'.[2] People with the power and means to carry out these crimes and then cover their tracks led to the systematic exploitation of innocent lives. Ganda Singh in his journal account of the partition days also notes that Shaukat Hyat Khan, who was the revenue minister in West Punjab, suspended the official of Lyallpur district due to 'neglect of duty' and 'instances of molestation of young girls by volunteers'.[3] Our national histories barely touch upon these national crimes which remain largely hidden and obscured behind the patriotic and nationalistic agenda. Collective, individual and community memories have little space in this, as it has the potential to subvert the meta-narratives weaved around a narrow nationalistic agenda.

Debating the Crimes

Gandhi's response to these crimes was - 'We must cleanse our hearts. But even if our hearts have not been cleansed, we can still do what is clearly our duty.

---

1   Khosla, *Stern Reckoning*, 206.
2   Ayesha Kidwai, 'Re-viewing Partition, Re-claiming Lost Ground: A Critical Recovery of the Recovery Operation,' paper delivered at the Kiran Nadar Museum of Art, New Delhi, 8 July 2014.
3   Ganda Singh, *A Diary of the Partition Days 1947*. Reprinted from *Journal of Indian History* XXXVIII, Part II (August 1960): 279.

Self-purification means that we purge our hearts'.[4] Indeed, following on from the violence that was unleashed after independence, there were attempts by the political leadership to quash and condemn the actions of the perpetrators. Prominent Sikh leaders such as Master Tara Singh (Akali Dal leader) and Udham Singh Nagoke (member of Punjab Legislative Assembly) issued a joint statement, appealing to both Hindus and the Sikhs to stop all retaliatory violence.

> We do not hesitate to admit that the Sikhs and the Hindus have also been guilty of the most shameful attacks upon women and children in the communal warfare, which is still continuing…We know Sikhs stooped to these low depths only in retaliation for what was done by the Muslims. But this is no justification for the Sikhs, who have falsified tradition… We tried our best and we are trying our best to prevent our brethren from falling into these low tactics. But it appears that most of the Muslims, Hindus and Sikhs have gone mad. Crime, then retaliation and retaliation again continued and there is no end to it…If we do not desire friendship of the Muslims and we may never befriend them, we may have to fight again, but we shall fight a clean fight - man killing man. This killing of women and children and of those who seek asylum must cease at once. We ask you to do so chiefly in the interests of your own communities' reputation, character and tradition and not to save the Muslims…[5]

What is interesting about the appeal above, is that while condemning the violence or communal warfare, there is at the same time a justification in the form of it being retaliation; it is 'mad' but necessary appears to be the contradictory message. Further, the idea of a 'clean fight' (between men) is acceptable but the killing of women and children is unacceptable. The tone of the appeal is, therefore, hardly conciliatory and harbours undertones of justifying the conflict between Sikhs and Muslims. The reality was that communal violence in August 1947 started much earlier and so did the discourse around abducted women and children. Events leading up to partition saw ever-increasing communal violence in Calcutta and Bihar, travelling west towards Punjab. One of the first times this is mentioned officially is in the

---

4   Speech at Prayer Meeting by Mahatma Gandhi, New Delhi, 24 January 1948, vol. 98, 299. Annotation from Collected Works of Mahatma Gandhi, accessed 20 June 2016, www.gandhiserve.org/cwmg/VOL098.PDF.

5   *The Pakistan Times*, 25 September 1947. The headline is Tara Singh condemns atrocities by Sikhs 'Guilty of most shameful attacks on women and children'.

session of the Indian National Congress in November 1946. Dr. Rajendra Prasad who was later to become the first President of independent India, moved a resolution that received wide support from prominent leaders of the Congress Party, including Jawaharlal Nehru:

> The Congress views with pain, horror and anxiety the tragedies of Calcutta, in East Bengal, in Bihar and in some parts of Meerut district. The acts of brutality committed on men, women and children fill every decent person with shame and humiliation. These new developments on communal strife are different from any previous disturbances and have involved murders on a mass scale as also mass conversions enforced at the point of a dagger, abduction and violation of women and forcible marriage.[6]

Clearly, there is a recognition that the nature of violence has changed and has now become broader; mass killings, which now also target women and children. It then goes on to elaborate on the nature of assistance that should be provided for these women, and so we see the beginning of the state adopting a paternalistic role in how to deal with these women.

> The immediate problem is to produce a sense of security and rehabilitate homes and villages, which have been broken up and destroyed. Women, who have been abducted and forcibly married, must be restored to their homes. Mass conversions, which have taken place forcibly, have no significance or validity and the people affected by them should be given every opportunity to return to their homes and the life of their choice.[7]

This resolution put forward by Prasad was adopted in November 1946, much before the events of August 1947, when the situation deteriorated even further. The discussion is also centred around the issue and importance of not recognising the conversions that had taken place. Importantly, the discourse here is around forcible conversions and not voluntary ones which, though there is no official count, many did convert to retain their ancestral lands or to avoid forced migration. Significantly, there is much ambiguity surrounding

---

6   Veena Das, *Life and Words: Violence and the Descent into the Ordinary* (Berkeley, CA: University of California Press, 2006). E-book version, 22.

7   Das, *Life and Words*, 22. Taken from the proceedings of the Indian National Congress 1946–47.

the circumstances under which some of these women converted. The Congress proceedings continue:

> During these disorders large numbers of women have been abducted on either side and there have been forcible conversions on a large scale. No civilized people can recognize such conversions and there is nothing more heinous than abduction of women. Every effort, therefore, must be made to restore women to their original homes, with the co-operation of the Governments concerned.[8]

A year later, there are echoes of this in the speeches delivered by Mahatma Gandhi.

> The Hindu and Sikh women carried away by force should be restored to their families. Similarly the Muslim women taken away should be restored to theirs. This task should not be left to the families of the women. It should be our charge...It is my belief that the police cannot do this. The army cannot do this...This is a task for the Governments to tackle...There is only one way of saving these women and that is that the Governments should even now wake up to their responsibility, give this task the first priority and all their time and accomplish it even at the cost of their lives. Only thus can these women be rescued. Of course we should help the Government if it requires help.[9]

This is in sharp contrast to what Gandhi was saying in September 1947, when he lauded pre-emptive suicides as sign of strength. Debali Mookerjea-Leonard argues that this served the purpose of combining 'death, national honour, patriarchal values, and communalized identities ... with a brutal and brutalizing nationalism that extols self-sacrifice'.[10] Gandhi labours the point:

8　Das, *Life and Words*, 22. Taken from the proceedings of the Indian National Congress 1946–47.

9　Post-Prayer Meeting Speech by Mahatma Gandhi in Hindi, 7 December 1947. Annotation from Collected Works of Mahatma Gandhi, vol. 90, no. 163, 191, accessed 20 June 2016, https://archive.org/details/Swaraj-Gandhi-1947-12-07Post Prayer Speech 1947-12-07.

10　Debali Mookerjea-Leonard, 'To Be Pure Or Not To Be: Gandhi, Women, and the Partition of India,' *Feminist Review* 94 (2010): 42.

I have heard that many women who did not want to lose their honour chose to die. Many men killed their own wives. I think that is really great, because I know that such things make India brave. After all, life and death is a transitory game. Whoever might have died are dead and gone; but at least they have gone with courage. They have not sold away their honour. Not that their life was not dear to them, but they felt it was better to die than to be forcibly converted to Islam by the Muslims and allow them to assault their bodies. And so those women died. They were not just a handful, but quite a few. When I hear all these things I dance with joy that there are such brave women in India.[11]

Legislating Purity and Un-purity

Much of this discussion eventually feeds into the state's policies in dealing with a highly emotive and sensitive issue. The official response to the abduction of women was to locate and repatriate them to their former homes. Remarkably, the voices of women are completely absent from this political discourse and National Assembly discussions.[12] The political leadership was supported by social workers on the ground and local police, working on both sides of the border. From the Fortnightly Reports, it is clear that the Ministry of Refugees and Rehabilitation was largely concerned with numbers and recording the number of women that were found and exchanged between India and Pakistan. This was a rather impersonal approach adopted by both countries and consequently, we know little about the details of the personal tragedies behind these numbers. The documents do not detail their individual accounts and they do not provide any information about the lives that were torn in the process. They merely serve the purpose of supporting politicians concerned with recovering the nations' lost honour. Below are two examples of these rather dispassionate and matter of fact accounts recording the recovery of abducted women.

> Restoration of converted persons to the Government of India. A Hindu
> girl named Sheela who had embraced Islam and was found to have been

11 Speech at Prayer Meeting, 18 September 1947, New Delhi. Annotation from Collected Works of Mahatma Gandhi, vol. 96, 388–9, accessed 20 June 2016, www.gandhiserve.org/cwmg/VOL098.PDF.

12 Michael Jauch, 'Witnessing Violence: Perspectives on Sa'adat Hasan Manto's "Khol Do" and Rajinder Singh Bedi's "Lajvanti",' *The Annual of Urdu Studies* (1998): 189–202.

living with a Muslim in the Punjab since the disturbances, was recovered and sent to India.[13]

A Muslim girl named Shafium Nisa, who had been abducted during the riots after the partition and taken to Singapore, was recovered from the custody of a Sikh and handed over to her father who had come over to Pakistan from India for this purpose.[14]

The documentation process finishes once the women have been recovered. But why would the state be concerned with anything more than knowing a woman has been recovered? It is enough that she has been relocated but what happens to them when they returned to their families and indeed, there is a question mark over how many were actually accepted back into their families. These issues were not dealt with and thus remain unrecorded and do not form part of the official history of partition and its true cost. Through other accounts by social workers, first-hand accounts of women, we know this process was not as seamless and as successful as both governments would have liked to show. The newspapers to some extent provide more detailed accounts of the circumstances under which they were abducted and/or rescued. Certainly, *The Pakistan Times*, which is supportive of the initiative taken by the government, provides more details on some of the cases.

Still another case related to the recovery of seven girls who had persisted in remaining there and has been married to some forcibly converted men. The parents and other men folk of these girls had been killed during the disturbances. They had declined to go back to their aged grandmother, but for the help of the State officials, these women as well as the forcibly converted men could not have been rescued.[15]

The first time the Governments of India and Pakistan decided to formally address the issue of women was on 6 December 1947, nearly four months after independence. Although there was evidence of abductions and rapes taking place, it only gradually became apparent that large numbers of women and children had been left behind on either side. At the Inter-Dominion Conference on 6 December, it was decided that the 'work of rescuing these

---

13 Fortnightly Report, 31 May 1950, File 21/CF/50 Vol X. Cabinet Secretary, MR&R, GoP.

14 8 August 1951, File 23/CF/5 – Vol XIV, MR&R, GoP.

15 *The Pakistan Times*, 20 August 1948.

women and children and also evacuating converts from "pockets" should be carried out in right earnest'.[16] The treaty signed by India and Pakistan detailed and echoed much of what had previously been said by Gandhi and Prasad:

1. Every effort must be made to recover and restore abducted women and children within the shortest time possible.
2. Conversion by persons abducted after 1 March 1947 will not be recognised, and all such persons must be restored to their respective dominions. The wishes of the persons concerned are irrelevant. Consequently, no statements of such persons should be recorded before magistrates.
3. The primary responsibility for recovery of abducted persons will rest with the local police who must put full efforts in this matter. Good work done by police officers in this respect will be rewarded by promotion or grant of cash awards.
4. MEOs will render every assistance by providing guards in the transit camps and escort for the transport of recovered persons from transit camps to their respective dominions.
5. Social workers will be associated with the scheme. They will look after camp arrangements and receive the abducted persons in their own dominions. They will also collect full information regarding abducted persons to be recovered, and supply it to the inspector general of police and the local superintendent of police.
6. The DLOs will set up transit camps in consultation with the local deputy commissioners and public workers and supply information regarding abducted persons to be recovered.
7. Co-ordination between different agencies working in the district will be secured by a weekly conference between the superintendent of police, the local MEO Officer, the DLO and the deputy commissioner. At this meeting, progress achieved will be reviewed, and every effort will be made to solve any difficulties experienced.[17]

Following this meeting, an agreement was reached with the Government of India for the promulgation of an ordinance to simplify the work of the recovery of abducted persons. The Government of India had put forward the

---

16 Taken from a report on the work done by the Ministry and the Pakistan-Punjab Refugees Council by W. V. Grigson, secretary, MR&R, 27 April 1948, NDC.

17 Kirpal Singh, *Select Documents on Partition of Punjab-1947: India and Pakistan* (Delhi: National Book Shop, 1991), 572–3.

Recovery of Abducted Persons Ordinance, 1949. The Government of Pakistan followed its lead. The draft ordinance ensured:

1. The establishment of camps for abducted persons;
2. The taking into custody of abducted persons by police officers;
3. The maintenance of discipline in camps;
4. The setting up of tribunals to determine whether a person detained is an abducted persons or not;
5. The handing over of abducted person; and
6. The termination of all proceeding for the production of any abducted person pending before a High Court or Magistrate at the commencement of the ordinance and the preventing of courts from questioning the detention of persons abducted.[18]

It is important to note that the interpretation of 'abducted person' meant a 'male child under the age of sixteen years or female of whatever age who is, or immediately before the 1st day of March, 1947 was a Muslim and who, on or after that, has become separated from his or her family and is found to be living with or under the control of a non-Muslim individual or family'.[19] This was of course an interesting distinction and difference, that women of any age were deemed as abductees and therefore required the state to intervene on their behalf whereas any male aged 16 and above was considered responsible enough to make his own decision. Recovery of women was also particularly targeted at women of child-bearing age.[20]

The Inter-Dominion Conference also outlined the agenda for the repatriation of women to their 'rightful' homes, regardless of what the women wanted. This involved the complex network of DLOs working with the local police, social workers and informants to locate and return women and children. As a result, Muslim women found in Indian Punjab were returned to Pakistan and Hindu/Sikh women in Pakistan were returned to India. Urvashi Butalia makes an interesting point that 'even for a self-defined secular nation (India) the natural place/homeland for women was defined in religious, indeed

---

18 Promulgation of an ordinance for the recovery of abducted persons, 23 April 1949. File 84/CF/47, MR&R, NDC.

19 GoI, Ministry of Law, 31 January 1949. Ordinance No. V or 1949. An ordinance outlining an agreement with Pakistan for the recovery and restoration of abducted persons. File 84/CF.47, Cabinet Secretariat, GoP. Courtesy of SARRC, Islamabad.

20 Pankhuree R. Dube, 'Partition Historiography,' *The Historian* 77, 1 (2015): 55–79.

communal terms, thereby pointing to a dissonance/disjunction between its professedly secular rhetoric... and its actively communal identification of women'.[21] More recently, Amartya Sen has been critical of the construction of these essentialised, or as Sen refers to as 'solitarist' identities, which negate the pluralities of individual identity and a common shared history.[22] Yet, this is exactly how these women (and indeed more broadly the nations) were defined, primarily by their religious identity. Kamla Bhasin and Ritu Menon interviewed Kamlabehn Patel, who had worked in the Lahore camp for four years, and was the Pakistani equivalent to Mridula Sarabhai. She recalls that the 'identification was done according to the countries they belonged to, this one is Indian, this one a Pakistani. Partition was internally connected with Islam, the individual, and the demand for a separate homeland. And since this label was attached, how could the women be free from it?'[23] It was of paramount importance to the new nations that these women be rescued, rehabilitated and returned to their rightful homes.

There were many appeals in the local media as well to rescue abducted women in India and Pakistan, including this one appearing in *The Pakistan Times* published on 23 December 1947. It states:

> An Inter-Dominion Conference was recently held in Lahore to consider the best method for accelerating the recovery of abducted women. The Conference felt that a good deal of selfless work had been done in recovering abducted persons but the time had now come to make an all-out effort to achieve the maximum results in the shortest time possible. No civilisation can ignore with impunity the sanctity attaching to a woman's person. It has already been declared by both the Governments that forcible conversions and marriages will not be recognised. The Governments of the Dominions of India and Pakistan have accordingly expressed their firm resolve to leave no stone unturned in rescuing the abducted persons and restoring them to their homes. Above all, the doubts and suspicions haunting these persons regarding the nature of the reception awaiting them in their homes must be categorically removed. The public leaders

---

21 Urvashi Butalia, 'Community, State and Gender on Women's Agency during Partition,' *Economic and Political Weekly*, 24 April 1993, WS16.

22 Amartya Sen, *Identity and Violence: The Illusion of Destiny* (London: Penguin, 2006).

23 Ritu Menon and Kamala Bhasin, 'Recovery, Rapture, Resistance: The Indian State and the Abduction of Women during Partition,' *Economic and Political Weekly* 28, no. 17 (24 April 1993): 2–11.

in both the Dominions have declared that these unfortunate victims of communal frenzy must be received with open arms. Every effort should, therefore, be made to erase their unfortunate experiences and give them happy homes. But more than that it will close a tragic chapter in the history of the recent disturbances.[24]

The newspaper article raises a number of issues that were the impetus behind this appeal and the need by both India and Pakistan to rescue and return abducted women and children. First, the issue of women's sanctity is highlighted in the article. This denotes that women are viewed as something more than ordinary individuals; they symbolise something that is sacred to the people. The idea of a woman's honour is inextricably linked with this concept. It was of vital importance that every effort had to be made in order to address and resolve this issue of abducted women. Second, the article highlights the need for firm resolve in rescuing and returning these women to their rightful homes. Why was it so important? Part of the answer clearly lies in the previous point, regarding the sanctity attached to women in what was at the time and still is a predominantly patriarchal society. In order to legitimatise the newly acquired freedom, there was a need for the state to assert its authority and one way it does this is by assuming the paternalistic role. This protective shield is only extended to those considered weak and vulnerable (women and children in this case) and thereby also reinforcing the masculine nature of the state. Third, there is an acknowledgement that these women may not be accepted back, but it was the duty of every citizen to accept them back. This presented a huge dilemma for the state, on the one hand it had to assert its authority and take a stance on this issue, but at the same time it was also compelled to deal with 'dishonoured' women. This worked well in principle; however, the work of the Recovery Ministry extended to ten years, during the course of which circumstances for many of the affected families changed.

More importantly, it is interesting that the need to close the chapter on this tragic event rests with the rescue and return of women. Again, we can go back to the point of the sanctity of women and what they symbolised. A few days prior, on 17 December, this drive to recover abducted women was the subject of reporting in the press once again:

In order to ensure that the peace, which is slowly but surely returning, be made permanent, it is imperative that these unfortunate women be

---

24 *The Pakistan Times*, 23 December 1947.

restored forthwith to their own people. As long as this is not done, real peace cannot return. We can reconcile ourselves to the loss of everything except honour and when our womenfolk are forcibly taken away from us, not only do they lose their honour, but we also, to whom they are related, lose it. Therefore it is but natural that we harbour ill-will towards the abductors. For the sake of good relations between Pakistan and India, this can be done by the restoration of abducted women. Let them make amends, as far as possible, for their past misdeeds.[25]

The last line here is particularly significant in highlighting the need to 'make amends for their past misdeeds'. Whose past misdeeds was the article referring to? Was it 'the states', the Governments', societies', the abductors' or indeed, the abductees? Or was the honour of women linked with the honour of all of them? By returning these women to their own people, it was in fact symbolising the restoration of not only their honour but also that of the nation; once this honour had been restored, the two nations could then in some way miraculously go forward. Yet, there is a contradiction here because this is an area shrouded in secrets about a dark past. How is it then possible to close a chapter without any acknowledgements of this bitter legacy? If anything, the exchanges between India and Pakistan during this process reveal the difficulty and distrust the two countries had with each other. For example, Begum Fatimah, who was the chief liaison officer of the Pakistan government, 'stated that the attitude of the Indian Government was not only non-cooperative but also very "insulting" and Pakistani women Liaison Officers were being daily harassed in the East Punjab where feelings were extremely hostile'.[26] In another incident, Mr Gopalaswami Ayyangar in the Indian Parliament had alleged that 2,000 women were in the custody of the Pakistani government. However, the Pakistani government retaliated by claiming that their enquiries reveal that the allegations were baseless and by sending an appropriate response to the Government of India 'informing them that such false reports and sweeping statements are not likely to improve the recovery of abducted persons'.[27]

---

25 *The Pakistan Times*, 17 December 1947.
26 Begum Fatimah arrested and released in East Punjab. *The Pakistan Times*, 31 August 1948.
27 Fortnightly Report, 15 March 1950. File 21/CF/50 Vol X. Cabinet Secretary, MR & R, GoP.

Embracing with Open Arms

The distrust among the two governments was of course also echoed with the families. Indeed, it was completely optimistic and idealistic to expect that families would openly take back these 'dishonoured' women. In reality, the task of simply rescuing and returning women to their homes was much more complex than had been anticipated. Propaganda was also used to create fear. For example, Kamla Patel says that the women were told that their relations were dead, that there was insufficient food for them, their families would reject them and so on; this deterred some of them from risking their lives again.[28] While there were multiple and complex reasons behind why some women did not want to go back, this did not prevent the state from making its position very clear, which was that they had to be recovered. Hindu and Sikh women, for example, feared that now that they were 'polluted' there was little point in going back as their families are unlikely to accept them.[29] Gandhi himself was quite clear on this issue and explicitly stated in his morning prayer meeting in December 1947:

> It is being said that the families of the abducted women no longer want to receive them back. It would be a barbarian husband or a barbarian parent who would say that he would not take back his wife or daughter. I do not think the women concerned had done anything wrong. They had been subjected to violence. To put a blot on them and to say that they are no longer fit to be accepted in society is unjust. At least this does not happen among Muslims. At least Islam is liberal in this respect, so this is a matter that the Governments should take up. The Governments should trace all these women. They should be traced and restored to their families.[30]

The idea that these women would be welcomed with open arms was rather optimistic of the governments, given the strong notions of *izzat* and family honour in Punjabi society. But it was clear that rehabilitation of women also included the rehabilitation of society: educating them and promoting this

---

28 Kamla Patel, *Torn from the Roots: A Partition Memoir* (New Delhi: Women Unlimited, 2005), 139.

29 Patel, *Torn from the Roots*, 173.

30 Post-Prayer Meeting Speech by Mahatma Gandhi in Hindi, 7 December 1947. Annotation from Collected Works of Mahatma Gandhi, vol. 90, no. 163, 191, accessed 20 June 2016, https://archive.org/details/Swaraj-Gandhi-1947-12-07 Post Prayer Speech 1947-12-07.

'good' deed as a form of cleansing and purification for past misdeeds. Later in December, Gandhi again addresses this issue:

> Today we are in such an unfortunate situation that some girls say that they do not want to come back, for they know that if they return they will only face disgrace and humiliation. The parents will tell them to go away, so will the husbands. I have suggested that a sort of home should be established for such girls which should take up the responsibility for their food and shelter and education, so that they can stand on their own feet. These girls are innocent. We must return all the abducted girls without any preconditions. If we want to retain our freedom we must learn decency of conduct. [31]

Even Nehru encouraged 'Hindu men to accept the women who were recovered and to not punish them for the sins of their abductors'.[32]

> Their friends and relatives should welcome them back and give them all comfort and solace after their harrowing experience. I am told that sometimes there is an unwillingness on the part of their relatives to accept the girls back in their homes. This is a most objectionable and wrong attitude for anyone to take and any social custom that supports this attitude must be condemned. These girls require our loving and tender care and their relatives should be proud to take them back.[33]

The underlying assumption was of course that once this great deed has been completed, the process of cleansing the nation of its violent and brutal past could be reconciled. What is quite intriguing about the first quote by Gandhi and even Nehru's appeal to 'Hindu men' is the way in which pain, abduction of women and reconciliation have been communalised. It has been given a religion, yet the crime remains the same and the wide-reaching impact this has on society also remains the same. This distinction between Hindus and Muslims is even more apparent in the speech by Gandhi:

---

31 Post-Prayer Meeting Speech by Mahatma Gandhi in Hindi, 25 December 1947. Annotation from Collected Works of Mahatma Gandhi, vol. 90, no. 260, 300, accessed 20 June 2016, https://archive.org/details/Swaraj-Gandhi-1947-12-26 Post Prayer Speech 1947-12-26.

32 Das, *Life and Words*, 56.

33 Speech by Nehru in Bede Scott, 'Partitioning Bodies: Literature, Abduction and the State,' *Interventions* 11, no. 1 (2009): 44.

I have received a long list of girls abducted from Patiala. Some of them come from very well-to-do Muslim families. When they are recovered it will not be difficult for them to be returned to their parents. As regards Hindu girls it is still doubtful whether they will be accepted by their families... And yet Hindu society does not look upon such a girl with respect any more. The mistake is ours, not the girl's.[34]

The task though was not simply of finding the girls and convincing families to take them back. What happens to them as a consequence of this 'recovery'? The violations which they experienced in many ways continued as they are subjected to more personal invasive checks, disempowered because they have no choice in the matter, and institutionalised until they are claimed by their families.[35] And if not claimed, they are then left in women's ashrams to dwell on their past. The humiliation, therefore, continues in the name of national honour.

Urvashi Butalia also makes the point that Muslim families were more willing to take Muslim women back than Hindu families, in part it seems due to different notions of purity and pollution.[36] Bhasin and Menon in their research make this assertion and suggest that 'recovery there [Pakistan] was neither so charged with significance nor as zealous in its effort to restore moral order'. The pressure to recover these women was from India rather than social or public compulsions.[37] 'It was women's groups which had to take the initiative to prod a callous and unresponsive government to do something about the plight of abducted women'.[38] However, it is difficult to make this assertion too strongly because these notions of *izzat* were prevalent in all Punjabi society and indeed they are still prevalent today, on both sides of the border. In fact, if we look through the discourse projected in *The Pakistan Times*, it appears

---

34 Post-Prayer Meeting Speech by Mahatma Gandhi in Hindi, 25 December 1947. Annotation from Collected Works of Mahatma Gandhi, vol. 90, no. 260, 300, accessed 20 June 2016, https://archive.org/details/Swaraj-Gandhi-1947-12-26 Post Prayer Speech 1947-12-26.

35 See further, Jauch, 'Witnessing Violence' and Veena Das, *Critical Events: An Anthropological Perspective on Contemporary India* (Delhi: Oxford University Press, 1995).

36 Butalia, 'Community, State,' WS20.

37 Bhasin and Menon, 'Recovery, Rapture,' WS10. The source of this information is Nighat Said Khan, who has done research on Pakistan experience.

38 Ayesha Jalal, 'Secularists, Subalterns and the Stigma of "Communalism": Partition Historiography Revisited,' *Modern Asian Studies* 30, no. 3 (1996): 689.

that the need to recover women there was no less vigorous than in India. There were many appeals made to expedite the recovery process, reports on missing women and their recovery. Sheikh Sadiq Hasan, who was a member of the West Punjab Assembly, was rather critical of Mr Ghazanfar Ali Khan, minister for Refugees, that the programme of recovery under him had not been very effective. He goes on to say:

> I appeal to the Press and the public men in Pakistan particularly in West Punjab, to create public opinion for a vigorous campaign for the recovery of the abducted women, while I would urge that non-Muslim women still stranded in West Punjab should be immediately restored to their people in the Indian Union.[39]

The need to recover these women was not significantly subdued or any less significant in Pakistan, compared to India, but certainly India had more of an obsession with the morality and the sanctity of women's bodies. There are signs of how women in Pakistan were welcomed and received back by families. From the reporting at the Refugee Women's Home in Lahore, we can see a reasonably good repatriation rate, 'at present the total number of women in the Home is 375 out of which only about 35 cases are of more than two months' duration, which is seen as a good indicator of how the abducted women are being received back into society by their relatives'.[40] Politically, both the Muslim League and the All Pakistan Women's Association were active in arranging the marriages of all unattached women, so that 'no woman left the camp single'.[41] In fact, the problems and dilemmas facing women were the same on both sides of the border. In the following interview with Tahira Mazhar Ali, many of the issues discussed are reiterated by her:

> I am sorry but nobody admitted that they were raped because of bad things. They had feared that maybe somebody would not marry them. Sarabhai knew more women because the establishment was with her and they helped her but we could not. Nobody told us, maybe there was a fear of getting a bad name, maybe she could not get married or she was already married and that her family would not accept her. Nobody mentioned this to us. Some of them did not come back. One of our relatives, she stayed there. She fell in love with a man and got married with him. Hassan

---

39   *The Pakistan Times,* 22 August 1948.
40   *The Pakistan Times,* 15 August 1948.
41   Bhasin and Menon, 'Recovery, Rapture,' WS10.

Abdal is our ancestral area. The women jumped into wells there. They were mothers, sisters, daughters and wives. They were all Sikhs. They committed suicide rather than be abducted by Muslims; this sort of thing happened on both sides. Some of them decided that they would settle here [Pakistan]. [The women said] why should we go back when our families did not accept us, what would we do then? No doubt Pakistan made a determined effort to recover those women. Most of them lost their honour and there was a lack of acceptance by society. But some these people talked about their past and how they were Sikhs before. I don't know whether they would talk about it now [due to the lapse in time].[42]

Moral Dilemmas

This process of recovering and restoring women was thus shrouded in a paternalistic approach endorsed by both governments. During the initial years of the exchanges that took place between India and Pakistan women's views were not taken into consideration; however, as the years progressed it became more difficult to forcibly repatriate these women. After all, this was years after the event and circumstances had inevitably changed from the time of the initial reports. In response to this, some changes did come about and special homes were set up at 'Jullundur and Lahore where "hesitant" girls will be kept for ascertaining their wishes as to whether they are willing to join their relatives in the country of claim or want to live with the abductors'.[43] However, we also see that there were disagreements on the management of the special homes which were set up in the two countries for keeping the so-called 'hesitant' cases.[44] The Government of Pakistan also lodged a complaint with India when they discovered that the Government of India had released thirty-four abducted women and fifty-nine children without first confirming their desires and wishes as was expected under the joint agreement. This unilateral action was therefore 'in clear violation of the Indo-Pak Agreement of May 1954, regarding the recovery of abducted persons'.[45] As a result of this concern, in 1955 a joint Fact-Finding Commission with the following terms of reference was set up:

---

42 Interview with Tahira Mazhar Ali, Lahore, September 2008.
43 Fortnightly summary for the period ending 30 September 1955. File no. 10/CF/55 XVI, Cabinet Secretary, MR&R, GoP.
44 Fortnightly summary for the period ending 20 August 1954. File 8/CF/54, Cabinet Secretary, MR&R, GoP.
45 Fortnightly summary for the period ending 30 June 1955. File no. 10/CF/55 XVI, Cabinet Secretary, MR&R, GoP.

1. To assess the extent of outstanding work of recovery in the two countries; and
2. To advise the two governments on measures to be adopted for speedy conclusion of recovery in both the countries.[46]

By 15 August 1955, 20,695 Muslim abducted persons were recovered from India and restored to Pakistan and for the same period 9,015 non-Muslim abducted persons were recovered from Pakistan and restored to India; the final figure was not much higher than that.[47] Even in the closing days of the programme, which is nearly ten years after partition, there are still women being repatriated and exchanged. Though the numbers are not as significant (see Table 8.1), nevertheless each one of these women has a story to tell, a past which has been disrupted numerous times, and often with little agency or control over events. How did these women feel about the prospect of being returned 'home'? Where was home now? And was there even any remote chance of returning home to pick up where they had left ten years ago? The official government records in the form of Fortnightly Reports barely delve into such complex questions; those are not the areas of concern as they would invariably expose the entangled and difficulties in policing morality.

Table 8.1: Summary for the Period Ending 30 June 1957

	Number of Muslim Abducted Women Recovered in India and Received in Pakistan	Number of Non-Muslim Abducted Women Recovered in Pakistan and Sent to India
1. January 1957	10	14
2. February 1957	12	22
3. March 1957	9	10
4. April 1957	16	15
5. May 1957	16	24

Source: File 13/CF/57 (17) Cabinet Secretary [as late as 1957] Fortnightly summary for the Cabinet for the period ending 30 June, 1957. Ministry of Refugees & Rehab, GoP, 8 July 1957.

Near the end of the programme, however, there was increasing awareness of the negative impact and disillusionment was setting in with the initiative. It was impossible to expect the social workers to remain so committed, resolute and detached from the project to not be affected by the emotional and morally

---

46 Fortnightly summary for the period ending 30 September 1955. File 10/CF/55 XVI, Cabinet Secretary, NDC.

47 The final figure is 20,728 Muslims and 9,032 non-Muslims. Fortnightly summary for the period ending 30 September 1955, Cabinet Secretary, NDC.

questionable nature of their actions. The women who were forced to be repatriated challenged the social workers. Social worker Anis Kidwai stated:

> People asked: Why are these girls being tortured in this way? ... [sic] What is the advantage of uprooting them once again? If making them homeless again is not idiocy, what is it? To take a woman who has become a respected housewife and mother in her [new] home, and force her to return to her old home and [or] her parents, is not charity but a crime. Forget this business: those [women] who are left in Hindustan [India] and those left in Pakistan are happy where they are ...[48]

Others questioned why the state was not there to protect them in the first place. This is of course a legitimate question and a lament by these women who were unquestionably let down by the state and society. Anis Kidwai's account was originally written in Urdu and remained unpublished until her friends took the task on and got it published in 1974. Her granddaughter later got this account translated into English. These accounts are invaluable because, through these first-hand experiences of the social workers, there is a more nuanced understanding of what was at play; there is at the same time a 'counter-memory' that provides 'voices that cannot easily be incorporated into the dominant referential frame provided by state and communities'.[49] Anis Kidwai increasingly grew ambivalent to the programme and, eventually prompted by Mridula Sarabhai's resignation,[50] the Government of India unilaterally discontinued the work of recovery and restoration of abducted persons and allowed their Abducted Persons Act, 1949, to expire by November 1957. Although the Government of Pakistan estimated that more than 50,000 Muslim women still had to be recovered from India,[51] it did repeal this act, eleven years after the issue of recovering women was first discussed.[52] The tacit agreement between the states of India and Pakistan to resolve the issue of 'female recovery' and thereby reassert their patriarchal approach concludes

---

48 Anis Kidwai, *Azadi ki Chhaon Mein* qtd. in Prose, 219–20. Anis Kidwai, *In Freedom's Shade*, trans. Ayesha Kidwai (Delhi: Penguin, 2011).

49 Dube, 'Partition Historiography,' 76.

50 See further, Aparna Basu, *Mridula Sarabhai: Rebel with a Cause* (Delhi: Oxford University Press, 1996).

51 Fortnightly summary for the Cabinet for the period ending 15 October 1957, File 13/CF/57 (17), Cabinet Secretary, MR&R, GoP.

52 Six-monthly summary of the Ministry of Rehabilitation for the Cabinet for the period ending the 30 September 1958, File 11/CF/58 (5), MR&R, GoP.

with a lapsing of the existing law. However, less explicit in this is the acceptance that increasingly it was difficult to convince women to uproot themselves or to forcibly repatriate them.

Almost from the beginning, it was apparent that the programme of recovering women was going to be fraught with difficulties. Leaving aside the wishes of what women may have wanted themselves, families were also reluctant to accept them back, having been 'soiled', dishonoured and who knows what else because many of these women chose to remain silent about this period.

With the passage of time, there has been a growing disenchantment and growing scepticism of the recovery programme. It has raised many moral and ethical issues for all concerned. It is here that the lines between the victim and perpetrator become blurred and what is in the interest of the nation compared with that of the individual becomes marginal. The feminist writers have of course been very critical of the 'patriarchal power' and misogyny that was evident, initially, on the part of the perpetrators, and then, in the ways in which the state handled the issue. The state's absolute sense of legislating around the lives of citizens, in this case the female citizens, sets a tone for the future. There is of course a legitimate case for humanitarian intervention, but there are many contradictions in the approach. Gandhi's initial praise of pre-emptive suicides by women is then re-scripted into accepting 'stained' women. Amrita Pritam's work, *The Skeleton*, fully exposes the re-scripting of the state narrative and the hypocrisy with which this is now justified. The story revolves around Poroo, who was abducted well before Partition and is rejected by her family when she manages to escape, as no one will marry her now that she is stained. However, when her sister-in-law is abducted during the 1947 violence, there is a state programme to accept and rehabilitate these women. Poroo is again encouraged to return to her family during this time, because it now has state backing along with religious sanction. The Ministry of Rehabilitation interestingly issued a pamphlet invoking the Laws of Manu to argue that 'a woman who had sex with a man other than her husband became purified after three menstrual cycles, and that her family should have no hesitation in accepting her back'.[53] The reality was that the state's endorsement or bringing its official legitimacy did not change the cultural resistance towards the innocent lives, which suffered in the process.

---

53   Scott, 'Partitioning Bodies,' 43.

Ahmad Salim

For Amrita Pritam[1]

My heart is in shreds here,
There, life also wanders in disarray.
On that side, the newly wedded are unwell,
On this side, a young woman also stands dishevelled.

In your village, honor is lost,
In my village, innocence is sold.
In your town, love is weighed,
In my town, dreams are sold.

Many lips have been sealed here,
Many have lost their lives there.
The Sassi[2] of my heart dies daily,
Your Punnu is also buried daily.

Distance doesn't understand the meaning of love,
Walls don't feel the pain of love.
Our separation is like a torn *chunni*,[3]
One shred here, one shred there.

---

1   Ahmad Salim from *Kunjan Moian*, trans. by Ami P. Shah, *Journal of Punjab Studies* 13, no. 1 and 2 (1989; trans. 2006): 95. Originally written in 1968.

2   *Sassi* and *Punnu* are the heroine and hero of a tragic romantic legend popular in the Punjab. Unable to live together in life, the two lovers are united in death.

3   The long scarf worn by women with traditional clothing, *salwar kameez*. It is often used in poetry as a metaphor for the honour and modesty of a woman.

9

Lost Innocence and Sold Honour

The previous chapter largely focused on the state's response to abduction and recovery of women during the partition period. Much of that discourse focused on the larger question of restoring the nations' honour and cleansing itself of past crimes, it is devoid of compassion and empathy and gives us little or no insight into the everyday experiences of women and how they dealt with this trauma. Fictional writers were the first to capture the human drama of partition, filling the gaps and omissions by historians who were dependent on documentary sources and thus restricted by what they could reveal. Writers like Intizar Hussain, Bhisham Sahni, Saadat Hasan Manto and Amrita Pritam were writing from their experiences of partition dislocation, having endured the break-up and its lasting implications on humanity. They were much more apt at capturing the nuances and the sensitivity of the subject matter under the guise of fiction. Historians, until more recently, have been quite reluctant to use literature as a source of social history. Bapsi Sidhwa, herself a writer, more critically argues that 'historians only quote the politicians and catalogue prejudices of the period. It is the novelists who try to convey the emotional truths of individual people'.[1]

The theme of abduction and recovery has been explored in several fictional accounts, including most notably by Amrita Pritam's *Pinjar* (The Skeleton); the classic Urdu short story, *Lajwanti*, by Rajinder Singh Bedi; and Saadat Hasan Manto's *Khol Do* (Open It). *Pinjar* focuses on Poroo/Hamida, who is abducted and forcibly converted, yet what is also apparent in the novel is the rejection of Poroo by her family after she was abducted and therefore deemed as being 'stained'. Similarly, *Lajwanti* is abducted but is 'recovered' and returned to her husband, Sundar Lal. But Sundar Lal finds it difficult to revert back to the life he once had. Lajwanti's desire to speak and share the experiences of what happened with Sundar Lal are rejected and silenced by him; he retorts, 'Let's just forget the past. You were hardly to blame for what happened. Society is at fault for its lack of respect for goddesses like you'.[2]

1   Interview with Bapsi Sidhwa in Alok Bhalla, *Partition Dialogues: Memories of a Lost Home* (Delhi: Oxford University Press, 2006), 237.

2   Rajinder Singh Bedi, 'Lajwanti,' in *India Partitioned: The Other Face of Freedom Vol*

Although Lajwanti was recovered and rehabilitated, 'she had also been ruined. Sunder Lal, on his part, had neither the eyes to see her tears, nor the ears to hear her painful groans'.[3] The past, though being lived in the present, in reality remains repressed. Lajwanti, though elevated to the status of a *devi* or 'goddess', has become increasingly like the muted idols that society worshipped.

The duality of the discourse surrounding the abduction and killing of women is most poignantly captured by the works of Manto, particularly in his book, containing the eponymous short story, *Khol Do*. The short story is laden with the trauma of partition, rioting and brutality where 'men pretended to act out of a sense of honour and piety' and 'at times co-religionists themselves turned out to be the perpetrators of crime'.[4] Among this, is the story of Sakina who has suffered at the fate of this; she has been brought to the camp hospital in an unconscious state.

> The doctor looked at the prostrate body and felt for the pulse. Then he said to the old man, pointing at the window, 'Open it.'
>
> The young woman on the stretcher moved slightly. Her hands groped for the cord that kept her salwar tied around her waist. With painful slowness, she unfastened it, pulled the garment down and opened her thighs.
>
> 'She is alive. My daughter is alive,' Sirajuddin shouted with joy.
> The doctor broke into a cold sweat.[5]

The father, oblivious to what the doctor had seen, only saw movement in his daughter's hands. The short story was published in *Naqoosh* in August 1948 and, while critically acclaimed, it generated some commotion within government circles.[6] The short story, while exposing the brutality, also provides a subtle counter-narrative that moves away from what Veena Das argues is a 'scripted tradition'.[7] In an age where it was preferable to die an honourable

---

1, trans. ed. Mushirul Hasan (New Delhi: Lotus Collection Roli Books, 1997), 179–91.

3   Bedi, 'Lajwanti,' 179–91.

4   Sudha Tiwari, 'Memories of Partition: Revisiting Saadat Hasan Manto,' *Economic and Political Weekly* XLVIII, no. 25 (2013): 54.

5   Saadat Hasan Manto and Introduction by Daniyal Mueenuddin, *Mottled Dawn: Fifty Sketches and Stories of Partition* (India: Penguin, 2011), 10.

6   Ayesha Jalal, *The Pity of Partition* (India: HarperCollins, 2013), 194.

7   Veena Das, *Life and Words: Violence and the Descent into the Ordinary* (Berkeley, CA: University of California Press, 2006). E-book version, 47.

death rather than to be dishonoured, where fathers killed their own daughters to avail this, here was a father shouting with joy that his daughter was still alive despite the obvious scars. Sensing the content of this to be a threat to public peace, the publisher *Naqoosh* was banned for six months, which signifies the early intolerance of dissent and criticism of state authorities.

While Manto was one of the earliest writers to expose this harsh reality of partition and independence, particularly from a feminist perspective, these issues have remained largely buried in subsequent years. Only some change emerged in the past fifteen years wrought by feminist writers and social activists like Butalia, Menon and Bhasin.[8] They have done much to highlight the darker side of partition and the impact this had on women and the wider amnesia surrounding the abduction and rape of women during 1947, allowing us to uncover these 'hidden histories' and bringing them into the public realm of discussion and debate. These works have challenged the conventional histories, which marginalised women and other subaltern groups. Combined with the fictional accounts, memoirs and autobiographical writing, these alternative, albeit richer, sources have enhanced our understanding of this neglected area, often filling in the gaps where official history fails. Yet there are still many gaps in the body of research. We rarely talk about women and partition without the lens of violence. We hardly touch upon the issue of caste and its impact or its relationship with partition. Pakistan, which comparatively had a much larger refugee crisis following independence, is largely examined through the prism of the Pakistan movement. Comparatively, we know little about the experiences of women in West Punjab. Feminist discourse there in recent years has been far more concerned about the impact of Zia's Islamisation of Pakistan rather than examining this from a historical perspective. Indeed, much of our current understanding about South Asian gender roles can be better contextualised by delving into the past and its legacies in shaping contemporary India and Pakistan. This chapter, therefore, attempts to unpick some of the issues raised in the previous chapter and bring in some broader experiences, particularly from the Pakistan perspective. This is based on first-hand accounts of interviews/ conversations with women over the past fifteen years; some of these women are what might be termed 'elite' class, but they certainly speak from the experience

---

8   See further; Urvashi Butalia, *The Other Side of Silence: Voices from the Partition of India* (New Delhi: Penguin, 1998) and Ritu Menon and Kamal Bhasin, *Borders and Boundaries: Women in India's Partition* (New Jersey: Rutger University Press, 1998).

of having endured and grown up in the period, which changed from colonial to post-colonial. There are also interviews with the '*aam log*', or women who form the fabric of society, but we rarely get to hear about these. Importantly, the work and voices presented here are largely from women in Pakistan. This is largely a conscious decision due to the scarcity of material representing the voices from West Punjab and Pakistan more broadly. Comparatively, much more had been written from an Indian perspective and there continues to be a lack of interest in women from Pakistan. However, the stories themselves will resonate across borders as they have no religion. The stories are of friendships turned into fear, forced to abandon homes but ultimately they are also of the tenacity and hope these women recovered. In the inevitable editorial process, the latter is important. Much of the material and written history around Partition focuses on the violence and projects women as victims. Indeed, much of what has been presented here has also focused on these issues, as there is no denying that this is the very essence of the pain and turmoil endured by the people.

Khurshid's Qissa

Khurshid Bibi migrated from Ludhiana district as a child.[9] In the extract from her testimony, she provides details of her flight from her village. Many aspects of the extract make it compelling reading; it is an account of children, their innocence lost and when they stopped just being children to being children of a defined religious community. Her account itself is depersonalised of any references to specific or named people and instead, they only have communalised identities. There are good and bad characters and while not judging the veracity of the account, one question every oral historian must ask is, 'how much of this is shaped by retrospective memory?' But the testimony also tells a communalised history. Although the story remains the same, the children's innocence is lost in the process and a new narrative has been embedded in its place. The psychological trauma of this is not even a consideration.

> When I was inside that village and came to Pakistan, we faced atrocities all the way. They invaded the village from all sides and started the massacre. They started firing bullets at people and burnt alive those that were hiding

---

9   Interview with Khurshid Bibi. Faisalabad, December 2002. Interview arranged with the assistance of Ahmad Salim, SARRC.

in their houses. They lifted the corpses of Muslims in the air on their blades. They did horrible atrocities. They set fire on such a scale as to kill each and every Muslim, even then few people escaped to Pakistan. I was also one of them.

Our house had been set on fire while we were hiding inside – roof was on flames, doors, windows and everything else was on flames. They dragged the females out with them and nobody heeded the children – most of us were lost and our mothers never saw us again. They took the females outside and loaded them on vehicles, left over children were ignored and not taken away. I not only saw all this but I equally suffered on that fateful day. I was present at that place. When the night came, someone took me and three other children with him – he was not from our family but someone else [a Sikh as she reveals afterwards]. People said to him that he should kill the Muslims kids. They teased us with their blades. They said to him that if he couldn't kill us, he had to leave that to them. While he was taking us with him many attempted to kill us on the way, but he said that he wouldn't kill us. We were four children, I [she was seven and a half years old then] had my younger sister with me and the other girl had her sister with her. There was some wisdom in my mind, which was transferred to me by my grandfather, who was a wise and renowned man. The lessons he taught and the advice he gave me helped me a lot on the way to Pakistan.

It was night and the gangs who had killed nearly all the Muslims by then, started looting and plundering their houses. While that man, who was a Sikh took us with him. On the way, he halted for some time and took the two other girls to a field and murdered them and at seeing this, great fear overwhelmed us. We ran for our lives, he followed us running. We saw a house with some people at a distance. We ran to that house and started crying over the atrocities done to us. The other girls were killed and we knew that we would also be killed in the same way. The people in that house forbade that Sikh from taking us away and requested him to leave us there – saying 'these kids neither have parents nor any caretaker, so please leave them with us, don't take them away'. He did as they requested and left us there. The people of that house took us to another village, where Muslim women had been taken. Even there we found no one who knew us. So, they took us back to their house and we lived with those Hindus for six months. There was no news of our relatives but we often heard that Muslim military would come during that month and take away Muslim women and children who were left behind. The Hindus didn't want to lose us and never let us out of the home. We were also afraid because we had already seen much of atrocities. We thought that this military of Muslims would kill us after taking us away because we were not so sensible. We were also afraid of the Hindus we lived with.

One day those Hindus sent us to bring water from the well and that's where the military saw us by chance. We Muslim kids were easily distinguishable from other kids as our noses and ears were pierced for putting on jewellery. The military men saw us; they stopped the jeep and came to us hesitatingly because they were not sure that we were Muslim kids. We also feared them. They asked the women with them to come forward and talk to us. Those women treated us with love and concern. When we told them that we were Muslims, they gave us more love and called the military people to take us to their vehicle. They military people treated us with great love and concern as well. When we sat in the jeep, everyone including those men started crying. But they made us feel better with their concern. We were taken to the camp in Ambala and we were wondering about possibilities of meeting any of our relatives who might still be alive.

During the six months we stayed there, we witnessed atrocities of Hindus and Sikhs towards Muslims. They murdered Muslims brutally and shattered their bodies to pieces with spears. Displayed the corpses in air on their blades and threw them on earth afterwards. Those were the rainy days and water became red with blood of the corpses lying unattended on the ground. When we started from there our feet got red with that bloody water. [Where was your grandfather at that time?] He was murdered at the time of attack. The attack was so ferocious that many women committed suicide due to its fear. They didn't want to get caught by Hindus so taking their children in their arms they jumped in the wells. Both the wells of our village were filled with dead women and children. We saw many of the dead bodies being taken out of wells. The dead body of Naziraan, our relative, was also taken out of a well.

The Train at Kamoke

Located in what became West Punjab, Kamoke was an important trade and factory centre where non-Muslims owned considerable property.[10] Almost all these factories were set alight on 22–23 August and most of the non-Muslim

---

10 G. D. Khosla, *Stern Reckoning: A Survey of Events Leading Up to and Following the Partition of India* (New Delhi: Oxford University Press, 1949, reprint 1989), 150.

population was also forced to flee. Sadly, Kamoke is also associated with one of the worst attacks and massacres on a refugee train. Most accounts suggest it happened on 24–25 September 1947 when the train was carrying around 3,000 non-Muslim refugees from West Punjab.[11] The train had been forced to stop overnight in Kamoke and the following day the train was attacked by mobs. There are accounts of this incident in the *Civil and Military Gazette*,[12] which reported 418 non-Muslim casualties following the attack which lasted for 40 minutes. According to *The Tribune* and Khosla,[13] almost all the passengers were killed while the girls were abducted. Gurbachan Singh Talib also mentions this incident; although the dates he provides are slightly different, it is most likely the same incident. In Talib's account, there were almost 5,000 passengers, and the police and military also joined in the attack and only made cursory attempts to stop the carnage.

Talib does provide the statement of Shrimati Laj Wanti, which was given to the chief liaison officer. She was a widow of Shri Manak Chand, age 23 years, caste Khatri and resident of Nurpur Sethi, district Jhelum. She narrates:

> The women-folk were not butchered, but taken out and sorted. The elderly women were later butchered while the younger ones were distributed. The children were also similarly murdered. All the valuables on the persons of the women were removed and taken away by the mob. Even clothes were torn in the effort to remove valuables. My son was also snatched away in spite of my protests. I cannot say who took him away. I was taken by one Abdul Ghani to his house. He was a tonga driver. I was kept in the house for over a month and badly used. I went to other houses to look for my son. I saw a large number of children but I was unable to find my son. During these visits I also saw a large number of Hindu women in the houses of the Muslim inhabitants of Kamoke. All of them complained that they were being very badly used by their abductors.[14]

---

11   See, for example, Khosla, *Stern Reckoning*, 151; Ishtiaq Ahmed, *The Punjab Bloodied, Partitioned and Cleansed* (Oxford; Karachi: Oxford University Press, 2012), 355; and *Civil and Military Gazette* (Lahore), Saturday, 27 September 1947.

12   See *Civil and Military Gazette* (Lahore), 26 September 1947 and 27 September 1947.

13   Khosla, *Stern Reckoning*, 151 and Ahmed, *Punjab Bloodied*, 355.

14   Gurbachan Singh Talib, *Muslim League Attack on Sikhs and Hindus in the Punjab* (Amritsar: Shiromani Gurdwara Parbandhak Committee, 1950). Introduction to the reprint by Ram Swarup. The volume is a reprint of an old book compiled in 1947 by Sardar Gurbachan Singh Talib, principal of Lyallpur Khalsa College,

Picture 9.1: The old train station at Kamoke

In the account, she goes on further to explain that she then spent one month staying in the house of Abdul Ghani. She was told that there would be no food for her in India and that she would be 'shot dead by the Indian Military because they were not fit for being returned to Hindu society and Hindu society was not prepared to take them back'. This type of propaganda was widespread and may explain why some women refused to go back.

> We were also told that we must state before the police and other authorities that we were not willing to return to India. The 150 women who were produced at the station, Kamoke, were taken in tongas to Gujranwala. Out of the women collected only 20 got up and said that they wanted to return to India. I was one of them. The remaining lot was put into the trucks and sent back to Kamoke by the Sub-Inspector of Police.[15]

Jullundur, and published in 1950 by the Shiromani Gurdwara Parbandhak Committee.

15   Talib, *Muslim League.*

Picture 9.2: View from the bridge at Kamoke train station

What is less clear in Laj Wanti's account, is why the few women who returned to India, chose to do so. Interestingly, these testimonies collected shortly after partition hardly touch upon the subject of why and how women made their choices. Most of them are accounts which conveniently fit into the existing narratives. During the conversations I had with some women in Kamoke, the accounts presented were understandably from a different perspective and at times quite confused and contradictory. For example, Sardar Bibi, who was a resident of Kamoke, recollects the same period, but from the interview the blurry space between victim and perpetrator is evident:

> Yes, they were from Kamoke. Because Pakistan had come into being, as I am telling you, Hindus migrated to India and the Muslims arrived here. The people of Gujranwala also joined with the local people when the train was being massacred and looted. [Did they take girls with them?] Yes, Pakistani women were humiliated, raped and their breasts were cut off in India. Many things happened here as well. The Muslims threw them in the wells; at that time, there were big wells around [here in Kamoke]. A young man came here after he killed a Hindu family; he killed small

children; women threw themselves in the well. We saw a lot. An old man lay down on the ground, but [the local] people did not even spare him.[16]

Escaping Terror

The accounts by both Laj Wanti and Sardar Bibi offer two experiences of one location but they differ and conflict in their outlook due to their own immediate experience and the lapse in time. The following two accounts are by Ayesha who migrated from Patiala, and Nazeeran who fled from Hoshiarpur. Although escaping themselves, they were still witness to the atrocities and carnage going on around them. But they are also testament to the fighting spirit and the human capacity for resilience.

> The Sikhs after attacking and burning other villages intended to attack our village. We escaped before the attack. One of our relatives' girls was raped and afterward they [Sikhs] tried to kill. When one of her uncles saw her, he spread his own *chadar* to her body to cover her. She survived and a doctor told us that she had twenty knife wounds in her body. They [Sikhs] also killed her children. There was one other girl who joined our caravan on the way. A Sikh abducted her along with her child. At night-time, she managed to escape and left her child in the Sikh's house. She concealed herself in a sugar field and eventually managed to find and join our caravan. She left her own child there...children and young boys were chopped off like vegetables.[17]

> May God forgive us; we could hear the cries and lamentations on the abduction of young girls because we used to live very close to the city that was the centre of violence. The day when we were supposed to be attacked by them, we gathered in a field. All our men encircled us and the children and we sat down there waiting for our fate. But before they could attack us, it started raining and we all dispersed to take shelters. After that, we made a deal with them and paid a lot of money to let us go safely. They allowed us to go but they accompanied us for a while and it was very horrific to travel under their gleaming swords. I got surprised to see the road full of blood and I asked my husband what it was. My terrified husband asked me to keep quiet and carry on with the journey.[18]

16   Interview with Sardar Bibi, Kamoke, September 2008.
17   Interview with Ayesha Bibi, Kamoke, September 2008.
18   Interview with Nazeeran Bibi, Lahore, April 2007.

Earlier in chapter four, I discussed the accounts of women who experienced familial violence and particularly the case of Thoha Khalsa; however, here I wanted to bring three accounts of women who all talked of the violent attacks, family accounts of fleeing these scenes of terror or being witness to the turmoil around them. Their experience reinforces accounts such as Thoha Khalsa. Furthermore, although some writers have linked this to the tradition of self-immolation in the Rajput community, these incidents were happening on both sides of the border and were not exclusive to any one religious community.

> I don't know much but I had heard stories of partition. When the caravan consisting of the inhabitants of our village moved towards Pakistan, they were very much afraid of the assailants. The major worry was about the women because they did not want to let their women taken by Sikhs. So, it was mutually decided that in case of an attack women will tie up their children with legs and will jump into the water; in any canal or well they will find nearby. The *lambardar* of the village had been travelling, on his horse, far ahead of the caravan to see if there were any attackers on the way. Once he returned waving his shawl, the caravan misunderstood it as a sign of danger. When women were about to jump he shouted 'my sisters do not jump, I have seen Pakistani army coming towards our caravan. Now the danger is over and we are in safe hands'. The women did feel much relief on hearing this news.[19]

> Yes, many wells filled with dead bodies of young girls who threw themselves (to save their honour) in Sultan Pura. That was nearby Amritsar. Our relatives used to live there. Many girls were humiliated and raped. Many wells swelled up with their dead bodies. They threw themselves for the sanctity of their honour. This all happened in a village nearby Amritsar, Dhariwal, Gurdaspur and Dina Nagar were all located side by side. The Sikhs were really bad people; the Hindus were not too much brutal. Now the Sikhs have developed good relations with the Muslims. We had many relatives there; they also migrated to Lahore.[20]

> I told you, one of our relatives was in the military. His family was migrating to Pakistan by the train. On his way to Pakistan, his sister who was very pretty was abducted. The girls' brother was Iqbal and due to the shock he became mad. The family tried hard to find her but remained unsuccessful.

---

19 Interview with Shareefan Bibi and Halima Bibi, Lahore, April 2007.
20 Interview with Balquees Begum, Lahore, September 2008.

Yes, he reported this incident. Everyone reported the missing of their girls, therefore the government tried to recover them when the incidents were reported. In a village Khan Pur, our relatives committed suicides. First, they countered the enemies but when their weapons run out they committed suicide. Women jumped into well and died. They were very brave girls. One of their daughters fired on the attackers. When all rounds of fires run out, they had no other option, so they committed suicide.[21]

Finding Solace

They searched everywhere and took their women and we took ours. They searched everywhere; they went to Gujranwala too. They took their women where they found them. Some Hindus and Sikhs came here and Muslims went to India…Eminabad, which is near to here, some Sikhs came here and took their women back to India. The Indian girls that were in Pakistan were returned back to India. They [Hindus or Sikhs] also took away my sister. We returned their two girls from Kamoke. Hindus came here and took their women back, while the Muslims brought back their abducted women. [What about your sister?] She is with us. Yes we found her. [Your sister talks about that time?] No, she has forgotten everything; I was the eldest and she was youngest. She got married and now has children and even grandchildren. She doesn't talk about this with anyone.[22]

The account above was from an interview done in Kamoke. It refers to the exchange and repatriation of abducted girls. Sardar Bibi's sister was recovered and managed to rebuild her life and although there is little information about the actual incident and the aftermath, the last line conceals many silences. In other cases, women were less open to returning, as was highlighted in Lajwanti's account earlier. As shown in the previous chapter, social workers who were responsible for recovering these girls often faced difficult and challenging moral dilemmas. This was especially difficult when they did not want to return. We can only speculate about the multiplicity of reasons behind why this was the case but some women had adjusted to a new life. Krishna Thapar, a social worker responsible for recovering girls, recalls:

---

21 Interview with Nadira Khanum and Zakira Fatima, Lahore, September 2008.
22 Interview with Sardar Bibi, Kamoke, September 2008.

> Sometime in 1950 I was required to escort 21 Muslim women who had been recovered to Pakistan. They did not want to return, but the Tribunal had decided that they had to go. They were young, beautiful girls and had been taken by Sardars [Sikhs]. They were determined to stay back because they were very happy. We had to use real force to compel them to go back. I was very unhappy with this duty – they had already suffered so much and now we were forcing them to return when they just didn't want to go. I was told that these girls are simply creating a commotion for nothing, their case has been decided and they have to be sent back...Those women cursed me all the way to Amritsar, loudly and continuously...It was complete helplessness, they had been transferred from one set of butchers (*kasais*) to another...they kept saying, 'Why are you destroying our lives?'[23]

In *Borders and Boundaries*, Menon and Bhasin met up with a woman in 1991; she had been forced to return to India, despite her desire to remain with her husband and three children. She refused to talk about her past, 'Leave it. What use is it recalling the past? Forget about it. I've banished it all from my mind. I lead a respectable life now, why look back to the past – even my children don't know anything about it'.[24] Some women indeed managed to put the past behind them and 'recover' from the trauma, but only by erasing it out of their memories. Yet these personal testimonies show that they are never completely erased, the events and thoughts do remain. By accepting the realities of their lives, some women perhaps found solace and reconciled. But Reshmi's account below shows that they did attempt to escape to bring about change.

> She did not want to come back; she has two children now. The Military men brought her back. They cunningly and forcefully left their children to her mother-in-law in India and took her away, first, in Amritsar then in Jullundur; then they wrote a letter to her brother who went to Jullundur and fetched her back to Lahore and then here to the village. Here she gave a birth to a baby girl. Men of the family intended to kill the baby because of the dishonour to family but we [women] did not allow them to kill her. She wrote a secret letter to her husband in India. When this secret came out, the men of the family beat her badly. Afterwards, they arranged her marriage and now she had got sons; even grandsons. [What

---

23 Interview with Krishna Thapar quoted in Menon and Bhasin, *Borders and Boundaries*, 91–2.

24 Menon and Bhasin, *Borders and Boundaries*, 95.

happened to the baby?] She died after a year. [Did she speak about the tragedy that happened with her that time?] She told us. She tried to come back. One day her previous husband took her to the nearest city. She got chance to talk with goldsmith. She requested him to send her and offered gold ring to him. He said I could not do this. People from Pakistan would take you back. She told me that she wanted to go to Lahore but could not find a chance.[25]

Nadira similarly recounts her experiences and memories of the challenges facing girls, who were abducted and recovered. Again, there are references to the shame and dishonour, but also importantly, that the girls were not to blame. There is also some hint of the communalised nature of the discourse, where one side is more to blame than the other. This form of 'blame displacement' can often be used to justify the actions but this changed none of the circumstances for the actual women who suffered. It merely functions to erase those memories.

> My aunt, who was abducted in India, had got children in India when she was recovered and brought back to the fold of the family. She again got married here in Pakistan. She was an innocent woman. She did nothing wrong…she was recovered after a long time and during that period she had got children there in India. [Does she talk about this episode?] Nobody could talk about such shameful incident. One of our relatives' daughter was left in India and was not allowed to come back here. She used to scream and cry desperately. Refugees who came from there told us about her miserable tale. She was a very pretty girl. She was abducted because of her beauty. God knows how she lived there. [This happened on both sides. Many Hindu and Sikh girls remained in this side of the Punjab.] This side, no, here nothing like this happened. I never heard about any Sikh girl being abducted here. Maybe some girls were left over here. The Muslims were not so cruel. They also killed Hindus and Sikhs. Refugees who reached India told us that the Muslims had been killing, attacking and looting their caravans. Everyone was involved in looting and killings. The Muslims were also involved in looting, but this type of incidents (abduction of Sikh women) did not happen here. Such incidents did not happen in our village. [Those girls in your family who were abducted during the partition, are they still alive?] Yes, one of them presently lives in Okara. She has got grandchildren now. They did not commit any crime, or wrongdoing. But they returned, got married here and now

---

25   Interview with Reshmi Bibi, Kamoke, September 2008.

have settled down. [Does she talk about those days?] No, we never asked her about such things; we feel shame in asking anything like that. They suffered, why should we disturb them by recalling their bad memories? [How did people of the family come to know all about this?] She must have talked with anybody; perhaps her own family, sisters or brothers. In fact, the entire family knows that they were abducted in India and were recovered after a long time. They were indeed abducted involuntarily and forcefully, otherwise girls did not have any relations with the abductors. [Both governments were trying to recover these girls.] Yes, because of such efforts these girls were recovered and they returned to their own homes. Some returned shortly while others took years to recover. Some girls came back within six months but others came back after many years. My sister-in-law came back after six years and other relatives came back after seven years and more.[26]

In an interview with Tahira Mazhar Ali, we discussed how the recovery of women was marred with difficulties, in large part due to the stigma and shame associated with being forcibly abducted and raped. She was actively working at the time to improve the condition of women and was familiar with the plight of women who were abandoned or then forcibly recovered by the government. The following extract by Ali also shows a disjuncture between government initiatives of recovering abducted women and the realities in then locating these women back to their 'rightful' homes.

I was working with Mridula [Sarabhai],[27] particularly after Jawaharlal [Nehru] asked for the return of the abducted Hindu women. I got myself immersed in the task of recovering those women. Mridula asked me to ask those women to come back to their homes. But many of those women did not want to face the family because of shame and sheer embarrassment they felt. Quite a few were accorded acceptability and some were happy and well settled in the households they were living. Such women, therefore, did not want to go back. Many did not recognise their girl simply because she had stayed in Muslim households, which was enough to cause a stigma for them. Same happened on this side also. That of course was a critical question and we could not make exceptions. We had to follow the policy. [Did you follow up on any

26 Interview with Nadira Khanum and Zakira Fatima, Lahore, September 2008.
27 Mridula Sarabhai was tasked with rescuing abducted women and returning them to their families following independence in India.

of the stories of those women?] No I did not. It was not the time to follow the stories. The time was such that following the stories was virtually impossible. Neither did Mridula follow the stories. It was a terrible time. The people had no homes or anything else to bank on. Our leaders had been telling them that there would be everything that they ever aspire. There would a heaven on earth. What a nonsense they were telling to the poor people.[28]

The state was obviously leading this initiative in recovering women and providing shelters for them. But the role of the voluntary social workers and the family is also important to ensuring the 'success' of this policy. The short account below by Balquess highlights the complexity of networks and relations at work to make it a success.

Their two daughters were abducted though after some time both were recovered; one of them even was pregnant that time. My mother arranged marriage for their younger daughter in Faisalabad. Many of our relatives live in Faisalabad, Gujranwala and Karachi. In the Sikh princely state of Kapurthala a Sikh Deputy [police] took away our *phuphi* [aunt]; she was a very pretty and married woman with two children. When we tried to bring her back, she refused to come back.[29]

Fatima Sughra shared a story about close friends. Again, the friends and family network is important in keeping this a closely guarded affair but in some ways at least it could be shared among close friends and family circles, presenting them with perhaps the only opportunity to talk about this. While the state is responsible for recovering the girls, the family is important in bringing them into the fold and protecting their honour. The silence around their past is important in ensuring their successful rehabilitation.

I know a case very well; a Syed family who came from Amritsar to Lahore, their daughter was abducted in Amritsar. When they came to know that Fatima Begum [an activist working for the recovery and rehabilitation of abducted Muslim women] had brought a truck of Muslim recovered women in Lahore, they learnt that their daughter was in the custody of a Sikh. The Sikh was nice man; he took over the girl from other Sikhs and kept the girl in his house like his sister. He helped the girl to be

---

28 Interview with Tahira Mazhar Ali, Lahore, April 2007.
29 Interview with Balquees Begum, Lahore, September 2008.

handed over the recovery team who finally sent her to Pakistan. Even
the Sikh man, who escorted her to the border to see off her, gifted her
sewing machine. He said: 'she is like my own daughter'. Eventually, this
girl reached home but the family never said anything about her abduction
and recovery to anyone, chiefly because of tarnishing their honour in the
society. At the end, the girl committed suicide but the family still never
disclosed anything to anybody. She did not speak to anyone; she was a
Syed Zadi [from the Prophet's lineage]. They had lots of *murids* [devotees].
They were pious and nice people. They were grateful to us because we did
not disclose this affair to anyone. [Did she come back happily?] Yes, in
fact she never disclosed to anybody what actually happened. There must
be many women like her. She was nearly 20. [How did the family allow
the abducted girls to come back?] One of my relatives adopted abducted/
missing kids and brought up them and gave them everything. She took
over two missing girls and brought up them like her own kids. Many
people adopted kids to make them their servants. Some women never
came back in Pakistan. One of my relatives was in the police. His family
was in India. During the partition-related-killing his wife jumped into
the well with two daughters to save honour...They preferred death rather
than humiliation. Many women recovered and settled and many others
lost everything. Many children lost their houses. Some were adopted by
good people and others were made servants by some bad individuals.
[Why do people not talk about the sufferings of that time?] Sixty years
have passed and people have forgotten many things. Many have already
passed away and others are too old now...Now people have settled.[30]

Reinventing Oneself

Shortly after partition and much before any attempts had been made to
understand the human tragedy of partition, Manto's writing provided us
with many sensitive and insightful accounts in his short stories.[31] *The Dutiful
Daughter*,[32] written through the perspective of liaison officer working to recover
women, highlights the challenges that people like Tahira and Mridula faced.
The abduction of girls did not just end with that event itself. Manto shows us
in *The Dutiful Daughter* that it forced many to sever old family relations, in this
case a woman refusing to recognise her old desperate mother. Partition forced

---

30   Interview with Fatima Sughra, Lahore, September 2008.
31   See further, Tiwari, 'Memories of Partition'.
32   Manto, *Mottled Dawn*, 73.

many to re-imagine their old family bonds in order to deal with the present. Afzal Tauseef, who was a Punjabi writer and experienced partition first-hand herself as a child, was more critical of the brutality of even those that one considered '*apne*' (our own).

> Besides abduction and rape, there was another tragic element of that situation. Those who remained safe from abduction and rape were exploited by their own people. On this aspect, a collection of my stories *Aman Wailay Milan Gay* is very relevant. It has been translated in Gurmukhi. A story from that collection perfectly explains this tragedy. It is about the girls who remained safe and had been sent to the countries they belong to. When these helpless girls reach Lahore, the welfare centre or the camps that were supposed to give them shelter started playing the role of a brothel. Irony reaches its zenith when the girls protest saying that they were better off when with the enemies. Anyway, this is a subtle and a serious issue and once you go deep you can see the true face of this society.[33]

Camps and centres for organisations were of course easy targets because they had a concentration of people in them. They could be preyed upon easily. Once recovered it was always preferable to be with a family but, as Butalia found, women lived in camps in some cities of Punjab, either because their families had never claimed them or because they had refused to go back to their families.[34]

> The ashrams became permanent homes... there they lived out their lives, with their memories, some unspeakable, some of which they were able to share with a similar community of women. And there many of them died.... As late as 1997 some women still remained in the ashram in Karnal; until today there are women in the Gandhi Vanita Ashram in Jullundur.[35]

Regardless of whether they remained in the ashram, went back to families, or refused to go back, even with these subtle silences, there is evidently an inability to break away from the past. This is most poignantly captured in *Khomosh Pani*,[36] which depicts the human drama and trauma of 1947 during the period of Muhammad Zia-ul-Haq's military dictatorship (1977–88) in

---

33 Interview with Afzal Tauseef, Lahore, April 2007.
34 Debali Mookerjea-Leonard, 'Jyotirmoyee Devi: Writing History, Making Citizens,' *Indian Journal of Gender Studies* 12, no. 1 (2005): 17.
35 Butalia, *Other Side of Silence*, 162.
36 *Khomosh Pani* (Silent Waters), Director Sabiha Sumar (2003).

Pakistan. Set during his rise to power in 1979, the two narratives are interwoven and gradually we begin to see the narrative threads unravelling but also the parallels between the two narratives become clear. The main protagonist of the film is Ayesha, and as the film progresses we see through flashbacks how she decided not to jump into the well to save her 'honour'. Dishonoured in her family's eyes, she was captured by Muslims, raped and ultimately married one of her captors before converting to Islam. Through the unfolding narrative, we see the scars of that painful period which is depicted by her fear of the village well and her refusal to go near it. The elders in the community are aware of this traumatic past but remain silent throughout, until one day Ayesha learns that her brother is visiting a Sikh gurdwara with other pilgrims from India. Through this turning point, Ayesha's son, Saleem, learns of his mother's past. But a radicalised Saleem in Zia's Pakistan is unforgiving and Ayesha ultimately jumps into that well. The violence depicted is not always actual but psychological and this manifests itself in a number of ways. The violence from her family and refusal to make that pre-emptive sacrifice, the enveloping political violence which targeted women like Ayesha, the silent trauma that haunted her throughout her life and then finally we see her own son disowning his mother, his own past. Saleem's gradual allegiance with Zia-ul-Haq's form of Islam and a rejection of his more moderate upbringing is the parallel narrative that shows the darker side of religious fervour. It also shows how since 1947, religion, nationalism, misogyny remain key characteristics in contemporary Pakistan as well as secular India.

Farkhanda Lodi, a renowned Punjabi/Urdu fictional writer, was in many ways able to articulate this silenced history in a more open and profound way. She suggests that there are still silences that exist around talking about women and the horrific crimes they were subjected to during the communal violence in 1947. The trauma associated with the upheaval and violence of 1947 has created a collective amnesia about the event. This has led to many people having only selective recall and choosing to consciously forget these harrowing and painful memories. The abduction of young girls was like an unspoken reality, something which existed but was hardly ever talked about because of the importance of women's honour. Yet silence is also prevalent in her family:

> My *bhabhi* [brother's wife] who was also my cousin and her family migrated from Kapurthala. When they came here they were wounded and shattered completely. None of them was killed but they were seriously injured… Only one woman from our relatives was abducted. But she never speaks about her abduction. We did hear, in our childhood, that she

was abducted and they brought her back, what happened to her during that time I do not know at all.[37]

Erasing those former memories and former self alleviates the fractures, though the problem for many of the partition refugees is that there has been no closure. The forced displacement following the violent and traumatic start led to permanent fractures because of the strained relations between India and Pakistan since 1947. Furthermore, there are cultural pressures which meant that in the case of what happened to women, there has been almost complete silence. When I interviewed Farkhanda Lodi she expressed her sadness at the suffering that women are subjected to, suggesting that women are forced to remain weak due their social and cultural conditioning. In her interview, she reflected on the plight of women in Pakistan and goes on to lament the fact that it is always women who bear the responsibility of suffering. She argues that it was not just strangers in the form of men from other communities but it was also those from within their own community.

> As you see our respectable culture does not allow us to speak about such things. That is why she never discusses this issue [referring to abduction] … She is weak, helpless and vulnerable. She has been forced to remain weak. It is the training; she gets this from her parents, culture and the social environment that develop in her a pitiable pathetic soul. Our system and society do not allow her to progress. So she is in pain, for me her life is a constant misery.[38]

Bapsi Sidhwa also agrees with this point, highlighting the pitiful position of women and use of the body as a tool to target the 'other'.

> It is the women who bear the brunt of violence that accompanies these disputes. They find their bodies brutalised. Victories are celebrated on the bodies of women. When women are attacked, it is not they *per se* who are the targets but the men to whom they belong. It is humiliating for a man to see his woman being abused before him.[39]

The abducted woman in Lodi's family eventually settled down and now has children and this is another reason why these memories of a traumatic past

---

37 Interview with Farkhanda Lodi, Lahore, April 2007.
38 Interview with Farkhanda Lodi.
39 Sidhwa, *Partition Dialogues*, 233.

are rarely discussed. As a mechanism for dealing with this past, families have, where possible, moved on and started a new life. These memories belong to a past that has been locked away and hidden, a secret history that is deemed too sensitive to discuss openly. Through these personalised histories and fictional stories, it is possible to gain some understanding of the ways women's lives were completely changed during those few months and years when the British left and left behind a fractured nation with a traumatic past. Displacement and resettlement was clearly a lengthy process, which tested people's resilience to overcome such trauma and rebuild their lives again. And even when lives were rebuilt, the state interjected and forcibly repatriated its citizens, prolonging and adding to the multiple tragedies women had to endure.

While Lodi touched on the issue of silence surrounding the discussion of this painful past, especially in relation to women, others often internalised those childhood memories. Having spent many years interviewing partition refugees, one theme that resonates constantly is how many people felt that it was a temporary measure and that once the law and order situation was brought under control they would return to their homes. But increasingly, the new nations of India and Pakistan were defined by the difference that added permanence to the border and more importantly to the division among the people. As Amitav Ghosh says 'if there is no difference, both sides will be the same; it will be just like it used to be before...what was it all for then? Partition and all the killing and everything?'[40]

---

40 Quoted in Meenakshi Mukherjee, 'Dissimilar Twins: Residue of 1947 in the Twenty-first Century,' *Social Semiotics* 19 (2009): 448.

Kafi by Sufi Saint Bulleh Shah (1680–1758)[1]

Bullah, I know not who am I
I know not its reason or rhyme
I neither belong to the Arab lands
Nor to the city of Lahore
I neither belong to Hindustan
Nor to the villages of hinterland
I am neither a Hindu nor a Musalman
Nor I live Nadaun

Bulleh, I know not who am I
I know not its reason or rhyme

Interview with Tahira Mazhar Ali, April 2007, Lahore

An interesting thing that happened in Wah is about an old woman, Mai Jiwan who used to bring vegetables to the homes of the people. When the partition plan was announced and the people who were non-Muslim were leaving the area including the sons of that woman, who intended to go to Delhi. People said in explicit terms "she belongs to us therefore we would not let her go." So the love and affection was there, that was why people said clearly that she has been living there for ages and we would not let her go anywhere. Her sons left her behind and after partition episode was over, they came and took her with them. She cried so much while leaving. But the question is "what did we achieve"? I am asking you people, someone should provide me the definition of freedom. Were we happy after the "freedom"? Instead, we witnessed tears and screaming women saying, "Would my son join me? My small son was left behind, would he ever come?" Obviously, such things cannot bring us happiness.

---

1   Harjeet Singh Gill, *Sufi Rhythms: Interpreted in Free Verse* (Patiala: Punjabi University, 2007), 115–17.

10

Dreams, Memories and Legacies

After seventy years of independence, the partition of India and its wider ramifications continue to resonate and reverberate. This is particularly palpable in the region of Punjab, which bore the brunt of the associated partition violence, resulting in millions of people being forced to migrate, forever severed from their ancestral lands. The generation that witnessed this grand project in history, which informs and defines the region, is fading away in numbers, but the small numbers that survive still talk about the events as if it were a recent memory. Najum Latif migrated from Jullundur as a child in 1947. When I met him in 2013 he emotionally recited this poem by Ustad Daman[1] to me in Punjabi, the language it was originally composed in. While reciting it, he had been transported back in time to the pre-partitioned Punjab. The sadness, the nostalgia and the loss were palpable:

> We may not speak but deep in our hearts we know,
> That you have lost, as we too have lost in this divide.
> With this false freedom, towards destruction,
> You ride, and so too do we ride.
> There was some hope, there is life to be found
> But you died, and so we too died.
> While still alive, inside the jaws of death
> You were hurled inside, as we were hurled inside.
> Fully awake, they robbed us till they had their fill
> You kept sleeping, leaving care aside, we too left care aside.
> The redness of the eyes tells the tale.
> That you have cried, and so we, too, have cried.

The painful loss and the lack of closure continue to haunt many individuals like Latif. For poets like Daman, who lived unassumingly by Badshahi Masjid in Lahore, there was ample material in post-colonial Pakistan to lament about.

---

1   Poetry: Ustad Daman. The Poet Laureate of Twentieth Century Punjab, Translated and Introduced by Fowpe Sharma, Revolutionary Democracy, Vol. XI, No. 2, September 2005. http://www.revolutionarydemocracy.org/ rdv11n2/ daman.htm [accessed 31 May 2016].

The remnants of this bygone era are everywhere, from the often-crumbling buildings to the often-melancholic memories, and serve to remind us of a different age and time: the food, the language, the dress, the vibrant and hearty Punjabi and the plains of the Punjab that connected people are now divided by a hostile boundary. There is a constant reminder of these divided histories while travelling between the two Punjabs; one only needs to casually observe the place names of shops which are frequently located in the 'other' Punjab. These are the small ways in which those who fled in 1947 have preserved their own ancestral histories, passing them through the generations that will be unfamiliar with the other half. The strict visa controls maintained by both the governments of India and Pakistan ensure that the ordinary people remain divided and estranged. This is a hard and harsh international border; it was imagined in the drawing rooms by the outgoing colonial power but it has been re-imagined by the nation-states today. It is a stark reminder of the animosity and mistrust the two nations have of each other, yet it also conceals other truths. The border is open for all foreigners yet it is the most restrictive for the very citizens of those two nations that it is located in. Indians and Pakistanis are the most scrutinised people at the border.

For the Love of Cities

The mass migration of people following Partition fundamentally altered the physical landscape. Delhi, the colonial capital, was transformed from an Urdu-speaking Muslim city in character to a city that housed the incoming Punjabi refugees that now lend much of their character to the city. Delhi retains its Mughal links through the extensive architecture that dominates the city but the people are heavily influenced by the Punjabi migrants.[2] Shaista Ikramullah, a prominent female Pakistani politician, after leaving the city wrote, 'For millions of people like me, to whom Delhi was synonymous with Muslim culture, a Pakistan without Delhi was a body without a heart'.[3] The economic and demographic transformation of the cities in Punjab was also to have a significant impact on the divided Punjab; it transformed small towns to cities and cities into regional and international economic centres.

---

2   Ravinder Kaur, *Since 1947: Partition Narratives among Punjabi Migrants of Delhi* (Delhi: Oxford University Press, 2007).

3   Raza Rumi, *Delhi by Heart* (New Delhi: HarperCollins, 2013), 49.

Demographically, the communally mixed Punjab was after independence unceremoniously 'unmixed' of 'other' communities to constitute two halves. Historically, Punjab had a strong pluralist and composite cultural tradition that despite challenges remained in the form of tolerance and co-existence. Numerical data and simple religious binaries conceal these tolerant lived spaces. There has been some necessary deconstruction of the role of colonialism and the formation of identities, particularly of these fixed religious categories.[4] The colonial obsession with ethnographic research and categorisation was to have a fundamental impact on politicising the people in the long term. But the problem with Punjab was that some localities, especially in Central Punjab, were much more diverse and mixed up, while others had a semblance of a majority community. Separating them into two halves was no easy task. Furthermore, after 1947, the impact of the total outmigration of the 'other' community had a huge impact on the local and regional economy because of the skills and contribution of these people. For example, in Ludhiana, skilled Muslim workers dominated employment in the flour and rice mills with 83 per cent; in the hosiery sector, Muslims accounted for 61 per cent; and in the textiles industry they accounted for 78 per cent of the workforce.[5] For many cottage industries, the result was closure. Furthermore, the new migrants coming from West Punjab, who had a different set of skills, did not compensate the skills that were lost with the migration of these workers.

Prior to independence, Lahore was the leading commercial and cultural heartland of Punjab (and indeed in North India) with an influential and affluent non-Muslim population; more popularly Lahore was seen as the 'Paris of the East',[6] and the cultural capital of North India. Amritsar, only a short distance from Lahore, depended much on the Muslim artisans that contributed to the

---

4   See further, Meeto (Kamaljit Bhasin-Malik), *In the Making: Identity Formation in South Asia* (Gurgaon: Three Essays Collective, 2007).

5   These figures are for the district, but most of the industry was located in the city. In Amritsar, Muslims accounted for 90 per cent of workers in scientific engineering, 83 per cent of wood workers and 79 per cent in the glassware sector. In Jullundur, 90 per cent of the workers in the hosiery industry were Muslim and in Ferozepur 80 per cent of the workers in the textiles industry were Muslims. K. L. Luthra, *Impact of Partition in Border Districts of East Punjab* (East Punjab: Board of Economic Inquiry, 1949).

6   See further, Ian Talbot and Tahir Kamran, *Lahore: In the Time of the Raj* (India: Penguin Random House, 2016).

vibrancy of the city.[7] During their deliberations of the Boundary Commission, Chester asserts that they were 'driven by the need to preserve Amritsar's economic and strategic position',[8] hinting that perhaps no one had anticipated the demographic and economic consequences of partition on Amritsar city.[9] The reality was that Amritsar suffered more than Lahore due to its geographic positioning as a border city; the large Muslim artisan class had left a big void in the labour market thus leading to its decline.[10] Furthermore, the sensitive international border between India and Pakistan ensured that the border areas, such as Amritsar, Gurdaspur and Ferozepur, now experienced economic decline.[11] Conversely Lahore, partly due to the lack of alternatives in Pakistan and its political importance, retained much of its former imperial glory, though it also suffered in the short term from the complete outmigration of Hindus and Sikhs who dominated the economic landscape of Lahore. In an interview with the writer and journalist Afzal Tauseef, she shared memories of Amrita Pritam, who had been a friend of hers and a former resident of Lahore.

> [Amrita Pritam] had a massive collection of books on literature. We also used to have good discussions. She herself was a victim to partition. She migrated from Lahore. She was very passionate about Lahore. It was her city rather you can say city of dreams for her. She was born in Gujranwala. She used to avoid this topic because it caused bitterness. Once I just asked her that could you sum up as to what happened to the love and affection, because so far we remember we had witnessed Muslims celebrating Diwali.[12] Even in my house, a *halwai* [sweet maker] used to make sweets and on *Eid*, Hindus and Sikhs used to come with gifts at our place and touch my grandmother's feet out of respect. This relationship was there for centuries. I asked her that could she imagine what happened to the hundreds of years old friendship and companionship. I witnessed this relationship in my childhood when there was no conflict and bitterness

---

7   Read further, Ian Talbot, *Divided Cities: Partition and Its Aftermath in Lahore and Amritsar 1947–1957* (Karachi: Oxford University Press, 2006).

8   Lucy Chester, *Borders and Conflict in South Asia: The Radcliffe Boundary Commission and the Partition of Punjab* (Manchester: Manchester University Press, 2009), 75.

9   Talbot, *Divided Cities*.

10 See further, Luthra, *Impact of Partition* and Talbot, *Divided Cities*.

11 Gurpreet Maini, *The Giant Awakens: Punjab Industry and Growth* (New Delhi: India Research Press, 2004).

12 Diwali is the festival of lights celebrating the victorious return of Rama and Sita to their kingdom.

in Punjab…Anyway, I asked Amrita ji that what had happened to that
friendship, love and social relations…Why Punjab? The centre of language
dispute (that Urdu is an Islamic language and Hindi is the language of
Hindus) was from U.P. Activists like Sir Syed was in that area and all
the other major issues were going on in that part of India. My question
is that, if it was a language dispute, why was U.P. not divided, why was
Punjab divided. If there was a political clash, Punjab was less involved.
Then why was it divided? We cannot find any root cause for the division,
whatever efforts we put in to find it.[13]

While writers like Tauseef and Pritam struggled to reconcile with the changes
wrought about by partition, other provincial towns like Ludhiana and Lyallpur
became industrial heartlands of divided Punjab in the changing landscape of
divided Punjab.[14] Both these towns previously had majority 'other' populations,
and consequently attracted fleeing refugees from the other side. The development
of the new Lyallpur canal colony in the late nineteenth century and the social
engineering that went along with the project has received relatively little
attention, given its dramatic impact on the region. Apart from Imran Ali and
David Gilmartin, the canal colonies still need to be explored more critically.[15]
Farmers, artisans and even some professionals from Central and East Punjab,
including Ludhiana,[16] were drawn by the economic opportunities in these newly
irrigated colonies that came to represent the most fertile lands in India.[17] Fifty
years later at the time of Partition, the non-Muslims re-migrated eastwards
once again to their 'original' ancestral homes from which their grandparents
and parents had earlier departed.[18] Adding to the attraction of Ludhiana was,

---

13   Interview with Afzal Tauseef, Lahore, April 2007.
14   Pippa Virdee, 'Partition in Transition: Comparative Analysis of Migration in
     Ludhiana and Lyallpur,' in *Partitioned Lives: Narratives of Home, Displacement
     and Resettlement*, eds. Anjali Gera Roy and Nandi Bhatia (Delhi: Pearson, 2007).
15   See further, Imran Ali, *The Punjab Under Imperialism, 1885–1947* (Princeton:
     Princeton University Press, 1988) and David Gilmartin, 'Migration and
     Modernity: The State, the Punjabi Village, and the Settling of the Canal Colonies,'
     in *People on the Move: Punjabi Colonial and Post-colonial Migration*, eds. Ian Talbot
     and Shinder Thandi (Karachi: Oxford University Press, 2004).
16   Read further, Moniza Alvi's poetry, *At the Time of Partition* (UK: Bloodaxe Books,
     2013).
17   Malcom Darling, *The Punjab Peasant in Prosperity and Debt* (Delhi: Manohar,
     1925; reprint 1977).
18   Darshan Tatla, 'The Sandal Bar: Memoirs of a Jat Sikh Farmer,' *The Panjab Past
     and Present* 29, nos. 1 and 2 (1995): 160–75.

however, the fact that it was on the main artery of North India, the Grand Trunk Road. It was therefore connected to all the major cities, (Delhi, Amritsar and Lahore) and thus was an important stop for refugees who were on the move and consequently attracted many refugees.

Internal migration has historically played an important role in the development of Punjab and, following partition, refugees and migrants have played a significant role in providing the basis for creating new industrial heartlands that have shaped new emerging cities like Lyallpur and Ludhiana and in regenerating the economy post-1947. However, it was the dominance of small-scale industry in Ludhiana that enabled it to emerge as East Punjab's leading industrial centre, quickly surpassing Amritsar and Jullundur. While small towns like Ludhiana eventually benefitted from the mass human displacement of 1947, there was also another side effect, which continues to resonate in contemporary India and Pakistan. Interestingly, when we discuss East Punjab today, we forget about the other parts, which constituted East Punjab in 1947, namely today's Haryana and Himachal Pradesh. These areas suffered equally and after Hindus, Muslims were often the second largest group. Muslims were significantly present in cities like Hissar (28 per cent), Gurgaon (34 per cent), Karnal (32 per cent) and Ambala (32 per cent) which are all re-formed and re-imagined in the post-partition era. Equally, there were significant concentration of Christians in cities like Lahore (3.2 per cent), Sialkot (3.72 per cent), Lyallpur (4.33 per cent), Gojra (9 per cent) and Gujranwala (2.24 per cent). The stories of Hindus in East Punjab and Christians in West Punjab, for example, then get subsumed in the wider history of partition.

While the urban landscape changed dramatically, lives were rebuilt and new homes were made, the emotional attachment that people had with cities such as Lahore and Delhi were a source of much literature. The following poem from Prem Kirpal who was a Lahori migrant to Delhi shows how his beloved city became a foreign land:

> My beloved City of Lahore
> Still Standing not far from Delhi
> Within quicker reach by air or train,
> Suddenly became a forbidden land
> Guarded by a sovereign state
> Of new ideologies, loves and hates.
> Homes were lost and hearts were bruised
> In both unhappy parts of Punjab.[19]

---

19 Prem Kirpal, 'Spirit's Musings' quoted in Pran Nevile, *Lahore. A Sentimental Journey* (New Delhi: Penguin Books, 2006), xxix.

Pran Nevile, a retired diplomat and writer in his later life, never forgot Lahore, the city of his youth. He reminisces, even today, 'my emotional attachment to this great city is as deep as ever. My memories of boyhood and youth are still fresh in my mind and are often a subject matter of conversation whenever I sit together with ex-Lahorias of my generation'.[20] However, Rumi in his eulogy to Delhi notes how many prominent writers from Lahore never came back to visit the city after migrating. These included figures such as Krishan Chandar, Rajinder Singh Bedi, Balwant Singh and Balwant Gargi; the trauma of seeing their beloved city transformed in the new world was perhaps too much for them.[21]

Aspirations

Similarly, Afzal Tauseef, a writer and journalist based in Lahore, moved to Quetta, after her family were killed, unable to come back to Punjab and Lahore until much later in life. The carnage left many members of her family dead during August 1947 and Tauseef is still puzzled about the root cause that led to such a painful division. She was forced to migrate following this massacre; displaced from her ancestral land, she has not to this day come to terms of being uprooted from her home. Her father, bitter from the experiences of partition and forced to flee, chose to remove himself completely from the Punjab he had known; instead, he went to Balochistan in Pakistan.

> I did not live here [Lahore] for too long because my father was so bitter about it. He opted for Balochistan and left Punjab forever. I came back to Lahore at the age of 25–26...So for me, my Punjab was my village, which then became a part of India. Living in Balochistan made me to forget Punjab and Punjabi language. But then I started rediscovering the Punjab. I was only nine years old and was too young to develop any personal opinion about such circumstances. I was just like a scared child simply following the instructions. My father was so dishearten and disappointed. He left a lot of land from three villages. He left it straightaway saying that: 'I don't want to live in here.'[22]

There was much bitterness in her experiences, understandably shaped by the massacre of her family, but then subsequently shaped by the new state of

---

20   Nevile, *Lahore*, xxix.

21   Rumi, *Delhi*, 51.

22   Interview with Afzal Tauseef, Lahore, April 2007.

Pakistan. The expectations of the new state were high and millions had paid the price for the creation of Pakistan and so the gradual deterioration of state institutions has created a class critical, a class that is trying to understand and reconcile itself to a bitter legacy of partition that has persisted for seventy years. The need to forget and move away from the place of trauma can be a useful tool to erase those painful memories. Meena Alexander, a poet and a novelist, in her autobiographical novel, *Fault Lines,* captures these subtle emotions beautifully: 'I am, a woman cracked by multiple migrations. Uprooted so many times, she can connect nothing with nothing'.[23] And so for many people, the only way to reconcile was to detach themselves from those sites of trauma, whether through physical dislocation or through emotional detachment.

Saadat Hasan Manto, a migrant from Samrala, Ludhiana, was never completely at ease in Lahore and died shortly afterwards in 1955. The confusions of identity and citizenship are themes which resonate in his work and as the ending of *Toba Tek Singh* unfolds we find the remnants of the many migrants that were torn between two spaces in no man's land. Manto struggled to come to terms with the intolerance and distrust. 'He could not accept the fact that suddenly some people saw him not as Saadat Hasan but as a Muslim'.[24] His stories often portrayed the absurdities of communities being forced to accept the new communalised and national identities. We see this most poignantly in the story about *The Dog of Titwal* in which the dog belongs neither to Muslims nor to Hindus and the exchange of patients of the mental asylum in *Toba Tek Singh*.[25] To mark Manto's birth centenary in 2012, Ajoka Theatre in Lahore developed a new play based on his writings *Kaun hai Yeh Gustakh?* (Who is this recalcitrant?). This recent tribute to Manto testifies to the importance that literature continues to play in bridging the divisions between the people of India and Pakistan. Shahid Nadeem, writer of *Kaun hai Yeh Gustakh?*, stressed the importance of cultural exchanges as he prepared for the play's performance in Delhi.[26] But writing in 2017, India

---

23 Jaspal Kaur Singh, 'Memory of Trauma in Meena Alexander's Texts,' in *Tracing an Indian Diaspora: Contexts, Memories, Representations*, eds. Parvati Raghuram et al. (New Delhi: Sage, 2008), 392.

24 Sudha Tiwari, 'Memories of Partition: Revisiting Saadat Hasan Manto,' *Economic and Political Weekly* XLVIII, no 25 (2013): 51.

25 Saadat Hasan Manto and Introduction by Daniyal Mueenuddin, *Mottled Dawn: Fifty Sketches and Stories of Partition* (India: Penguin, 2011).

26 Interview with Shahid Nadeem, Ajoka Theatre, Lahore, January 2013.

and Pakistan have once again closed the doors for such exchanges and a more confrontational and aggressive mood is noticeable.

One of the earliest writers to tackle the subject of partition, Manto was pioneering in tackling dark subjects. 'His most memorable characters are products of the illicit social exchanges' and 'whether he was writing about prostitutes, pimps or criminals, Manto wanted to impress upon his readers that these disreputable people were also human, much more than those who cloaked their failings in a thick veil of hypocrisy'.[27] Again, the importance of humanity above religion and state is prevalent in the subjects and their stories. It is also highly questionable whether someone like Manto could exist and be tolerated in today's Pakistan and India. 'Times are tougher than they were in his time and we are now more intolerant as a nation,' says his daughter Nusrat.[28]

Salim Akhtar in his essay poses the question, 'Is Manto Necessary Today?' For Akhtar, unquestionably writers like Manto are essential in providing the 'courage to face bitter truth, to analyse it and to express it openly. He fought all his life for the right to speak the truth. He endured not only the censure of religion and the courts but also, eventually, the rejection of his fellow progressives'.[29] These freedoms are indeed constantly under threat in both contemporary India and Pakistan. In Pakistan, for example, a young lady, who gained popularity through social media, was murdered by her brother for dishonouring the family. Arsalan Khan quoted in *Al Jazeera* and commenting on Qandeel Baloch's tragic murder highlights 'a culture of toxic masculinity in Pakistan in which men's reputations are bound up with their ability to control the bodies and lives of their daughters, sisters, and wives. We think of women as the keepers of family and national honour, and so they are endlessly scrutinised for upholding the values of sexual modesty and propriety, and are relentlessly policed to ensure that they do not transgress those norms'.[30] What struck me about the commentary by Khan was that it could quite easily have been applied to the Partition-related violence what women were subjected

---

27 Ayesha Jalal, *The Pity of Partition* (India: HarperCollins, 2013), 26.
28 Sarfraz Manzoor, 'Saadat Hasan Manto: "He Anticipated Where Pakistan Would Go,"' *The Guardian*, 11 June 2016.
29 Salim Akhtar quoted in Stephen Alter, 'Madness and Partition: The Short Stories of Saadat Hasan Manto Alif,' *Journal of Comparative Poetics*, Special edition on Madness and Civilisation, no. 14 (1994): 92.
30 Alia Chughtai, 'Pakistanis on Qandeel Baloch: The Problem Is Society,' *Al Jazeera*, accessed 18 July 2016, http://www.aljazeera.com/indepth/features/2016/07/qandeel-baloch-honour-killing-problem-society-160717212155778.html.

to or even Delhi in 1984, Gujarat in 2002 and so on. But the point is that as nations, neither India nor Pakistan has really progressed particularly when we assume that women are integral to national and familial honour and thus are subjected to stringent norms of behaviour, which are not applicable to men. In an interview with Tahira Mazhar Ali, she pointed out the more systematic and political faults that have prevented progress:

> Was it a freedom? We have to be very clear as to what does it mean by freedom. When the British left, we had some idealism. But nothing was done. All lies and eyewash had been promoted brazenly. Constructions of the buildings all around in the name of development that is what has been done in the name of freedom. Unless poor people have a share in the resources, rich and poor have equal opportunities, only then one can say that there is freedom. My contention is that we have not got freedom. There is no freedom.[31]

Much of the bitterness emanates from the lack of those freedoms that people were promised. Freedom or its Urdu equivalent, *azaadi*, was very powerfully used in agitations at Jawaharlal Nehru University in 2016 and echo much of what Ali was saying ten years earlier. Interestingly, the *azaadi* chant used by Kanhaiya Kumar (who was at the centre of the JNU controversy) originated from a feminist discourse by Kamla Bhasin, who had, in turn, improvised this slogan from Pakistani feminists. It boldly demanded freedoms: 'From patriarchy: Azaadi; from all the hierarchy: Azaadi; from endless violence: Azaadi; from helpless silence: Azaadi'.[32] Like Ali, it was not simply a question of freedom but a freedom *from* the injustices which still plague society and disempower them from achieving *real* freedom. The idea of freedom is not merely then an act of political freedom and is certainly not a freedom from thought in the increasingly forced homogenisation of society. It entails actual and real freedoms, freedoms which allow the citizens to exist without fear of persecution, fear of raising critical voices, fear of consumption and cultural practices, fear from oppression and, above all, freedom from having a question mark at their very existence just for being. These questions of rights and freedoms still remain largely unresolved in contemporary India and Pakistan.

---

31 Interview with Tahira Mazhar Ali, Lahore, April 2007.
32 Nirupama Dutt, 'Hum kya chahte? Azaadi!' Story of slogan raised by JNU's Kanhaiya, *Hindustan Times*, Chandigarh, 5 March 2016.

Ali goes on to expose the differences between what Jinnah had envisaged and what became the reality. The disappointment in her voice was palpable, as was Najum Latif when he recited Ustad Daman's poem. She argues:

> Yes, of course they failed the people. They had disappointed the people. It was good that Jinnah passed away very early otherwise heaven knows what these people would have done to him. The Mullahs already denounced him as non-Muslim. Jinnah was a good man. He came from a very sophisticated society of Bombay. He had been mixing with Parsees and other communities. But in Punjab when we raise these relevant questions as to how this country should be managed suggesting the ways and means to ameliorate the lot of the poor, we are branded as the Indian agents or the Soviet agents etc. On the eve of partition, CID was sitting at the door of my house...In 1945-46 the Communist Party had passed resolution that Muslims of India must have a separate homeland and I was asked to go and deliver the copy of the resolution to Mr. Jinnah who was staying at Mamdot Villa. I rode my bicycle and went there. When I met Mr. Jinnah he said a bit pointedly, "you are with Congress and not with us". I said, "Jawaharlal talks about whole of India whereas you talk about Muslims only". He said, "I know you have apprehensions that you would not be able to meet your non-Muslim friends but I promise you that you will be able to come to India whenever you like, as I will come to Bombay every year". Now when anyone talks about mending fences with India he/she is branded as renegade whose ideology has gone astray. But I fail to understand that ideology. You will have to meet more competent people than me.[33]

Urvashi Butalia also continues to raise this issue of injustices. Bringing the experiences of Dalits, she highlights the way in which their experiences do not neatly fit into the broad meta-narratives. She recounts one story: 'My entire dowry came from there. My friends' dowries came from there'. And I asked her how she escaped the violence when it was all around her. And she said, 'We're not Hindu or Muslim, we are Dalit'.[34] At that moment, there was a realisation for Butalia that caste played a role in the movement of refugees and the ways in which they faced violence. This was not a homogenised experience. And those experiences continue into the contemporary age, where the injustices remain despite freedom from colonial rule.

---

33   Interview with Tahira Mazhar Ali, Lahore, April 2007.
34   Urvashi Butalia, keynote address. Presented at the International Conference on Teaching History, Calcutta, 30 July to 1 August 2015, accessed 21 May 2017, http://www.historyforpeace.pw/news/keynote-address-urvashi-butalia/.

What We Remember, How We Remember

A future student of history would wonder how hundreds of thousands of people suddenly made up their mind to abandon their homes and belongings for ever without even hope of crossing the border, let alone the certainty of rehabilitation later. The woeful tale of the stampede and orgy that followed in the wake of the partition of the country would be forgotten in course of time, but while memory serves, tears would always burst whenever the tragedy is recalled.[35]

I start with the above quote, which is taken from a small publication detailing the Punjab industries following partition because it encapsulates so much that is tragic about the partition. It highlights the human suffering, the violent (and at times genocidal) forced migration, and although the pain may eventually subside, the quote above also touches upon the individual's capacity to recall those painful memories. Indeed, for some people, it was better to forget and to live in amnesia. Mushtaq Soofi in a recent article in *Dawn* quoted Brecht's poem, 'when the wound stops hurting what hurts is the scar',[36] and it is this 'scar' that continues to mark Punjab, the spectre of a violent beginning which continues to loom over a divided home. But what happens once survivors pass away with the passage of time? Does that mean we forget about it? Is it no longer necessary to remember the event? Or, does it become even more important to ensure that these memories are not lost with that generation? Many in the past have questioned why surprisingly there has not been a meaningful partition memorial of some sort to commemorate the lives lost, those that survived and also to promote peace between India and Pakistan. Veena Das has also questioned this complete absence of public discourse around Partition and 'public anxieties around sexuality and purity'.[37] Furthermore, there has been nothing in the form of public hearings to allow for stories of mass rape and murder to be public,[38] to allow for truth and reconciliation which has been done elsewhere. There is no form of 'putting history on trial'.[39] These are cathartic processes which have been completely absent in South Asia.

---

35 R. Dhiman, *Punjab Industries* (Ludhiana: Dhiman Press of India, 1962), 24–5.

36 Mushtaq Soofi, 'A Spectre Haunts Punjab!' [Online] *Dawn* (2013).

37 Veena Das, *Life and Words: Violence and the Descent into the Ordinary* (Berkeley, CA: University of California Press, 2006). E-book version.

38 Das, *Life and Words*, 19.

39 Das, *Life and Words*, 19.

Picture 10.1: The small monument at the Indian border dedicated to the 10 lakh Punjabis who died unsung in 1947. This was funded and petitioned by the Folklore Research Academy in Chandigarh and was inaugurated on 31 December 1996

There are some small memorials: there is the Martyrs Monument in the purpose-built capital of Indian Punjab, Chandigarh, which commemorates the people lost during the freedom struggle and the partition of Punjab. In Pakistan, there is Bab-i-Pakistan in Lahore which was developed on the Walton Camp site which was one of the largest refugee camps in Punjab and commemorates the millions who were made homeless and destitute. There is also a small privately built peace memorial on the Indian side of the Wagah/ Attari border but these initiatives barely receive wide-spread coverage and most of the public is unaware of their existence. The push for a meaningful peace museum or memorial has been mooted for some time, but it has largely been driven by peace activists, online campaigns and occasionally endorsed by the political leadership on both sides of the border. These initiatives include Aman ki Asha, Friends without Borders, Indo Pak Bangla Friendship (one of the many Facebook forums) and Asiapeace, which was started by the Association for Communal Harmony in Asia in 2001, as part of a sustained and coordinated campaign to promote peace and harmony in South Asia. But these initiatives remain tangential and minuscule, although importantly, they do maintain and encourage dialogue across borders. More recently a concerted effort has been made by The Partition Museum Project to establish a People's Museum.[40] Kishwar Desai, an Indian author and columnist, started the project in 2015 and launched this to commemorate 70 years of independence. Ironically, one of the events organised to launch the project was co-funded by the British Council. The colonial linkages are never far away, and even after seventy years the ex-colonial power contributes towards commemorating an event created by its policies. Moreover, during a recent trip to The Partition Museum, the patriotic overtures and strong sense of nationalism were discernible in curating the exhibition. For this to be more meaningful, some balance in apportioning blame must be visible.

Anindya Raychaudhuri argues that a partition museum would certainly help in healing and educating while at the same time 'helping in the project of nation-building by promoting an informed citizenry'.[41] But Raychaudhuri's article is also titled 'demanding the impossible', which highlights how difficult the task of developing a memorial for partition has been. The natural place for a memorial or museum has always been at the Attari/Wagah border in

---

40 www.partitionmuseum.org, accessed 9 August 2016.
41 Anindya Raychaudhuri, 'Demanding the Impossible: Exploring the Possibilities of a National Partition Museum in India,' *Social Semiotics* 22 (2012): 175.

Picture 10.2: Bab-e-Azadi, the Gateway to Pakistan, Attari-Wagah border

Picture 10.3: Inaugurated in 2007 the new look Attari-Wagah border which is the only official land crossing between India and Pakistan

Punjab. Thousands of people use this space to travel across the no-man's land that Radcliffe created. Yet, few would notice the small symbolic memorial to the people who died in 1947 at Attari, India; but even this small effort is crumbling away among the transformation of Attari checkpoint.

There has obviously been some urgency to establish a memorial because those who witnessed these events first-hand are a fading generation, and with seventy years approaching we turn to another milestone. Personal testimonies of first-hand accounts have been collected by a number historians (used extensively in this work) and now, increasingly, by oral history projects within the diaspora communities.[42] The 1947 Partition Archive based in America is one example, but other smaller projects have also been conducted in the United Kingdom and oral testimony collections are preserved in Leicester, Cambridge and London, for example. Some initiatives also exist in the subcontinent such as the Citizens Archive of Pakistan (CAP), a repository for Partition oral histories (and other projects) and is the brainchild of the Academy Award winning documentary maker, Sharmeen Obaid Chinoy. In India, CAP worked closely with the Delhi-based NGO Routes2roots on the 'Exchange for Change' project that encouraged interaction between children to demystify the 'other' by learning about their shared history and culture. The Nehru Memorial Library and Museum in New Delhi also has a collection of interviews related to the freedom movement. More recently, a joint project between ITU, LUMS and Habib Universities in Pakistan and Harvard University in the United States brings together a plethora of material to form a digital archive. But there is a vigour with which these projects are currently being conducted in the diaspora that is not found in either India or Pakistan. This may be partly explained through the exposure that the diaspora community has to other memorials, museums and commemorations, especially to the Holocaust. There is evidently some cultural transfer taking place, including an increased interest in documenting 'hidden histories', in multicultural Britain at least.[43] Crucially though, it is the changes in technology that have made this

---

42 Ian Talbot and Darshan Singh Tatla, eds., *Epicentre of Violence: Partition Voices and Memories from Amritsar* (Delhi: Permanent Black, 2006).

43 For example, I worked on two such projects, *The Punjab: Moving Journeys* (Royal Geographical Society, 2008) and *Coming to Coventry* (The Herbert, 2006). Both projects were about incorporating minorities into mainstream history in public spaces. These provide the impetus needed to explore and document partition narratives from a people's perspective and form part of the new drive towards a people's history.

possible. Since I first started my research in this area, I have advanced from cassettes, to micro cassettes to digital recordings. The citizen journalist can now collect and record material on a smart phone and share instantly with a global community among others, social media. This was not possible even as recently as 2001, when I first embarked on this journey. Artists, writers and people can work together despite the hard borders and made possible through technology. The virtual space is now as important as the actual space and it is here that there is at least some hope in the collaborative and open discussion.

Reimagining the Land, Language and Religion

While the partition of Punjab addressed the needs of the Muslims of India, the territorial division itself has created a much more unintended outcome, that of a more communalised and fractured post-colonial Punjabi identity. As noted earlier, Punjab was made up of three main communities, Hindus, Muslims, Sikhs and a smaller number of other minorities. Rammah powerfully argues that the Muslim–Hindu–Sikh mix in Punjabi society ceased to exist once Punjab was divided.[44] The 1947 partition, and subsequently, the linguistic reorganisation and further division of East Punjab in 1966, has created territories which are now associated with three 'unmixed' religious communities. Thus, Pakistan Punjab is predominately Muslim; Indian Punjab is dominated by the Sikhs, and Haryana and Himachal Pradesh (previously part of East Punjab) are now dominated by the Hindus. The princely states of Punjab, like the rest of British India, were carved up and 'integrated' into India or Pakistan, a seemingly 'bloodless revolution. Post-1947 Punjab(s) today reflect the fault lines created in colonial India and remain divided religiously and linguistically. Scholarly work, unfortunately, tends to remain divided too, but recent research has started to challenge this dominant discourse of Punjabi society that is still quite complex given that huge population transfers have taken place. What is interesting in the case of East and West Punjab, is how both areas dropped reminders of division from their name and retained only Punjab. In order to create new histories and new re-imagined homelands, East Punjab was simply known as Punjab from 1950 and although West Punjab remained until the emergence of the one-unit in 1955, it was mostly the shortened version of Punjab that was used from the 1950s onwards. Compare this with Bengal: while Bangladesh was formed as a new entity, West

---

44   Safir Rammah, 'West Punjabi Poetry: From Ustad Daman to Najm Hosain Syed,' *Journal of Punjab Studies* 13, nos. 1 and 2 (2006): 215.

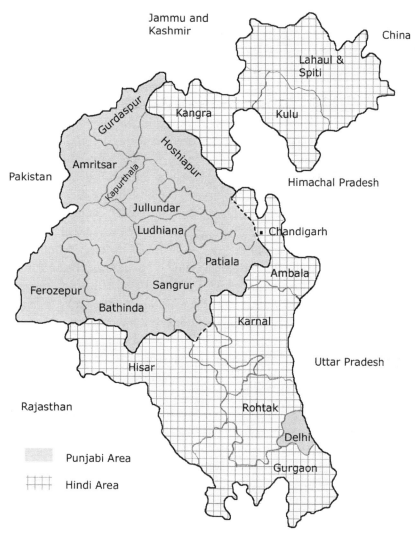

Map 10.1: East Punjab after 1966

Bengal has retained the stark reminder that there was once, also, another half.[45]
By erasing the West and East, both Punjabs have sought to erase a past history
and create a new homeland in which the primary identity has become religion.

---

45 I am thankful to Dr. Yaqoob Khan Bangash for bringing up this point in a panel
discussion at the Lyallpur Sulekh Mela, February 2017. Although, since writing
this, Chief Minister Mamata Banerjee also now wants West removed from
Bengal. http://www.thehindu.com/news/national/other-states/Assembly-drops-
West-renames-State-as-Bengal/article14596751.ece. Accessed 5 October 2017.

One of the most important features of any ethnic group is language; it binds and brings the cultural history of those people together to form a cohesive group of people with a shared sense of its past. Punjabi, interestingly, was never given state patronage; this is true for the Mughal period, Ranjit Singh's reign and also under the British. The preferred state or official language was Persian and Urdu.[46] Farina Mir argues that part of the problem under the British was the plurality of the scripts used to write Punjabi; all three scripts (Indo-Persian, Gurmukhi and Devanagari) were used but none of them dominated.[47] Yet, despite this anomaly, Punjabi continued to be the language of the masses and reached into wider Punjab (from Peshawar to Delhi), albeit in different dialects but broadly comprehensible. But it is the plurality in written Punjabi that causes friction and provides the space for further divisions in the post-colonial context. It is within this milieu that the language, the people and the land become further subdivided to reflect both national and, in the case of Sikhs, subnational identities. This produces three distinct outlooks: Hindi, Hindu, Hindusthan; Urdu, Muslim, Pakistan; and Punjabi, Sikh, Khalistan.[48] The Hindu Punjabi has therefore been absorbed into the wider *Hindutva* project; the Muslim Punjabi (in West Punjab) has abandoned the Punjabi language in favour of the more 'Islamic' Urduised identity; and interestingly, it is the Punjabi owning and speaking Sikhs that have become synonymous with the Punjab and Punjabi identity. Yet in reality, it is also the mother tongue of the majority of Pakistanis and non-Sikh Punjabis in India.

The connection of language and religion has therefore come to define the post-colonial landscape in Punjab. While these are simplified stereotypes of the divided people, more broadly, they are symptomatic of the communalised politics of the subcontinent and more specifically, they are much more peculiar to the Punjab region. For example, Tariq Rehman has shown how, 'soon after the creation of Pakistan, Punjabi vanished as a University subject. Because of its association with Sikhs and due to the state's promotion of Urdu, Punjabi was relegated to the periphery'.[49] It is difficult to think of another region in the subcontinent that has shunned its own linguistic and ethnic history in favour of a national or religious identity. The pluralistic land of Punjab that epitomised people like my own parents' generation are fewer and fewer. My

---

46 Anshu Malhotra and Farina Mir, eds., *Punjab Reconsidered: History, Culture, and Practice* (New Delhi: Oxford University Press, 2012), xxix.

47 Farina Mir, *The Social Space of Language: Vernacular Culture in British Colonial Punjab* (London: University of California Press, 2010).

48 Virinder Singh Kalra, 'Punjabiyat and the Music of Nusrat Fateh Ali Khan,' *South Asian Diaspora* 6, no. 2 (2014): 179–92.

49 Rammah, 'West Punjabi Poetry,' 216.

Picture 10.4: The multilingual sign indicates the closeness of Lahore but yet this is a distant city for most Indians

father's generation is hardly to be found now in Indian Punjab; as a child, I never found it strange that my father made most of his notes in the Indo-Persian script despite being a Sikh. As Bhardwaj notes, 'in East Punjab, Urdu became a casualty of Punjabi'.[50] The prescriptive orthodoxy symbolising Sikhism today is also unfamiliar to many. My mother, a practising Sikh, had embraced 'other' practices to epitomise the pluralistic tendencies associated with the Punjab that I am familiar with. Similarly, Bhardwaj has tried to

---

50 Ajay Bhardwaj, 'The Absence in Punjabiyat's Split Universe,' *The Hindu*, 15 August 2012.

unearth some of the hidden histories of a composite Punjab, which belies the dominant narrative. He recalls this story:

> Behind my grandparents' house in our village Akalgarh, in district Ludhiana, is a narrow street. To this day it is called *Rajputan de Gali* (the street of the Rajputs). This is where the influential community of 'Rajput Muslims,' as they were addressed, lived before Partition. The villagers' reference to the *Maseet Wala Gurdwara* (literally the mosque turned gurdwara) is yet another symbol of the once powerful presence of Muslims in Akalgarh. Similarly, there is a pond called *Taru Shah da Toba*, named after a wandering fakir Taru *Shah*, who preferred to stay on in our village. Over the years his shrine in the old graveyard has grown in size and stature. Yet there are no Muslims in the village.[51]

Partition has enabled this rewriting of history that is now constructed through a lens that is linear and mono-religious in its outlook. Both India and Pakistan have been trying to erase and rewrite their shared past; the forced migration resulted in the separation of people and lasted a few months, but the project to rewrite these histories has been more complex and subtle. Churnjeet Mahn in a recent project has been exploring this cultural amnesia towards contested sites and how Sikh and Muslim sites co-exist in post-1947 along the Grand Trunk Road.[52] Retelling this story in the post-1947 Punjab also means erasing 'other' histories. But as Bhardwaj highlights, these new imagined localities still retain a connection with its previous history despite renaming of places. For example, in Lyallpur, old Sikh localities are still known as Guru Nanak Pura and Guru Gobind Pura, despite the out-migration of all the Sikh community. Malhotra and Mir's work interestingly tries to delve into some of these complexities which have shaped contemporary Punjab(s). Memory and nostalgia for a glorious past continues to resonate beyond the divided boundaries, as they note, 'For many of the Partition's refugees, while the physical relationship with land/people was irrevocably lost, their "Punjab" would live on in their imaginaries, and in the new world they constructed for themselves'. For example, names given to refugee colonies of Delhi are Gujranwala, Bhera or Punjabi Bagh or the other is conversation opener, 'tussi pichhon Kithon de ho?' (where are you from?), which is a clear reference to

---

51　Bhardwaj, *The Hindu*, 15 August 2012.
52　See the project website: www.thegtroad.com.

where are you from before partition.[53] Naming places after former villages, towns or cities helps embed and memorialise the past in the present. It is a form of preserving our own history despite new borders, and while East and West Punjab have erased this reminder people still memorialise their past histories in these small but significant ways. This, of course, is contrary to what has been happening at the national level in India and Pakistan, where both countries have been busy erasing colonial place names and renaming them with their heroes from a mythical past and resisting any challenges to current state narratives. A good example of this is the resistance to a campaign to have Shadman Chowk in Lahore to be renamed Bhagat Singh Chowk to commemorate the revolutionary hero of undivided Punjab and the place where he was hanged. In contemporary Punjab(s), an atheist like Bhagat Singh has increasingly become a contested figure for all those who want to own him.[54]

Interestingly Ajay Bhardwaj, a documentary filmmaker, has been attempting to capture this hazy space of shared and composite culture of Punjab. In his films, he captures the voices of a marginalised idea of *Punjabiyat* (Punjabi-ness, especially through language), which becomes replaced by contending identities through the establishment of two new nation-states. In his film, *Milange Babey Ratan De Mele Te* (Let's Meet at Baba Ratan's Fair), Bhardwaj takes you through a journey that pieces together remnants of a pre-partitioned Punjab in which identities were fluid and people blended together in fairs and Sufi shrines. More recently, Yogesh Snehi has been exploring the lives of two Sufi shrines in East Punjab which remain peripheral in otherwise dominate discourses.[55] While in Pakistan, writers such as Haroon Khalid have been delving into the composite culture and history of West Punjab.[56] These are small attempts to 'recover' these lost spaces and traditions in order to bring them into the mainstream; his work alludes to the presence of the past in the present.

Making New Histories

This regional history highlights the transformation and legacies of that moment in time, when greater Punjab disappeared and was instead replaced by communalised

---

53 Malhotra and Mir, *Punjab Reconsidered,* xxv–xxvi.

54 See further, Talbot and Kamran, *Lahore,* Chapter 7; *and* Chris Moffat, *Infinite Inquilab: Celebrating a Revolutionary Past in Pakistan's Present. The Caravan. A Journal of Politics and Culture,* 1 August 2013.

55 Yogesh Snehi, 'On the Margin of Religious Discourses,' *Café Dissensus,* no. 34 (2017).

56 Haroon Khalid, *In Search of Shiva: A Study of Folk Religious Practices in Pakistan* (New Delhi: Rupa, 2015); *Walking with Nanak* (New Delhi: Tranquebar, 2016).

Punjab(s), of a time when the 'great men' decided what the fate of millions of people should be. The tragic and longer-term consequences of this violent beginning have overshadowed the trauma and forced migration experienced by millions of innocent people who were never asked about their desires and dreams of what *azaadi* should look like. While the process of carving up India was pre-planned, the exchange of population was not; though disruption and violence was expected, the ability to deal with this was inadequate and while New Delhi and Karachi celebrated their new existence, neither thought this would be the source of such hostility between the two countries. The legacy of decolonisation in India has therefore had ramifications far beyond merely transferring power. This was not just a physical separation but a division of people, emotions, ancestral lands and properties; it was a partitioning of people whose primary identifier now was their religious identity, while their caste, class, linguistic or ethnic identity had been receded, albeit temporarily. The process had started in colonial Punjab, with increasing communalisation of identities. Revivalist groups, like the Arya Samaj, were important in awakening and constructing essentialised religious identities among people who had previously adopted a more pragmatic attitude. And it is within this context, that more broadly, it is about the transformation of a region which has not just been demographically altered but that also now tells us a different history. It is now a new and different history that fails to adequately acknowledge the shared cultural roots and traditions of the broader ethnic identity.

In the making of these new histories, one aspect that stands out in the new globalised world is the widespread impact of migration. Earlier in the chapter, there was a brief discussion of how refugees often find small ways of preserving their histories and memories in their 'new' homes. This has allowed them to remain connected with the past, which is forever fractured. Others, however, decided to completely break with history and chose to migrate abroad. There is evidence that this great migration led to further migrations, both internally to other states and abroad like post-war Britain, which at the time was short of labour and was an attractive option for those looking to escape the trauma of Partition.[57] According to estimates by Tan and Kudaisya, 'between 8 and 10 per cent of all Sikhs had migrated overseas by the end of the 1950s and another 30 per cent were living within India but outside Punjab in towns and cities of adjacent provinces and in the capital of Delhi'.[58] And it is within the diaspora that much of the recent

---

57   Tan Tai Yong and Gyanesh Kudaisya, *The Aftermath of Partition in South Asia* (London: Routledge, 2000), 231–2.

58   Tan and Kudaisya, *The Aftermath*, 231-2.

scholarship on memory, trauma and partition has been emerging. Though they escaped the immediateness of the sites that were associated with the violence and dislocation, the memory associated with the land has not escaped. The generation that has grown up listening to stories of partition has prompted some people to at least explore this history. Bhalla, a US-based physicist, 'grew up listening to these stories from her grandmother who remained traumatized till her death. She regretted not having recorded them and this prompted her to start the *1947 Partition Archive'.*[59] The oral history project has been busy collecting first-hand accounts from a fading generation.

The loss associated with Partition is also made worse by any lack of closure or any form of official recognition for what happened. People were forced to flee and many thought they would return to their home but most never did and this sudden fracture was never allowed to heal properly. The suffering, therefore, has largely been a private matter, until more recently with the digital revolution allowing people to share their stories across the borders and religious boundaries. But it is the dreams, memories and legacies of partition that Balraj Sahni, a prominent Indian actor and a migrant from Rawalpindi, captures so evocatively in his poem and continues to haunt many. It was written during his visit to Amritsar in 1951 and it draws on much of the pain and loss associated with partition:

> You are those with a country; you are those with homes
> We are homeless; we are estranged
> You smiled and took us to your breast
> We cried and took consolation
> The faded stars, twinkled once again
> What we did not hope for, was made possible by your warmth
> May my city live, and its people thrive
> We came and pray for this as we now depart
> All our pockets are empty!
> We carry nothing with us as we leave.
>
> Half a heart repines here
> Half a heart lies neglected there.
> The paths, for which our hearts once beat
> For those paths we became strangers.
> What of our becoming human beings,
> We have turned into Hindus, Sikhs, and Muslims.[60]

---

59   Sameer Arshad, 'Partition Stories, in First Person,' *The Times of India*, 27 October 2013.

60   Balraj Sahni, 'Mera Pakistani Safarnama', trans. Gibb Schreffle, *Journal of Punjab Studies* 13, nos. 1 and 2 (1963; trans. 2006): 89.

Select Bibliography

India Office Library and Records, London

Bahawalpur State Affairs
Malerkotla State Files
Moon Collection
Mudie Papers
Political and Judicial Records

National Archives of India, New Delhi

Dr Rajendra Prasad Papers
Malerkotla State Files
Ministry of Rehabilitation
Ministry of State

Nehru Memorial Museum and Library, New Delhi

All India Women's Conference
Dewan Chaman Lall Papers
Hindu Mahasabha
Ministry of Rehabilitation
Papers of Nawab of Malerkotla
Rameshwari Nehru Papers
Renuka Ray Papers
S. P. Mookerjee Papers
Sunder Lal Papers

Punjab State Archives, Chandigarh

Liaison Agency Files

Punjab State Archives, Patiala

Malerkotla State Records

South Asian Research and Resource Centre, Lahore

Pakistan-Punjab Refugees Council Papers

National Documentation Centre, Islamabad

Ministry of Refugees and Rehabilitation
Cabinet Secretary

Newspapers

Asian Age
Civil and Military Gazette (Lahore)
Dawn (Karachi)
India Today
Outlook
The Hindu
The Hindustan Times
The Pakistan Times
The Times of India
The Tribune (Chandigarh)
Tribune (Lahore)

Oral Interviews*

Abdul Haq, Montgomery Bazaar, Faisalabad, January 2003.
Abdul Rahman, Lyallpur Cotton Mills, Faisalabad, February 2003.
Afzal Tauseef, Lahore, April 2007.
Ajay Singh, Ahmedgarh, Malerkotla, August 2001.
Atiq-ur-Rehman, Jama Masjid, Field Ganj, Ludhiana, March 2002.
Ayesha Bibi, Kamoke, September 2008.
Balquees Begum, Lahore, September 2008.
Bashiran Bibi, Harcharan Pura, Faisalabad, February 2003.
Bhagwant Kaur, Sabzi Mandi, Ludhiana, March 2002.
Bibi Amir Fatma, Gill Village, Ludhiana, March 2002.
Chaudhari Rehmat Ullah, Harcharan Pura, Faisalabad, December 2002.
Farkhanda Lodi, Lahore, April 2007.
Fatima Sughra, Lahore, September 2008.
Ghulam Nadi, Gobind Pura, Faisalabad, February 2003.
Gian Chand Ahuja, Model Gram, Ludhiana, April 2002.
Gurnam Singh, Sabzi Mandi, Ludhiana, March 2002.
Haji Kazim, Jhang Bazaar, Faisalabad, February 2003.

---

* All names of interviewees have been changed to protect the identity of the people, unless these are already public figures.

Hajji Mohammad Shafi, Harcharan Bazaar, Faisalabad, December 2002.
Halima Bibi, Lahore, April 2007.
Isher Singh, Ahmedgarh, Malerkotla, August 2001.
Jagat Singh, G. S. Auto, Ludhiana, March 2002.
Jaswant Singh, Industrial Area B, Ludhiana, March 2002.
Kabir, Jhang Bazaar, Faisalabad, February 2003.
Khurshid, Raza Abad, Faisalabad, February 2002.
Khurshid Bibi, Lyallpur, December 2002.
Kushi Mohammed, Malerkotla, August 2001.
Mai Manta, Sabzi Mandi, Ludhiana, March 2002.
Malik Mohammed Yousaf Ludhianvi, Ghulam Mohammad Abad, Faisalabad, January 2003.
Mehr, Harcharn Pura, Faisalabad, December 2002.
Mohammad Sadeeq, Katchery Bazaar, Faisalabad, February 2003.
Nadira Khanum, Lahore, September 2008.
Nand Lal, Saidan Chowk, Ludhiana, April 2002.
Nazeeran Bibi, Lahore, April 2007.
Nirmal Singh, Malerkotla, August 2001.
Puran, Model Town, Ludhiana, February 2003.
Rana, Chiniot Bazaar, Faisalabad, February 2003.
Ratten Singh, Model Gram, Ludhiana, February 2003.
Reshmi Bibi, Kamoke, September 2008.
Sakina Bibi, Madina Town, Faisalabad, January 2003.
Sardar Bibi, Kamoke, September 2008.
Sarwan Singh, Lal Bazaar, Malerkotla, August 2001.
Shahid Nadeem, Ajoka Theatre, Lahore, January 2013.
Shareefan Bibi, Lahore, April 2007.
Sohan Lal Pahwa, Managing Director, Avon Cycles, Ludhiana, April 2002.
Tahira Mazhar Ali, Lahore, September 2008 and April 2007.
Zakira Fatima, Lahore, September 2008.

Printed Primary Sources

Anwar, A. A., *Effects of Partition on Industries in the Border Districts of Lahore and Sialkot* (Lahore, 1953).
Government of India, *Census of India 1941*.
Government of India, *After Partition* (Delhi, 1948).
Government of India, *Census of India 1951*.
Government of Pakistan, *Note on the Sikh Plan* (Lahore, 1948).

Government of Pakistan, *Rashtriya Swayam Sewak Sangh in the Punjab* (Lahore, 1948).

Government of Pakistan, *The Sikhs in Action* (Lahore, 1948).

Government of Pakistan, *Census of Pakistan 1951*.

Government of Pakistan, *Census of Pakistan 1961*.

Government of Punjab, *Report on the Department of Industries, Punjab for the Year Ending 31st March 1930* (Lahore, 1930).

Government of Punjab, *Punjab District Gazetteers, vol. XXV Part B, Lyallpur District, Statistical Tables* (Lahore, 1935).

Government of Punjab, *Annual Report on the Working of the Factories Act, 1948, for the year 1950–54* (Simla).

Government of Punjab, *Five-Year Industrial Development Programme for the Punjab 1951–1956* (Lahore, 1952).

Government of Punjab, *Report on the Working of Municipalities in the Punjab During the Year 1949–50* (Jullundur, 1952).

Government of Punjab, *Census of Manufacturing Industry, 1955* (Punjab, 1955).

Griffen, Sir Lepel H., *Chiefs and Families of Note in the Punjab Vol. II* (Lahore, 1940).

Hasan, M., Gen ed., *Report on the Industrial Survey of Ludhiana District* (Lahore, 1942).

Khan, K. I. A., *A Description of the Principal Kotla Afghans* (Lahore, 1882).

Khan, S. U., *The Journey to Pakistan: A Documentation on Refugees of 1947* (Islamabad, 1993).

Luthera, K. L., *Impact of Partition on Border Industries* (Punjab, 1949).

Mansergh, N., Lumby, E. W. R., and Moon, Sir P., eds., *Constitutional Relations between Britain and India: The Transfer of Power 1942–47 [12 Volumes]* (London, 1970–83).

Penny, J. D., ICS, *Final Settlement Report of the Jhang and Gugera Branch Circles of the Lyallpur District* (Punjab, 1925)

Prakash, O., *An Economic Survey of Industrial Labour in the Punjab, Publication No. 14* (Punjab, 1952).

Randhawa, M. S., *Out of the Ashes – An Account of the Rehabilitation of Refugees from West Pakistan in Rural Areas of East Punjab* (Chandigarh, 1954).

Rao, Bhaskar U., *The Story of Rehabilitation* (Delhi, 1967).

Sadullah, M. M., *The Partition of Punjab 1947: A Compilation of Official Documents, 4 Vols* (Lahore, 1983).

Sharma, B. R., *Punjab District Gazetteers, Sangrur State* (Chandigarh, 1984).

Singh, Brig. R., *The Military Evacuation Organisation 1947–48* (New Delhi, 1962).

Singh, T., *Land Resettlement Manual* (Simla, 1952).

Suri, V. S., *Punjab State Gazetteers, Ludhiana* (Chandigarh, 1970).

Zafar, R. (compiler), *Disturbances in the Punjab 1947: A Compilation of Official Documents* (Islamabad, 1995).

Published Material

Books

Ager, A. ed. 1998. *Refugees: Perspectives on the Experience of Forced Migration.* New York, London: Pinter.

Ahmed, I. 2012. *The Punjab Bloodied, Partitioned and Cleansed.* Oxford, Karachi: Oxford University Press.

Akbar, A. S. 1997. *Jinnah, Pakistan and Islamic Identity: The Search for Saladin.* London: Routledge.

Ali, I. 1988. *The Punjab Under Imperialism 1885–1947.* Princeton: Princeton University Press.

Amin, S. and D. Chakrabarty. eds. 1996. *Subaltern Studies IX: Writings on South Asian History and Society.* Delhi: Oxford University Press.

Anand, B. S. 1961. *Cruel Interlude.* Bombay: Asia Publishing House.

Ansari, S. 1992. *Sufi Saints and State Power: The Pirs of Sind, 1843–1947.* Cambridge: Cambridge University Press.

Bal, G. 1995. *Development and Change in Punjab.* New Delhi: National Book Organisation.

Banga, I. ed. 1997. *Five Punjabi Centuries: Polity, Economy, Society, and Culture 1500–1990.* Delhi: Oxford University Press.

Basu, A. 1996. *Mridula Sarabhai: Rebel with a Cause.* Delhi: Oxford University Press.

Bhalla, A. ed. 1994. *Stories About Partition of India 3 Volumes.* New Delhi: HarperCollins.

Bigelow, A. 2010. *Sharing the Sacred: Practicing Pluralism in Muslim North India.* New York, Oxford: Oxford University Press.

Bourke-White, M. 1949. *Halfway to Freedom: A Report on the New India in the Words and Photos of Margaret Bourke-White.* New York: Simon & Schuster.

Brass, P. 1997. *Theft of an Idol: Text and Context in the Representation of Collective Violence.* Princeton: Princeton University Press.

Brass, P. 2003. *The Production of Hindu–Muslim Violence in Contemporary India.* Seattle: University of Washington Press.

Butalia, U. 1998. *The Other Side of Silence: Voices from the Partition of India*. New Delhi: Penguin.

Campbell-Johnson, A. 1985. *Mission with Mountbatten*. London: Hale.

Chatterji, J. 1994. *Bengal Divided: Hindu Communalism and Partition, 1932–1947*. Cambridge: Cambridge University Press.

Chatterji, J. 2011. *The Spoils of Partition: Bengal and India, 1947–1967*. Cambridge: Cambridge University Press.

Chattha, I. 2011. *Violence, Migration, and Development in Gujranwala and Sialkot 1947–1961*. Karachi: Oxford University Press.

Chawla, D. 2014. *Home Uprooted: Oral Histories of India's Partition*. New York: Fordham University Press.

Chester, L. 2009. *Borders and Conflict in South Asia: The Radcliffe Boundary Commission and the Partition of Punjab*. Manchester: Manchester University Press.

Copland, I. 1999. *The Princes of India in the Endgame of Empire, 1917–1947*. New Delhi, Cambridge: Cambridge University Press.

Corfield, C. 1975. *The Princely India I Knew: From Reading to Mountbatten*. Madras: Indo British Historical Society.

Darling, M. L. 1977. *The Punjab Peasant in Prosperity and Debt*. New Delhi: Manohar.

Darling, M. L. 1979. *At Freedom's Door*. Oxford: Oxford University Press.

Das, D. 1972. *Sardar Patel's Correspondence Vol. IV 1945–50*. Ahmedabad: Navajivan Publishing House.

Das, S. 1991. *Communal Riots in Bengal, 1905–1947*. Delhi: Oxford University Press.

Das, V. ed. 1983. *The Word and the World: Fantasy, Symbol and Record*. New Delhi: Sage.

Das, V. 2006. *Life and Words: Violence and the Descent into the Ordinary*. Berkeley: University of California Press.

Deschaumes, G. G. and R. Ivekovic. eds. 2003. *Divided Countries, Separated Cities: The Modern Legacy of Partition*. Oxford: Oxford University Press.

Dutt, N. ed. and translation. 2010. *Stories of the Soil: Classic Punjabi Stories*. India: Penguin.

Engineer, A. A. 1991. *Communal Riots in Post-Independence India*. India: Sangam.

French, P. 1997. *Liberty or Death: India's Journey to Independence and Division*. London: HarperCollins.

Gallagher, J., G. Johnson and A. Seal. eds. 1973. *Locality, Province and Nation: Essays in Indian Politics 1870–1947*. Cambridge: Cambridge University Press.

Gaur, I. D. 2008. *Martyr as Bridegroom: A Folk Representation of Bhagat Singh.* New Delhi: Anthem Press.

Ghai, P. V. 1986. *The Partition of the Punjab, 1849–1947.* New Delhi: Munishiram Manoharlal Publishers.

Gilmartin, D. 1988. *Empire and Islam: Punjab and the Making of Pakistan.* London: I. B. Tauris.

Gopal, S. 1990. *Selected Works of Jawaharlal Nehru Vol. IXA.* New Delhi: Oxford University Press.

Gosal, G. S. and G. Krishan. 1984. *Regional Disparities in Levels of Socio-economic Development in Punjab.* Kurukshetra: Vishal Publications.

Grewal, J. S. 1999. *The Sikhs of the Punjab.* New Delhi: Cambridge University Press.

Guha, R. ed. 1997. *A Subaltern Studies Reader: 1986–1995.* Minneapolis: University of Minnesota Press.

Hansen, A. B. 2002. *Partition and Genocide: Manifestation of Violence in Punjab 1937–47.* New Delhi: India Research.

Hasan, M. 1997. *India Partitioned: The Other Face of Freedom.* New Delhi.

Hasan, M. 1997. *Legacy of a Divided Nation: India's Muslims since Independence.* New Delhi: Roli Books, Lotus Collection.

Hasan, M. ed. 2000. *Inventing Boundaries: Gender, Politics and the Partition of India.* New Delhi: Oxford University Press.

Horowitz, D. L. 2001. *The Deadly Riot.* Berkeley: University of California Press.

Jalal, A. 1985. *The Sole Spokesman.* Cambridge: Cambridge University Press.

Jalal, A. 2013. *The Pity of Partition.* India; Princeton: Princeton University Press.

Kabir, A. J. 2013. *Partition's Post-Amnesias: 1947, 1971 and Modern South Asia.* New Delhi: Women Unlimited.

Kakar, S. 1996. *The Colors of Violence: Cultural Identities, Religion, and Conflict.* Chicago: The University of Chicago Press.

Kamra, S. 2002. *Bearing Witness: Partition, Independence, End of the Raj.* Calgary.

Kaul, S. ed. 2001. *The Partition of Memory: The Afterlife of the Division of India.* New Delhi: Permanent Black.

Kaur, R. 2007. *Since 1947: Partition Narratives among Punjabi Migrants of Delhi.* Delhi: Oxford University Press.

Keller, S. 1975. *Uprooting and Social Change.* New Delhi: Manohar Book Service.

Khalique, H. and R. Kohli. 2002. *Unfinished Histories: Stories of Separation and Belonging from the South Asian Diaspora*. Islamabad: Alhamra.

Khan, Nawab I. A. 2000. *History of the Ruling Family of Sheikh Sadruddin Sadar-I-Jahan of Malerkotla*. Patiala.

Khan, N. S., R. Saigol and A. S. Zia. 1994. *Locating the Self: Perspectives on Women and Multiple Identities*. Lahore: ASR Publications.

Khan, Y. 2007. *The Great Partition: The Making of India and Pakistan*. New Delhi: Penguin.

Khosla, G. D. 1989. *Stern Reckoning: A Survey of Events Leading Up to and Following the Partition of India*. New Delhi: Oxford University Press.

Kidwai, A. 2011. *In Freedom's Shade*. Translated by Ayesha Kidwai. Delhi: Penguin.

Low, D. A. and H. Brasted. eds. 1998. *Freedom, Trauma, Continuities: Northern India and Independence*. Delhi: Sage.

Ludden, D. ed. 1996. *Making India Hindu: Religion, Community and the Politics of Democracy in India*. Delhi: Oxford University Press.

Mahajan, S. 2001. *Independence and Partition: The Erosion of Colonial Power in India*. New Delhi: Sage Publications.

Maini, G. 2004. *The Giant Awakens: Punjab Industry and Growth*. New Delhi: India Research Press.

Malhotra, A. and F. Mir. eds. 2012. *Punjab Reconsidered: History, Culture, and Practice*. New Delhi: Oxford University Press.

Malik, I. H. 1985. *Sikander Hayat Khan (1892–1942): A Political Biography*. Islamabad: National Institute of Historical and Cultural Research.

Manto, S. M. 2011. Introduction by Daniyal Mueenuddin. *Mottled Dawn: Fifty Sketches and Stories of Partition*. India: Penguin.

Mazumder, R. 2003. *The Indian Army and the Making of Punjab*. Delhi: Permanent Black.

Meeto (Kamaljit Bhasin-Malik). 2007. *In the Making: Identity Formation in South Asia*. New Delhi: Three Essays Collective.

Menon, R. and K. Bhasin. 1998. *Borders and Boundaries: Women in India's Partition*. New Delhi: Kali for Women.

Menon, V. P. 1956. *The Story of the Integration of the Indian States*. Calcutta: Longmans, Green & Co.

Menon, V. P. 1957. *The Transfer of Power in India*. Calcutta: Longmans, Green & Co.

Mir, F. 2010. *The Social Space of Language: Vernacular Culture in British Colonial Punjab*. Berkeley: University of California Press.

Moon, P. 1998. *Divide and Quit.* New Delhi: Oxford University Press.

Nadvi, K. and S. M. Naseem. eds. 2002. *The Post-colonial State and Social Transformation in India and Pakistan.* Oxford: Oxford University Press.

Nanda, B. R. 2003. *Witness to Partition: A Memoir.* New Delhi: Rupa & Co.

Nanda, J. 1948. *Punjab Uprooted: A Survey of the Punjab Riots and Rehabilitation Problems.* Bombay: Hind Kitabs.

Nevile, P. 2006. *Lahore: A Sentimental Journey.* New Delhi.

Panayi, P. and P. Virdee. eds. 2011. *Refugees and the End of Empire: Imperial Collapse and Forced Migration during the Twentieth Century.* Hampshire: Palgrave.

Pandey, G. 2001. *Remembering Partition: Violence Nationalism and History in India.* Cambridge: Cambridge University Press.

Pandit, M. L. 1985. *Industrial Development in the Punjab and Haryana.* Delhi: B.R. Pub. Corp.

Panikkar, K. N. ed. 1991. *Communalism in India: History, Politics and Culture.* New Delhi: People's Publishing House.

Pasha, M. Z. and S. A. Shahid. 1996. *From Sand Dunes to Smiling Fields History of Lyallpur Now Faisalabad.* Faisalabad: Kitab Markaz.

Patel, K. 2005. *Torn from the Roots: A Partition Memoir.* New Delhi: Women Unlimited.

Perks, R. and A. Thompson. 1998. *The Oral History Reader.* London: Routledge.

Rai, S. M. 1965. *Partition of the Punjab: A Study of Its Effects on the Politics and Administration of the Punjab 1947–56.* Bombay: Asia Publishing House.

Roy, A. G. and N. Bhatia. eds. 2007. *Partitioned Lives: Narratives of Home, Displacement and Resettlement.* Delhi: Pearson Longman.

Rumi, R. 2013. *Delhi by Heart.* New Delhi: HarperCollins.

Sahni, B. 2001. *Tamas.* New Delhi: Penguin.

Singh, Khushwant. 1956. *Train to Pakistan.* London: Chatto & Windus.

Singh, Khushwant. 1977. *A History of the Sikhs Vol. 2: 1839–1974.* Delhi: Oxford University Press.

Singh, Kirpal. ed. 1991. *Select Documents on Partition of Punjab-1947: India and Pakistan.* Delhi: National Book Shop.

Singh, P. and S. Thandi. 1999. *Punjab Identity in a Global Context.* New Delhi: Oxford University Press.

Singh, S. and I. D. Gaur. eds. 2008. *Popular Literature and Pre-modern Societies in South Asia.* Delhi: Pearson Longman.

Symonds, R. 1950. *The Making of Pakistan.* London: Faber & Faber.

Symonds, R. 2001. *In the Margins of Independence: A Relief Worker in India and Pakistan 1942–1949*. Karachi: Oxford University Press.

Talbot, I. 1988. *Punjab and the Raj*. New Delhi: Manohar Publication.

Talbot, I. 1996. *Khizr Tiwana: The Punjab Unionist Party and Partition of India*. Surrey: Curzon Press.

Talbot, I. 2006. *Divided Cities: Partition and Its Aftermath in Lahore and Amritsar 1947–1957*. Karachi: Oxford University Press.

Talbot, I. ed. 2007. *The Deadly Embrace: Religion, Violence and Politics in India and Pakistan 1947–2002*. Karachi: Oxford University Press.

Talbot, I. and G. Singh. 1999. *Region and Partition: Bengal, Punjab and the Partition of the Subcontinent*. Oxford: Oxford University Press.

Talbot, I. and D. S. Tatla. 2006. *Epicentre of Violence*. Delhi: Permanent Black.

Talbot, I. and S. Thandi. eds. 2004. *People on the Move: Punjabi Colonial and Post-colonial Migration*. Karachi: Oxford University Press.

Tan, T. and G. Kudaisya. 2000. *The Aftermath of Partition in South Asia*. London: Routledge.

Tandon, P. 2000. *Punjab Century 1857–2000*. New Delhi: Rupa.

Taylor C. Sherman, William Gould and Sarah Ansari eds. 2014. *From Subjects to Citizens: Society and the Everyday State in India and Pakistan, 1947–1970*. Cambridge: Cambridge University Press.

Thompson, P. 1988. *The Voice of the Past*. Oxford: Oxford University Press.

Tucker, Sir F. 1950. *While Memory Serves*. London: Cassell.

Vakil, C. N. 1950. *Economic Consequences of Divided India: A Study of the Economy of India and Pakistan*. Bombay: Vora & Co.

Varshney, A. 2002. *Ethnic Conflict and Civic Life: Hindus and Muslims in India*. New Haven: Yale University Press.

Weiss, A. M. 1991. *Culture, Class, and Development in Pakistan: The Emergence of an Industrial Bourgeoisie in Punjab*. Lahore: Vanguard.

Wolpert, S. 1984. *Jinnah of Pakistan*. Oxford: Oxford University Press.

Woolgar, M. 1997. *Mountbatten on the Record*. University of Southampton: Hartley Institute.

Yong, T. T. 2005. *The Garrison State*. New Delhi: Sage.

Zakaria, A. 2015. *The Footprints of Partition*. New Delhi: HarperCollins.

Zamindar, V. 2008. *The Long Partition and the Making of Modern South Asia: Refugees, Boundaries, Histories*. India: Penguin Viking.

Zeigler, P. 1985. *Mountbatten: The Official Biography*. London: Collins.

Journals

Ahmed, A. S. 1990. 'Refugee Voices: Memories of Partition 1947.' *Journal of Refugee Studies* 35 (3): 262–64.

Ahmed, I. 2002. '1947 Partition of India: A Paradigm for Pathological Politics in India and Pakistan.' *Asian Ethnicity* 3 (1): 9–28.

Aiyar, S. 1995. '"August Anarchy" The Partition Massacre in Punjab 1947.' *South Asia* 18 (Special Issue): 13–36.

Alam, J. and Sharma, S. 1998. 'Remembering Partition.' *Seminar* (461): 98–103.

Ansari, S. 1995. 'Partition, Migration and Refugees: Responses to the Arrival of Mohajirs in Sind 1947-8.' *South Asia* 18 (Special Issue): 95–108.

Arora, A. C. 1982. 'Malerkotla Succession 1871-72: Its Reflections on the British Policy.' *The Panjab Past and Present* 16: 252–59.

Bacchetta, P. 2000. 'Reinterrogating Partition Violence: Voices of Women/ Children/Dalits in India's Partition.' *Feminist Studies* 26 (3)Fall: 567–85.

Bhalla, A. 1999. 'Memory, History and Fictional Representations of the Partition.' *Economic and Political Weekly* 34 (44) 30 October – 5 November: 3119-28.

Brara, R. 1994. 'Kinship and the Political Order: The Afghan Sherwani Chiefs of Malerkotla (1454-1947).' *Contributions to Indian Sociology* 28 (2): 203–41.

Brass, P. 2003. 'The Partition of India and Retributive Genocide in the Punjab 1946-47: Means, Methods and Purposes.' *Journal of Genocide Research* 5 (1): 71–101.

Butalia, U. 1993. 'Community, State and Gender on Women's Agency during Partition.' *Economic and Political Weekly* (April): WS12–WS21+WS24.

Campbell-Johnson, A. 1997. 'Mountbatten and the Transfer of Power.' *History Today* 47 (9) September.

Copland, I. 1988. '"Communalism" in Princely India: The Case of Hyderabad, 1930-1940.' *Modern Asian Studies* 22: 783–814.

Copland, I. 1995. 'The Integration of the Princely State: A Bloodless Revolution?' *South Asia* 18 (Special Issue): 131–51.

Copland, I. 1998. 'The Further Shores of Partition: Ethnic Cleansing in Rajasthan 1947.' *Past and Present* 160 (August): 203–39.

Copland, I. 2000. 'The Political Geography of Religious Conflict: Towards an Explanation of the Relative Infrequency of Communal Riots in the Indian Princely States.' *International Journal of Punjab Studies* 7 (1) January-June: 1–27.

Copland, I. 2002. 'The Master and the Maharajas: The Sikh Princes and the East Punjab Massacres of 1947.' *Modern Asian Studies* 36 (3): 657–704.

Gill, T. S. 1997. 'Punjabi Literature and the Partition of India.' *International Journal of Punjab Studies* 4 (1) January–June: 85–100.

Gosal, G. S. 1965. 'Religious Composition of Punjab's Population Changes 1951-61.' *Economic and Political Weekly* 17 (23 January): 119–24.

Jalal, A. 1996. 'Secularists Subalterns and the Stigma of "Communalism": Partition Historiography Revisited.' *Indian Economic and Social History Review* 33 (1) January–March: 93–103.

Jalal, A. 1998. 'Nation, Reason and Religion: Punjab's Role in the Partition of India.' *Economic and Political Weekly* 33 (12) 8 August: 2183–90.

Kabir A. J. 2002. 'Subjectivities, Memories, Loss of Pigskin Bags, Silver Spittoons and the Partition of India.' *Interventions: International Journal of Postcolonial Studies* 4 (2) July: 245–64.

Kalra, V. S. 2014. 'Punjabiyat and the Music of Nusrat Fateh Ali Khan.' *South Asian Diaspora* 6 (2): 179–192.

Kaur, D. 2006. 'Sukhwant Kaur Mann: Preserving Cultural Memory Through Fiction.' *Journal of Punjab Studies* 13: 247–53.

Kudaisya, G. 1995. 'The Demographic Upheaval of Partition: Refugees and Agricultural Resettlement in India.' *South Asia* 18 (Special Issue): 73–94.

Major, A. 1995. 'The Chief Sufferers: The Abduction of Women During the Partition of the Punjab.' *South Asia* 18 (Special Issue): 57–72.

Malik, I. 1998. 'Pluralism, Partition and Punjabisation: Politics of Muslim Identity in the British Punjab.' *International Journal of Punjab Studies* 5 (1) January–June: 1–27.

Menon, R. and Bhasin, K. 1993. 'Recovery, Rapture, Resistance: The Indian State and the Abduction of Women during Partition.' *Economic and Political Weekly* 28 (17) 24 April: 2–11.

Mookerjea-Leonard, D. 2010. 'To Be Pure or Not To Be: Gandhi, Women, and the Partition of India.' *Feminist Review* 94: 38–54.

Nandy, A. 1999. 'The Invisible Holocaust and the Journey as an Exodus: The Poisoned Village and the Stranger City.' *Postcolonial Studies* 2 (3): 305–329.

Pandey, G. 1997. 'Community and Violence: Recalling Partition.' *Economic and Political Weekly* 9 (August): 2037–45.

Pathak, H. N. 1970. 'Small Scale Industries in Ludhiana.' *Economic and Political Weekly* 5 (28): 1091–97.

Purewal, N. K. 1997. 'Displaced Communities: Some Impacts of Partition on Poor Communities.' *International Journal of Punjab Studies* 4 (1) January-June: 129–46.

Rahman, T. 1997. 'Language and Ethnicity in Pakistan.' *Asian Survey* 37 (9) September: 833–39.

Raj, D. S. 1997. 'Partition and Diaspora: Memories and Identities of Punjabi Hindus in London.' *International Journal of Punjab Studies* 4 (1) January-June: 101–27.

Rammah, S. 2006. 'West Punjabi Poetry: From Ustad Daman to Najm Hosain Syed.' *Journal of Punjab Studies* 13 (1&2): 215–28.

Raychaudhuri, A. (2012). 'Demanding the Impossible: Exploring the Possibilities of a National Partition Museum in India.' *Social Semiotics* 22: 173–86.

Roy, A. 1990. 'The High Politics of India's Partition: The Revisionist Perspective.' *Modern Asian Studies* 24 (2): 385–408.

Scott, B. 2009. 'Partitioning Bodies: Literature, Abduction and the State.' *Interventions* 11 (1): 35–49.

Sims, H. 1990. 'Issue Salience and Regime Responsiveness: The Politics of Reclamation in Two Punjabs.' *Journal of Commonwealth and Comparative Politics* 28 (July): 183–200.

Singh, K. 1997. 'Partition of Punjab: The Women's Fate.' *The Sikh review* 45 (524): 29–35.

Singh, M. 2002. 'Surgical Instruments Industry at Jalandhar: A Case Study.' *Economic and Political Weekly* 3 (August): 3298–304.

Singh, S. 1990. 'Bicycle Industry since Independence: Growth, Structure and Demand.' *Economic and Political Weekly* 25 (34): M98–M109.

Tatla, D. S. 1995. 'The Sandal Bar: Memoirs of a Jat Sikh Farmer.' *The Punjab Past and Present* 29 (April-October): 160–75.

Tewari, M. 1999. 'Successful Adjustment in Indian Industry: The Case of Ludhiana's Woollen Knitwear Cluster.' *World Development* 27 (9) September: 1651–1671.

Tiwari, S. 2013. 'Memories of Partition: Revisiting Saadat Hasan Manto.' *Economic and Political Weekly* XlVIII (25): 50–58.

Virdee, P. 2009. 'Negotiating the Past: Journey through Muslim Women's Experience of Partition and Resettlement.' *Cultural and Social History* 6 (4): 467–83.

Virdee, P. 2013. 'Remembering Partition: Women, Oral Histories and the Partition of 1947.' *Oral History* 41 (2): 49–62.

Waseem, M. 1997. 'Partition Migration and Assimilation: A Comparative Study of Pakistani Punjab.' *International Journal of Punjab Studies* 4 (1) January-June: 21–41.

Whitehead, A. 2000. 'The Partition of India' (Discussion with B. Sidwa and U. Butalia). *History Workshop Journal* 50 (Autumn): 230–38.

Yong, T. T.1995. 'Punjab and the Making of Partition: The Roots of a Civil-Military State.' *South Asia* 18 (Special Issue): 177–92.

Yong, T. T. 1997. '"Sir Cyril Goes to India": Partition Boundary-making and Disruptions in the Punjab.' *International Journal of Punjab Studies* 4 (1) January-June: 1–20.

Index